SALAH

KING OF EUROPE

THE MAKING OF A LIVERPOOL LEGEND

SALAH

KING OF EUROPE

FRANK WORRALL

JOHN BLAKE

Published by John Blake Publishing,
The Plaza,
535 Kings Road,
Chelsea Harbour
London, SW10 0SZ

www.facebook.com/johnblakebooks
twitter.com/jblakebooks

First published in paperback in 2018
This updated edition published in 2019

Paperback ISBN: 978 1 78946 266 1
Ebook ISBN: 978 1 78946 024 7

British Library Cataloguing-in-Publication Data:

A catalogue record for this book is available from the British Library.

Design by www.envydesign.co.uk

Printed and bound in Great Britain by Clays Ltd, Elcograf S.p.A.

1 3 5 7 9 10 8 6 4 2

John Blake Publishing is an imprint of Bonnier Books UK
www.bonnierbooks.co.uk

CONTENTS

CHAPTER 1

ACKNOWLEDGEMENTS

Many thanks: Sarah Fortune, James Hodgkinson, Toby Buchan and all at JBP, Dominic Turnbull, Ben Lazarus, Jo Porter, John Maskey, Liverpool fans Jo Hernon, Roy and Pat Stone, Neil and Dylan Bason and James Edwards, Charlie Wyett, Danny Bottono, Andy Clayton, Steven Gordon, Ian Rondeau, Ben Felsenburg, Alex Butler, Tom Henderson Smith, David and Nicki Burgess. Not forgetting: Angela, Frankie, Jude and Natalie, Frank and Barbara, Bob and Stephen.

THE REAL THING

SATURDAY, 26 MAY 2018
KIEV, UKRAINE

It was billed as the Mo versus the Ego, the final showdown between two of the four players who had produced the best football on the planet over the previous ten months. No Lionel Messi and no Neymar, but Mo Salah and Cristiano Ronaldo would be expected to provide irrevocable proof of their worth; that they deserved to be in that quartet of geniuses. For Ronaldo, it would be a chance to show he *still* should be considered among the best, as talk of his supposed decline had spread far and wide.

For Salah, it was a chance to show he was worthy to be considered *among the very best* after all the plaudits that had fallen his way in a remarkable debut season for his new club. Underlying all that was a sub-plot involving two European heavyweights and two heavyweight managers, all battling for footballing hegemony in the world's most important club tournament's showcase, the Champions League final. Salah v Ronaldo, Liverpool v Real Madrid, Jürgen Klopp v Zinedine Zidane and England's Premier League v Spain's La Liga. This was the final that had the UEFA bean counters and spin doctors licking their lips: it was the *perfect final* in their eyes given the tradition and levity of the clubs and the X Factor of its key contestants.

But who would emerge triumphant? Would Salah come out on top, or would Ronaldo still reign? Or would another player emerge from the pack and wreck what should have been the highlight of Mo's career? A strong and uncompromising player called Sergio Ramos, renowned for his direct and ruthless challenges, who would leave Mo's dreams in tatters – and the man himself in tears? We didn't have to wait long to find out the answer in Kiev. But sixteen days earlier in London, Liverpool manager Klopp's speech at the Football Writers' Association awards had provided a moving insight into why the effortlessly modest and selfless Mo Salah will always be a fan favourite both as a player and as a likeable, decent human being. Mo is a superstar but lives as a simple person.

THURSDAY, 10 MAY 2018
THE LANDMARK HOTEL, LONDON

Klopp was unable to attend the awards ceremony but had an inkling his star man might just pick up the Player of the Year gong voted for by the cream of the nation's football writers. So he sent down a transcript from Liverpool to London with the speech he would have made if he had been there. It showed his affection for Mo Salah and his respect for the man and the body of work from that debut season that marked him out as a truly good man, a humble character and a wonderful footballer. It was a moving speech and almost brought a tear to the faces of hardened hacks that night. This is what Jürgen had to say:

Your winner – Mr Salah is either with you now or on his way – depending when this message is read out. It is typical of Mo's character that he was so keen to attend. And I don't mean greedy for awards – but being gracious and good mannered to make every effort to be there in person and thank you for the honour.

There's not much I can say about what he does 'on the pitch' that you guys haven't already seen and written about. The fact you have voted for him as your 'Player of the Season' reflects that you have witnessed his incredible quality as a footballer.

But it's his qualities as a person that should not be overlooked.

I read and hear about him being a wonderful role model for Egypt – North Africa – for the wider Arabic world and for Muslims. This of course is true – but he is a role model FULL STOP. Regardless of race or religion – country or region of birth. The only 'labels' we should put on Mo are what a good person he is and what a fantastic footballer he is – and by the way – the first part of that is more important in life than the second.

Mo is someone who sets an example of how to approach life and how to treat others. Around Melwood – with his teammates and the club staff – he is gentle and humble despite being the international superstar he is now. The attention and acclaim has not changed him even by 0.01 per cent.

He arrived at Liverpool humble and warm and this is the same boy who comes to be with you all tonight to accept your generous recognition. Although, maybe a little more tired and weary of selfies and autographs – so keep that in mind please.

Mo – if you are there in the room now – we are very proud of you and thankful for what you have done for this team and club – and of course we look forward to sharing many more seasons with you at Liverpool.

In a season when Manchester City have been outstandingly good – and played outstandingly well, football from another planet – you have won the two major awards. The one voted for by your fellow professionals and now the one voted for by the football writers.

You are World Class Mo – truly world class – and what's even more exciting, for you, for Liverpool and for the public who get to watch you play – you can and will get even better.

As character references go, you won't better that. Klopp had hit the mark – as everyone who knows Mo Salah will tell you. He is not your archetypical Premier League star in his mid-twenties who likes to be in the limelight, in the nightclubs and showing off his flash cars. This is a man who prefers the simple life and spending his time away from Anfield with his wife Magi – a biotechnologist, who was his childhood sweetheart – and their daughter Makka. Of that simple lifestyle, he would say, 'I love Italian food, especially pasta with tomato sauce and rice. I spend my spare time with my family. And practising my favourite sport, PlayStation. But I have to confess...Salah in the video game is stronger than the real one.'

The couple married in 2013 and Makka was born two years later in Westminster Hospital when Mo played for Chelsea. Both Mo and Magi are practising Muslims, with Magi seen wearing a hijab on a rare public outing at Anfield, and that faith helps explain Salah's innate decency. 'He is someone who embodies Islam's values and wears his faith on his sleeve,' Miqdaad Versi, the assistant secretary general of the Muslim Council of Britain, said. 'He has a likeability. He is the hero of the team. Liverpool, in particular, has rallied around him in a really positive way. He is not the solution to Islamophobia, but he can play a major role.' Makka was named after the Muslim Holy City and the site of the first revelation of the Koran.

Mo's solid faith is also apparent on the pitch: he celebrates goals by raising his hands up and bowing to Allah with his face on the ground. And he even gave his blessing to a chant the Liverpool fans came up with in which they joke that they would convert to Islam if the goals continued to pile up. He tweeted his liking to the chant, which was sung to the tune of Dodgy's 'Good Enough', with these words:

If he's good enough for you, he's good enough for me.
If he scores another few, then I'll be Muslim too.

If he's good enough for you, he's good enough for me.
Sitting in the mosque, that's where I wanna be!
Mo Salah–la–la–la, la–la–la–la–la–la–la.

Mo has also revealed his beliefs in a message he put out to young people, telling them to always have hope and to keep going, whatever setbacks they may face, advising them to: 'Always feel your heart. Be loyal to yourself. Always believe in your ability and in your goals. This is the only way you will be able to reach them. During this journey, always respect your mates and your opponents. Respect other people – their origin, religion, and nationality. And finally, never stop improving yourself. When someone tells you you're fast, make sure, the next day, you show them you can run faster.'

Haytham Abokhalil, a pro-Muslim Brotherhood human rights activist, said Mo's success, 'gives confidence to our youth that it can be the best if it has the appropriate possibilities and opportunities.'

WHERE IT ALL BEGAN

Mo Salah's story begins 3,500 miles away from Liverpool, in Nagrig, a small farming village, near the city of Basyoun, in the Gharbia Governerate of Egypt. It is eighty miles north of the country's capital, Cairo, and is where Mohamed Salah Ghaly was born on 15 June 1992. It is where many years later, after he had earned untold riches as a footballer, he would return to pay for a medical centre, a school for girls, a sewage treatment plan and an ambulance station. He also bought gym equipment for the community centre named after him and paid for an all-weather football pitch to be built at Mohamed Ayyad Al-Tantawy school, where he studied.

It is little wonder that wherever you go in Mo Salah's homeland his face is plastered on walls and buildings. Streets have been named in his honour and he has given hope to young Egyptians who now believe they can make something of their lives, as their hero has done. Mo has donated millions of pounds to make life easier and better for the people who live in the place that gave him a start in life and, along with this beginning, the hunger and determination to become a great footballer.

The Mayor of Nagrig, Maher Shatiyah, gives us an insight into just how much help Salah has provided to the town, and talks of his philanthropic character, explaining that: 'Salah is a refined person who, despite his popularity, has never forgotten about his town. He has provided many forms of assistance, the first of which was a series of foodstuff outlets under the municipality's management, as well as the town's first ambulance unit.' He added that Mo also gives around £2,000 a month to help struggling families get by.

Nagrig is where a modern-day fairy tale begins, a true rags-to-riches tale, and Mo Salah would never forget his roots and the people he left behind. Stories of his altruistic gestures are legend wherever you go in or near his hometown. There is also the tale of how when his father's house was robbed, Mo convinced Mr Salah senior to drop the criminal charges when the villain was caught. Still more surprisingly, he gave the robber money and offered to help him search for a job.

Matrawy Abu Habsah, a teacher from Nagrig nearly broke

down as he spoke to the online news organisation *Middle East Eye* about Salah. He said: 'I can't tell you how much he means to us, honestly. What he's done for us and for Egypt, I just can't explain it at all. I'm just tearing up speaking about him. Mohamed doesn't like to speak about the charitable work he has done or the money he donates. He doesn't like the spotlight and he doesn't make a fuss wherever he goes. I saw Mohamed yesterday at a funeral and I asked him how he was and he just thanked God.'

Meanwhile, Ahmed Daef Sakar, the governor of Gharbia, once called Salah's father to thank him for 'All the charitable work [his son] has done to serve his country. He is a great role model to be followed by young people and is loved by millions around the world because he paints happiness on their faces.'

'Mo still returns to Nagrig, every Ramadan, to present prizes to local kids,' Mohamed Bassyouni, a childhood friend, told the *Mail*. 'He plays table tennis and pool. When he comes back, he signs every autograph, stands for every picture. He hasn't changed.'

Mo's attitude to life was shaped by his parents – a salesman and a housewife. They encouraged him to work hard and to follow his dreams. A brother and sister completed the family unit and Mo has only happy memories of his childhood; the family never had money to burn, but all their needs were provided for and it was a happy home. Mo was not a natural academic and found solace in football, playing endlessly in the streets with his pals. His dad, Salah Ghaly, worried about his schooling but realised the boy was bent on being a footballer, and eventually offered him his wholehearted support. He too had been a keen footballer as a boy, but only at amateur level.

Of his schooldays, Mo said, 'I was not a very good student. I was thinking only about football and this was the reason to be there.' When he wasn't out playing in the street, or for the youth team, he was watching games on TV. Football was fast becoming his everything, his one and only dream and goal.

His father and two uncles had played football for the youth club in Nagrig and Mo followed in their footsteps. Eventually, Mo was spotted by a scout representing El Mokawloon, a professional club based in Cairo. 'His talent clearly showed from the beginning,' said Ghamri Abdel-Hameed el-Saadani, who was the juniors' coach at the Nagrig Youth Centre, where Mo started playing aged eight. Now his commitment to a footballing future would really be tested – as that meant a 160-mile daily round journey from Nagrig to the Egyptian capital. At the age of fourteen he had to catch three buses each way for a ten-hour round trip to train with El Mokawloon. 'I'd have to transfer buses three, four, sometimes even five times just to arrive at training and then back home again,' he remembered. That exhausting schedule would continue for five days a week for years.

Finally, his precocious talent was recognised and rewarded and the draining journeys would come to an end. The club have lodgings built into the main stand of their Osman Ahmed Osman Stadium and Mo was allocated accommodation. He would lodge in a basic and simple room, number 510, which overlooked the pitch. It may not have been luxurious but for Mo Salah it was wonderful: the view itself was inspirational to a sensitive, contemplative boy like himself.

In May 2010, now eighteen, he finally made the senior team at the club. At first, he turned out at left-back and was mostly used as a substitute. But soon the club realised they had a star in the making and, from training, also sussed the boy had the natural ability to play as a forward. He scored his first senior goal during a 1–1 draw against major Egyptian club, Al Ahly. 'Mohamed was willing to sacrifice everything,' Hamdi Nooh, a former Egypt international who was Salah's first coach at El Mokawloon would say. 'When he came, it was too much left foot. I looked at him and said, "You have to use your right." He replied, "OK, sir!" Always the same answer, always polite. The next morning, he is there: practise, practise. I called his father when he used to go home. I told him to keep a timetable: no staying up late to watch TV. No getting out of bed late. He didn't. He lived as he should. He would pray and then go to sleep early. I am not the man who made him but I know he listened to me. He listened to everyone.'

Salah played regularly for the club from 2010 to February 2012, when the Port Said Stadium disaster prompted the Egyptian FA to cancel the rest of the season. He was recruited by Basel after they arranged a March 2012 friendly against Egypt's U23s. Salah came on at the break, scored twice and joined the Swiss club that April. He had scored eleven goals in thirty-five appearances for El Mokawloon and was named the Confederation of African Football's Most Promising African Talent of the Year for 2012.

But Europe – and the big time – were now calling.

Salah told his father that he was anxious about leaving Egypt but he had worked so hard and put in so many hours travelling in those early years at El Mokawloon that he knew he had to go. It was another essential step to achieving his dream of becoming a footballing world superstar. In April 2012, Mo signed a four-year contract with the Swiss outfit. He made his Champions League debut in the same year and also starred for the club in the Europa League. Mo helped Basel to reach the semi-finals of the latter competition in May 2013.

It was his displays against Tottenham and Chelsea in the tournament that would make the big English teams – and Barcelona in Spain – pay attention to his potential. In the quarter-finals, Basel would beat Spurs on penalties after the two ties ended in 2–2 draws. Mo would not be on the scoresheet in the first leg at White Hart Lane at the start of April 2013, but caused Tottenham problems all night with his tricky runs down the right.

He was on target in the return fixture the following week. Clint Dempsey had put Spurs ahead but Salah was there with one of his trademark goals to equalise, beating a defender on the right, running central and then dispensing the ball in the bottom left-hand corner of the goal with that deadly left foot. The match went to extra time after goals from Aleksander Dragović and another for Dempsey, but ended all square at 2–2. It was the Swiss hosts who then won the day by keeping their nerve in the subsequent penalty shoot-out. They won 4–1 on penalties but Salah was not called upon to take one. It was his best moment in club football to date – and now he had the semi-finals and, hopefully, the final to make an even bigger name for himself.

Mo and Basel would lose in the semis – but it would be the performance Salah gave in both legs that would prove critical for his future. For the opponents were Chelsea, his next footballing destination. Mo played well in the first leg in Switzerland but it would not be his night. He was booked twelve minutes from time, did not get on the scoresheet and Chelsea departed with a 2–1 win. With a David Luiz free kick winning the game for the Blues.

In the return leg at Stamford Bridge, Salah really shone, earning praise from then Chelsea boss Rafa Benítez and leaving a lasting impression on the club's bigwigs, who were involved in transfers, both incoming and outgoing. Basel lost 3–1 to three second-half goals but Salah had given them hope when he found the net just before the interval. He slotted the ball home past Petr Čech and looked like the natural goalscorer he is. Cool and calm, no worries and no mistake, and no doubting the outcome. Chelsea killed off Mo's dream of being in the final in Amsterdam, but he had made his presence felt – and sent a message to the footballing giants who were circling for his signature.

Was destiny calling him to Chelsea? It certainly seemed that way as the following season's Champions League fixtures brought him up against them yet again, this time in the Group stage of Europe's premier club event. Basel would not progress from the group, but Mo would score twice against them. That was enough for the London club to splash out for his signature the following January. He had scored three times against them in four European fixtures and left their backline dazed at times with his hazy runs down the right.

In September 2013, Salah scored a sizzler at Stamford Bridge, lashing the ball past Petr Čech to give Basel hope of a shock win. It made Chelsea boss José Mourinho sit up and take notice: this was his first European match in charge since he returned to manage the club after his spell at Real Madrid. Salah levelled it at 1–1 after Oscar had put the Blues ahead. Marco Streller won the day for Basel, his late header making it 2–1 on the night. It was Chelsea's first Champions League group stage defeat at the Bridge since October 2003 and Salah's display was all the more impressive, as he had given Ashley Cole a night to forget. Years later Cristiano Ronaldo would name Cole as his most difficult opponent, so for Salah to take him to the cleaners that night was quite an achievement.

Mourinho was impressed with the young Egyptian and his respect grew still more when Mo hit the winner as Chelsea lost 1–0 in Switzerland in the return group fixture. He raced on to a pass from the left wing and coolly hit the ball home past the despairing Čech. This was a major result in Basel's history – beating an English giant in Europe at home, and now it was twice in succession they had floored Chelsea.

It didn't get much better than this for Salah in Switzerland. He was the hero of Basel, the talk of Europe and the No. 1 transfer target for the team he had put to the sword. It is not hyperbole to suggest that this was the night Mourinho decided he would sign Mohamed Salah for Chelsea – and the sooner the better. Not a bad night's work by the boy who would go on to become known as 'The Egyptian King'.

But it wasn't just in Europe that Mo would play a significant role for himself and Basel. He was a key figure as the team soared to domestic glory by winning the 2012–13 Swiss Super League and he was named Swiss Player of the Year for that season. Mo made his final competitive Basel appearance in a game against Lucerne in December 2013. He ended his time at the club having scored twenty goals in seventy-nine appearances.

But it was those standout performances against Chelsea that would rocket him towards the big time. The West London club had been spellbound by how he would cut in from the right wing with his left foot to torment their defenders. This would become his trademark procession to goal – speeding down the right, then twisting past opponents and moving into the centre-forward slot as he headed towards the keeper, finally delivering the coup d'état with that potent left foot.

In January 2014 he said goodbye to Basel for good as Mourinho emerged with the Chelsea chequebook. The real big time loomed and he would now pass through Chelsea, Fiorentina and Roma to polish his talent before finally arriving 'home for good' at Liverpool, and that mesmeric, if ultimately heartbreaking, Champions League final of 2018.

NIGHTMARE IN KIEV

So back to Kiev and the Champions League final in May 2018, which ended with Mo in tears and out of the contest after just thirty minutes. We had been warned that Real Madrid, and Marcelo in particular, did not fancy coming up against him. Egypt legend Mohamed Aboutrika had said the left-back was 'terrified' of Mo. Aboutrika pointed to Salah's previous skinning of Marcelo as the initial root of Marcelo's fear.

The Brazilian and Mo had competed against each other in the 2012 London Olympics. Mo had come on as a sub and was key to Egypt's fightback after they had been 3–0 down.

He scored as Egypt eventually lost 3–2. They met again in the 2015–16 Champions League when Salah caused the Real defender problems in a Roma shirt. Aboutrika, Egypt's captain at the 2012 Olympics, told beIN SPORTS MENA: 'Liverpool have a big chance to win the Champions League against Real Madrid. I witnessed on that pitch what Salah can do to Marcelo during the Olympic Games. I was playing with Egypt against Brazil. Marcelo is terrified of Salah. I noticed the same thing in the Champions League when AS Roma played against Real Madrid.'

And Michael Owen has also spoken with awe about how Salah was making him and fellow former Liverpool strikers look average in comparison. Owen said in *The Mail on Sunday*, 'Maybe, as Klopp suggested last week, we shouldn't be too surprised at the rise and rise of Mohamed Salah. After all, his stats at Roma were impressive, with 19 goals last season. That said, he is beginning to make me and the likes of Robbie Fowler, Fernando Torres and Luis Suárez look average. Salah has perfected the art of seeing the game in slow motion, allowing himself time to pick the right finish, even when the real-time speed is 100mph.'

Yet the threat to Madrid was eliminated early on by the full-blooded challenge of Sergio Ramos who cruelly barged in to wreck Salah's big night in Kiev. Mo's contribution to the biggest game of his career lasted just half an hour. He had set off on one of his trademark driving runs towards goal only to be pulled to the ground by Ramos. Did Ramos mean to hurt Salah? He denies it. What is clear is that as Mo's arm was locked as they tumbled to the ground, his shoulder would shudder under the impact of their joint body weights. Many fans have no doubt that Ramos should have been sent off – a straight red, believing that the constant reruns of the incident confirm this, but the referee did not see it that way. Ramos wasn't even cautioned. Ramos would later claim it was an accident; nevertheless TV cameras on the night would capture him smiling as Mo trudged off.

Klopp would later comment on the challenge, saying, 'Of course it was a big moment in the game. I know if you say something like that after a game you lost, it sounds like you are a little bit a bad loser, but it was, for me, kind of a harsh challenge. It's like wrestling a little bit and it's unlucky then that Mo fell on his shoulder.'

This should have been Salah's night. But it was not to be. Ramos had executed a shuddering challenge and Liverpool would wilt without their star man. It is a telling statistic that when Mo was on the pitch Liverpool had nine attempts on goal: then, up until half-time, with him gone, they had none. Their confidence was shot. Ramos would end the night grinning inanely with the Cup while Salah's night ended in tears. Liverpool would lose 3–1, with a Gareth Bale wonder goal and two clangers by Loris Karius.

But maybe they really lost when Salah was taken out of the game. It was a cruel end to a wonderful season for Mo Salah. But he would be back. The Egyptian King would rule Europe sooner rather than later, no doubt about that: his No. 1 mission now was to dethrone Ramos and Real Madrid.

CHAPTER TWO

THE BLUES AT CHELSEA

Mo Salah's time at Chelsea would be short – and far from sweet. José Mourinho brought him to Stamford Bridge in the winter transfer window of 2014. He arrived in the January for a fee said to be around £12 million and made the club's history books as the first Egyptian to join. But that was the only real mark he would make in a year's stay before being farmed out on loan, and it was hardly his fault that he failed to make an impression.

Mourinho had secured his signature and then criminally underused the player. Salah simply did not get a fair crack of the whip at the Bridge. It made you wonder if Mo had been signed above José's head. Certainly there were rumours that was the case, and he would hardly have been the first player to be brought into Chelsea without the manager's consent. More likely, I was told, was that Mourinho had nodded his approval to the transfer, put the lad through his paces and then bombed him out because he hadn't adapted to his straitjacket tactical methodology quickly enough.

Over the years the Portuguese manager would become famed for his wanting to sign only players who were, in his eyes, the finished article. He did not seem to have the patience to develop a youngster through to that point. Mo needed only to have cast an eye over Mourinho's similar treatment of another youngster at Chelsea. As Mo was arriving at Chelsea, Kevin De Bruyne was leaving. José had sanctioned the latter's transfer to Wolfsburg in the very window he was signing Salah.

Both Salah and De Bruyne would go on to become world-class players, but at Chelsea they both suffered at José's hands. It is now viewed as a huge mistake by Chelsea to have not developed the potential that both Mo and Kevin, the stand-out Premier League performers in the 2017–18 season, had possessed. But that error may help us comprehend why Mo Salah's stay at Chelsea was not a successful one.

That £12-million fee could have risen to £16 million if Salah had reached certain appearances and achievement targets. So it probably stayed at £12 million. He moved from Basel to much fanfare and the Chelsea fans were looking forward to him making a positive impact, particularly as he was replacing their Player of the Year, Juan Mata, whom Mourinho was flogging to Manchester United. It was not as if Salah was a comparative novice: he had done well in Switzerland and, at that stage, had scored seventeen goals in twenty-seven games for his country.

Chelsea also knew about his knack of scoring goals –

he had hit the net in his last three games for Basel against them, including in both Champions League group matches earlier that season. Chelsea announced his imminent arrival with a short statement: 'Chelsea can confirm an agreement has been reached with FC Basel for the transfer of their 21-year-old attacking midfielder Mohamed Salah. The move is subject to the Egyptian international agreeing personal terms and completing a medical examination.'

Ironically, Liverpool had also expressed an interest in signing him at the time – but the word was that they had balked at the £12-million fee, believing Salah was worth more in the region of £8 million. He departed Basel with the team at the top of the Swiss Super League and left on good terms, as his goals had helped them get there.

Three days after their initial statement, Chelsea issued another, confirming Salah had signed and giving more details of the deal, stating:

Chelsea Football Club today completed the signing of Mohamed Salah from FC Basel. The Egyptian international signed a five-and-a-half-year contract and will wear the Number 15 shirt. Upon signing, Salah said, 'I'm very happy to sign for Chelsea, such a big club in the world. I hope I can make the Chelsea supporters happy and have a good career at the club for many years to come.' A quick, inventive attacking-midfielder, Salah moves to Stamford Bridge having played against us twice for Basel in the group stages of this season's Champions League, when he scored in both matches, as well as in last season's Europa

League, when he was also on target in the second leg of our semi-final. The 21-year-old's versatility ensures he is comfortable playing on either flank or occupying a more central role behind a striker.

Someone at Stamford Bridge clearly had a perceptive eye to visualise Salah playing 'a more central role' – the role he would gravitate towards from the left wing as his career progressed. Whether that person was Mourinho remains unclear.

Salah made his Chelsea debut in the Premier League a couple of weeks after arriving at the Bridge. He came on as a sub for Willian in the seventy-eighth minute 3–0 home win over Newcastle, receiving generous applause from the Chelsea faithful. They knew he had great potential after those goals for Basel against their team and hoped he could reproduce his fine form and develop within a winning team.

Mourinho gave him a further one minute of action in the 1–1 draw at West Brom three days later; he replaced Ramires in the eighty-ninth minute. Then he got a full forty-five minutes in the 2–0 defeat at Man City four days on from the draw at the Hawthorns, this time taking over from Samuel Eto'o. It was hardly a barnstorming start to his Blues career but then again that was hardly his fault. Mourinho, in his most cautious mode, was only willing to allocate his new boy odd minutes here and there. José could be the most controversial of managers when the mood took him, but also the most conservative. He believed firmly in his tried and trusted ways. He was not one for spontaneity or taking a gamble unless he and his team were really up against it.

Two months after joining Chelsea, Mo scored his first goal for them. It was his fourth appearance for the club – and his fourth as a substitute. In those four games, he had managed a total of eighty-one minutes playing time out of a possible 360. He replaced Brazilian ace Oscar in the sixty-seventh minute. The goal came against Arsenal in a 6–0 thumping at Stamford Bridge on 22 March 2014. It was Chelsea's biggest win against the Gunners and an unhappy way for Arsène Wenger to celebrate his thousandth game in charge of the team. It was Wenger's joint biggest defeat as Arsenal boss, along with the 8–2 thrashing at Man United. It was also Mourinho's biggest win as Chelsea manager.

Salah was glad to get his chance, delighted with his goal and happy to be part of a match marked with so many landmarks. He had beaten the abject offside trap Arsenal had set and confidently shot home past Gunners' keeper Szczęny. Chelsea were now four points clear at the top of the table from Liverpool, with seven games to go. To give him his due, Mourinho did involve Salah in all those remaining games, albeit in a sub's role.

But the Chelsea boss would only say, 'He's settling in and doing OK', when asked about his new signing from Basel. Mourinho was never afraid of being in the spotlight, the type of manager who would not hold back about individual players when talking to the press, and critical of them for not doing as he wanted.

Even after that 6–0 win over Arsenal, the talk at the post-match interviews was about why he had left the dugout early at the end of the game and rushed down the tunnel. He said it was so he could ring his wife to tell her the score. The spotlight, yet again, was on him, not the players. In that sense, Mo Salah should have had nothing to worry about. At least his new manager was not criticising him in public.

Mo was doing his darnedest to make an impression at the Bridge, but it was not easy when he was limited to so few minutes. Mo was on the bench for the Crystal Palace game, the one directly after that win over Arsenal. This was becoming frustrating: he had moved from Basel with the promise that he would get his chance – that he would be given a run in the team. Yet it seemed he had signed to become an impact player from the bench: a super-sub role. He expressed his frustrations to friends but continued to work hard in training.

Then, suddenly, he was in the team, and he stayed there until the end of the season. That is not quite as impressive a stat as it sounds – Salah started the final six Premier League matches, beginning with the home fixture against Stoke on Saturday 5 April and concluding with the away clash in Cardiff on Sunday 11 May. That debut start against Stoke saw him score his second goal for the club and give an impressive performance.

The win also took his new club back to the top of the Premier League table. Mo's goal came on the half-hour mark after some excellent play by Willian. The Brazilian beat his man and crossed the ball to the far side of the box. It fell to Nemanja Matić, who cut the ball back to Salah. Instinctively, Salah lashed the ball home with a brilliant left-foot shot that gave Asmir Begović no chance in the Stoke goal. Salah also won a penalty for his team, after he was fouled by Andy Wilkinson in the box, and Frank Lampard scored from the rebound after his spot kick was initially saved. It looked as if Mo had finally arrived at the Bridge. He had performed wonders and looked the part, driving in from the left wing.

The Chelsea diehards were certainly impressed with him, many believing he represented the future of the club. They took to social media and the message boards in large numbers to laud the new boy. One said: 'Salah was amazing yesterday and I think him, Hazard and Willian and the rest of the blues crew can make it and get the title.' Another added: 'Salah looked decent yesterday'. While another Blues fan commented: 'Salah looks like being a great buy. The way he linked up with Willian was excellent. Salah, Willian and Hazard – what a forward line!'

Even Liverpool fans got in on the act, expressing their sadness that he had signed for Chelsea instead of the Reds. One said: 'As a Liverpool fan it hurts so much to see Salah doing so well.' And another added: 'Why did we not pay up for Salah? Why the indecision? You could see how good he was against Stoke – we've dropped an almighty bollock!' While another fan of the Reds added: 'I am going to cry. Salah was ours but Chelsea stole him from us!'

The season ended with a more optimistic Mo, although Mourinho still refused to guarantee him a regular starting spot when the pair met as part of the regular progress chats José had with his squad before they headed off on summer holidays. Then, in the July of 2014, Mo got an unexpected shock when informed that he may have to return to Egypt to carry out military service. He was said to have had his registration for an education programme rescinded by the Minister of Higher Education in his home country. If that was correct he would have been forced to return to Egypt as his travel visa was conditional on his taking part in the education programme.

The excellent Egyptian football and news outlet *KingFut* was claiming that national team director Ahmed Hassan had already spoken to Salah about it and the player was distraught. 'Salah has expressed his shock about the decision,' the reporter said. 'He told me that he is trying to represent Egypt in the best way possible. Is this the best response from the country?' The *Metro* website summed up the worrying situation, saying: 'The decision could mean should Salah return to Egypt – where his family is still based – he will not be permitted to leave again until he has completed a period of national service, which could add up to anything between 12 and 36 months. A meeting is due to be held between the Minister of Higher Education, the Egyptian FA and the national team coaching staff to find a solution.'

The news had Chelsea fans up in arms. The player had made an impression towards the end of the season – and now, just as he was set for a first full season, he could be lost for more than a year. Thankfully, for all concerned, that planned high-level meeting smoothed things over. The issue had become such a headline-maker that the Prime Minister Ibrahim Mahlab also turned up at the discussion with his Minister of Higher Education and the Egyptian national manager Shawky Gharieb. The outcome was that Salah, now twenty-two, was told he would not have to return home to join his country's armed forces.

THE BLUES AT CHELSEA

Everyone breathed a sigh of relief and Mo was now clear to join his teammates on Chelsea's pre-season tour to Austria, where he would be joined by the club's three summer signings: Cesc Fàbregas, Diego Costa and Filipe Luís. He had already made an impact pre-season by scoring in the club's 3–2 friendly win at AFC Wimbledon.

Now he wanted a clear run at making a name for himself at Chelsea when the season proper began. The club had finished third in his first season, but he was as ambitious as Mourinho in wanting to be part of a team that would, hopefully, win the Premier League. That third-place finish had meant Chelsea had not won a trophy for the first time in three years while their eighty-two-point total was their worst under Mourinho, who had moaned about not having a striker with a 'killer instinct'. He rectified that by bringing in the combative Diego Costa, but if he had been a tad more patient he would surely have found he already had that man on his books in Salah. José went for the finished article rather than investing in youth and potential.

With the arrival of Costa and luminaries such as Hazard and Willian on the books, what had looked hopeful for Salah now looked much more of a challenge. How was he to get regular playing time when Mourinho would surely turn to his bigger money stars first? It was a dilemma he tried to put to the back of his mind on the pre-season tour but when the 2014–15 campaign got underway it was something Mo had to face head-on. It would be his first full season at Chelsea and, despite the threat he faced for his place from the other strikers, he was motivated, keen and raring to go. He had changed his squad number from

15 to 17 for the start of the season and hoped it would help improve his luck. No chance of that. For the next six months Mo Salah would be almost criminally underused by his manager. There was just a regular spell on the sidelines as Mourinho relied on his big-money, big-name buys to get results.

It would be 14 September before Mourinho called upon him, and that was only to start on the bench in the 4–2 home win over Swansea. He was brought on as a substitute eight minutes from time. Mourinho did start him twice in Carling Cup matches against Bolton in September and Shrewsbury six weeks later. This didn't mean he had turned a corner – the boss regularly threw in youngsters and squad players in this competition. Mo was young and obviously viewed as a squad player.

This treatment was disheartening for a young man who had been promised a fair crack of the whip; who had left Switzerland ready to make his name in the English top-flight only to be banished to the peripheries. The player got another rare start when Sporting Lisbon came to town in the Champions League in December, but then he was plonked back on the bench for what was clearly a more important fixture – the Premier League meeting with Spurs on 1 January 2015.

Things were going from bad to worse and the situation wasn't helped when Mourinho, true to type, laid into Salah publicly, also remonstrating with his teammate André Schürrle. It came when the duo played in the 2–1 Carling Cup win at Shrewsbury. A clear sign that Mo's confidence was low came when he shot and it ended up as a throw-in, he was so far off target. Afterwards Mourinho told reporters, 'I expect players to give me problems. I love problems. But a lot of them didn't and they've made it easy to choose my team for Saturday. If players who played ninety minutes two days ago were fantastic I expect people who are not playing a lot to raise the level to create me problems. They didn't create me big problems.' Asked if Schürrle and Salah in particular had disappointed him, Mourinho answered, 'Yes.'

José then added that Salah and Schürrle could learn from the example of one of his favourites, veteran striker Didier Drogba. He said, 'I was worried when they equalised but we go through and Didier played a massive part in that. Hopefully he will be good for the weekend but we will have to see because right now his character is stronger than his body. Maybe what he has done today is through his character – not his body. That's what makes players special, and any of the young players lucky enough to play alongside him should learn from that.'

Surely an arm around the shoulders and a quiet word would have been far more effective. As an exercise in encouraging and developing young players, Mo was effectively back to square one with the Portuguese manager. Those six starts at the end of the previous season had proved to be a false dawn.

This was the reality. Mourinho clearly viewed him as, at best, an impact sub, and it was surely telling that he would not score again in his short-lived career at the Bridge. Mo wasn't a player who performed better with a kick up the backside in private or in public but, unfortunately, that was

Mourinho's favoured tactic. Salah was a kind, humble guy who much preferred to talk things through one-to-one in order to find an amicable solution. Not so José.

No matter, to his credit Mo never moaned publicly or rocked the boat. He continued to put in the hard yards in training and hoped his manager might give him a proper chance to show what he could do. It never came and the only goals he would score from August 2014 to his departure at the end of January 2015 would be for his country. When he returned home he found love and encouragement. He played in three African Nations Cup ties for Egypt in October and November 2014 and scored a goal in all three.

Mo may have been one of life's good guys but he was also certainly no mug. By January 2015 he knew what the score was at Chelsea. He wasn't getting many chances and he asked himself whether that would be likely to change in the immediate future. He thought not and even a call-up to the first team on the twenty-fourth of the month did not make him change his mind. He started in the FA Cup tie with Bradford City at the Bridge that day, and it would be his last game for the Blues.

It was no fairy-tale ending, though. Chelsea crashed 4–2 to the League One outfit and Salah had been withdrawn with twenty minutes to go. Mourinho had not been impressed with him, or his teammates. José declared himself 'ashamed' and 'embarrassed' by the loss. He added, 'It is a disgrace for a big team to lose to a small team from a lower division. Me and the players must feel ashamed.' The atmosphere in the Chelsea dressing room was 'like a morgue', I was told, with Mourinho 'yelling and telling his team they had been crap'.

Enough was enough for Mo Salah. Within eight days he had gone from Chelsea and it would only be away from Mourinho that he would find his feet again and become the world-class star many predicted even back then. On 2 February 2015, it was announced he would be moving to Italy and Serie A side, Fiorentina.

Florence in the springtime had a nice feel about it and now, being able to express himself in a much happier atmosphere, Mo blossomed again. The player who had hit the heights in Basel had returned. There was one happy sidebar to that unfulfilled first season at Stamford Bridge: Chelsea would go on to win the Premier League title and Salah would receive a Premier League winners' medal. It wouldn't be an official one and Mo wouldn't count it as one when he looked back on his time at the club. The medal would be a replica paid for by Chelsea on the orders of Mourinho.

José revealed all the squad would get an official medal or a replica – including Mo, who had appeared in just three league games that season. 'Not all of them will get an official medal. But yes, we are going to buy medals,' Mourinho said. 'We are going to buy replicas of the cup. And, obviously, for me the champions are those who played every minute like John Terry, but also people like Schwarzer who were not involved.

'Salah, Schwarzer, Lewis Baker...all of them who started the season with us. They have been invited to the last match and the Player of the Year dinner. They belong to us. We are not sure they can be there, but at least they know we feel they belong to the title.'

As a parting gesture, it was pretty admirable. But Mo had started a new chapter: he was enjoying himself in Italy and making waves with his brilliant attacking play. He would have a ball in Serie A – initially in Florence, but more especially in Rome.

CHAPTER 3

RENAISSANCE MAN

Salah escaped the claustrophobia of José Mourinho's second Chelsea reign at the start of February in 2015. On the second of the month he agreed to go out on loan to Florence in Italy. The length of the deal was unusual: such loans normally expired after six or twelve months, but the Fiorentina contract saw Mo sign up to them for eighteen months. He would later view that time-frame 'a mistake' and it would cause unpleasantness with the Italian club when he asked to quit early. But for now, everything was rosy. He was quitting the inclement London winter weather for a more temperate climate, and the city of Florence, with its architectural delights and wonderful vistas, was in itself worth the transfer.

The capital city of the Italian region of Tuscany was considered the birthplace of the Renaissance and had been called 'the Athens of the Middle Ages'. To a peaceful, nature-loving man like Mo Salah this was a great attraction and he knew that his wife would also find much to enjoy in the cosmopolitan atmosphere within the city. It would perhaps not be too sentimental to suggest that Salah's own renaissance, after being choked by Mourinho, began in Florence.

An immediate indication of Salah the contemplative, humanist being, came when he told Fiorentina he wanted to wear the Number 74 shirt. The bosses looked at him puzzled – until he explained it was his way of paying tribute to the number of victims of the Port Said Stadium riot in 2012. He told reporters a little more about the decision at his official unveiling. Mo said, 'A few days ago the third anniversary of the tragedy of Port Said was commemorated and it seemed right to pay homage to the seventy-four victims.' He elaborated, explaining that it was three years ago to the day that seventy-four fans had died in violent clashes between rival supporters of Al-Masry and Al Ahly. Then he added, 'And to be clear, no one has ever asked me to put this number on the jersey. It's something I felt inside and chose to do it.'

He said he wanted to remain with Fiorentina for 'as long as possible' and added:

I want to win championships and cups and do well for the team. I feel good here. Before coming I talked to Ahmed Hegazi [Egyptian centre-back who played for Fiorentina at the time and who would go on to later sign for West Bromwich Albion] who reassured me about the environment and the team – there are players who have done great things like Batistuta and Baggio in Florence and the Italian championship is excellent. I spoke English at Basel and Chelsea but I hope to learn Italian soon, next week I will start a course. I know I am not the finished article; there are many areas in which I can improve. But I'm only twenty-two and am confident I can improve here in Florence with this team. I can also play in several positions – at Basel I played in a 4–3–3 on the right or left wing, but also as a second striker.

How quickly he settled in Florence could be gauged by the fact that he scored six goals in seven games. That statistic is probably as damning an indicator as you could ask for on his former boss Mourinho, who had been reluctant to give him his chance in Mo's first full season at Stamford Bridge. Even back in 2015, he was a goal machine and Fiorentina, like Basel previously, were the beneficiaries.

Chelsea, meanwhile, had taken the Colombian winger Juan Cuadrado from Fiorentina as part of the deal that took Salah to Florence. Who got the better of the deal? Well, Salah was loaned while Cuadrado weighed in at a hefty £24 million with similarly hefty wages agreed within his four-and-a-half year deal. And just seven months later Cuadrado found himself farmed out on loan to Juventus, returned to Chelsea and played in a few friendlies, then headed back to Turin, now on a three-year loan. He officially joined Juve in May 2017. What a signing he had turned out to be for Chelsea – while Salah, who was twice the player, started to sparkle in Florence.

Salah grabbed his first goal for Fiorentina less than a fortnight after his arrival, in the 3–1 win at Sassuolo. Mo netted in the thirtieth minute and then turned provider for Khouma Babacar a couple of minutes later. Two weeks later he was on target with his first European goal for the club – and this was a strike which reverberated across Europe back to Stamford Bridge. Chelsea have an intense rivalry with Tottenham, so Mo's strike was all the sweeter for Blues fans, as it meant they had beaten Spurs 3–1 on aggregate in the Europa League, helping them advance to the Round of 16 stage.

The papers back in the UK also had a field day, telling how a so-called Chelsea reject was hitting the high notes. The *Express*, for instance, said: 'The Egyptian pounced on Jan Vertonghen's lax defending to put the tie beyond doubt after Mario Gomez had opened the scoring. It was Salah's third goal since moving from Chelsea on deadline day as part of Juan Cuadrado's switch to Stamford Bridge. Gómez broke free midway through the second half to bury his one-on-one effort under Hugo Lloris, who was then stranded for Salah's strike as Vertonghen dithered on a clearance.'

And *The Telegraph* summed up the nonsensical nature of Salah's Italian exile, reporting: 'Mohamed Salah, deemed not good enough by José Mourinho, produces killer goal to end Spurs' hopes. Mario Gómez's 54th minute goal emphatically shifted the momentum in favour of La Viola. Salah then provided the definitive contribution of the night to complete an agonising evening at the Stadio Artemio Franchi and Pochettino must lift his players quickly.'

Eurosport commented on what 'a handful' Salah had been, saying: 'Salah scored Fiorentina's second, beating Jan Vertonghen to finish emphatically into the top corner. The Egyptian, on loan from Chelsea was a handful for Spurs all evening.'

While destroying Tottenham's Europa League hopes – and Mauricio Pochettino's of a first trophy – Salah had inadvertently helped his parent club. Chelsea would play Spurs a few days later in the League Cup final. Perhaps still suffering from that Europa League hangover, Spurs crashed 2–0 at Wembley, allowing John Terry to lift the cup. Mo was on target again just a few days later – scoring another important goal for his new club in the 1–0 Serie A victory at Milan giants Internazionale. He fired home ten minutes after the interval and the result meant Fiorentina had jumped into the Europa League spots in the league. Both sides had progressed in the Europa League and Inter had also won their last three league matches.

Many footie fans in the UK watch the Italian league on satellite or Channel 4 and they were in no doubt that Salah would have shone had he stayed at the Bridge. One fan commented, 'Mou underestimated Salah, never give him the chance to prove himself. Never trusted him but I wonder why he trusts Willian (average player) or Oscar (shaky player) and not Salah. If Salah had joined Liverpool he would have been a great success. But Chelsea bought him just to prevent him from going to Liverpool.' And another claimed, 'Should have joined Liverpool. He would have been perfect for our fast pacy attacking style of football.'

An even more impressive feat lay around the corner. For

on 5 March, Salah grabbed a brace in the 2–1 Coppa Italia triumph at mighty Juventus. He couldn't have endeared himself more to the fans in Florence – Mo Salah was now a hero in his adopted city, officially. There was more to come. Further goals against Sampdoria, Empoli and Parma helped Fiorentina finish fourth in Serie A, above Napoli and both Milan sides.

In between those strikes and the glory climax to the campaign there had been one big disappointment, when Salah and his teammates crashed 3–0 at home to Juve in the return leg of the Coppa Italia. The club had big hopes of progressing after the first leg but reality hit home hard when the giants came to town. The win sent Italian champions Juve through to the final, much to Salah's dismay. He had dreamed of ending his first season in Italy in a domestic final, but it was not to be. Juve were now on course to complete the treble. They had a fourteen-point lead at the top of Serie A and were in the Champions League quarter-finals. And, in a sign of the squad money can buy, they beat Fiorentina soundly without the injured Carlos Tevez, Andrea Pirlo, Paul Pogba and Stephan Lichtsteiner.

Salah had shone in the first leg but struggled to get going on this occasion. Every time he had the ball he was surrounded by two or three defenders, with even strongman Giorgio Chiellini coming out of his centre-back role on to the left wing to choke Mo's progress. Mo was a speed king, but speed can only get you so far when two or three men are bearing down upon you.

The final goal of Salah's Florence odyssey arrived when Parma came to town on Monday 18 May 2015. It also came from his right foot as he struck the ball into the bottom right-hand corner of the net from six yards out. It was his ninth goal for the club in twenty-six matches in all competitions and helped them achieve that Europa League spot. His final match came days later but he only lasted twenty-seven minutes after complaining that he felt sick. As he walked off the pitch, the Fiorentina fans rose to applaud him, and he received what locals described as 'a rousing ovation'. The excellent Fiorentina fans' website, *violanation.com*, had this take on the day's events, stating: 'The atmosphere afterwards was something to behold, with the Viola supporters – who had packed the stadium for a nearly meaningless end of season finale – showering the team and the players' families with affection. Whatever happens going forward, this was a wonderful moment after a long and emotional season, one richly deserved by this group and coach after 3 consecutive 4th place finishes.'

Those fans probably wouldn't have awarded Salah such a pleasing reception if they had known that he planned to ditch them and the club – and move instead to their bitter rivals, Roma. In what was a potential personal legal nightmare, he refused to return to Florence on loan and insisted on changing to Rome. The problem was that he, Chelsea and Fiorentina had jointly agreed the loan would last eighteen months, not the six he had just completed.

So you could understand the Florentines' anger and dismay that the player seemed to want to double-cross them. It isn't being legally contentious for us to suggest that Salah had his head turned by the interest from the giants of Italian football after his sensational spell in Florence. It wasn't just Roma – the Milan clubs and even Juventus were linked with him. But it later emerged he did have the final say on whether an extension – which would take the loan to the initial eighteen-month deal – should be agreed. However, Fiorentina at the time did not simply sit back and accept the situation when he told them he was not returning.

Things got nasty when Fiorentina said they were ready to take legal action to solve the dispute to 'protect the club's rights'. 'Through his representative, the player has rejected our improved contract offer and expressed his desire to join another club,' the club's statement read. 'He has also informed us that he does not intend to respond to our request for him to report back for pre-season training. As a result of the above, we have placed the matter in the hands of our lawyers so that they may assess all possible courses of action in order to protect the club's rights.'

Salah's agent, Ramy Abbas, then released a statement of his own, claiming the moral high ground, stating: 'We referred to the document signed by all parties in January, which is clear, crystal clear, and it's regrettable that Fiorentina are now talking about legal proceedings. It's very sad to see a great club like Fiorentina make such pathetic attempts to renege on their agreements, and their written contractual obligations. Salah would like to play for a club with different moral and professional values.'

Fiorentina now approached FIFA over the affair, alleging breach of contract. Salah argued his consent was needed before an extension to the Fiorentina loan could be agreed – and FIFA backed him, dismissing the claim. There was even a suggestion that Chelsea were involved in breaking the deal but there was no truth in this, either. Indeed, even when the matter ended up before the Court of Arbitration for Sport (CAS) in June 2017, both Salah and Chelsea FC were cleared of any wrongdoing. The Court's verdict read: 'CAS has dismissed the appeal and confirmed the decision issued by the FIFA dispute resolution chamber on May 26, 2016 (FIFA DRC) in which Fiorentina's claim for compensation of €32 million was rejected. The CAS panel found that the player did not breach the employment agreement by returning to Chelsea FC after June 30, 2015 and that Chelsea FC did not induce the player to terminate the employment agreement without just cause.' Accordingly, it dismissed the appeal and confirmed the FIFA DRC decision.

The matter had finally been put to bed, with both Salah and Chelsea exonerated. Given the verdicts of FIFA and CAS, Mo had been perfectly within his rights to leave Florence – and now he would end up at Roma, where his career would hit new heights. First up he had to return to Chelsea, who held his registration, and agree with the London club his next move. Chelsea rubber-stamped a new loan deal with the Italian club, which included a mandatory option to buy, and he was on his travels again.

Should Mourinho have stepped in then to keep him at the Bridge? Well, he had just won the league with Chelsea and probably thought he had no need of Salah's talents at that stage. After all, his players were champions – and so was he. No one could have guessed that within six months Mourinho would be gone from Chelsea, sacked a second time, and the club would be in turmoil, struggling mid-table. They certainly could have done with Mo Salah then, but at that stage it was too late, he was settled in Rome – and the Italians had a right to buy on him. What a shambles the English champions were responsible for.

Over in Rome, it did not take long for Salah to make his mark. He joined the club on a season-long loan for a 5-million-euros fee (roughly £4.3m at the time). The figure quoted to make the deal permanent was 15 million euros (£13 million). Mo explained exactly why he had chosen to join Roma, saying, 'It's very simple. I want to win with this team, with a club that is so popular in my home country and in this great city with which it's impossible not to fall in love.'

Roma also expressed their delight on their website, saying the twenty-three-year-old was 'the best Egyptian player in the world right now'. And Mo made his new fans happy by saying he believed the team could win the Scudetto from Juventus. He said, 'I think everybody here has ambition and everybody wants to win the title. That would be good for us and very good for the fans. Everybody will do their best to make the fans happy.'

Salah was already well known in Italy after his spell at Fiorentina and the general feeling was that Roma had got themselves a bargain and a player who could fire them to great heights. In his first season at the Stadio Olimpico Mo made forty-two appearances and grabbed a credible fifteen goals to become the club's top scorer on both the league and all other competitions. Of those, fourteen goals came in thirty-four games in Serie A – which was what Roma had brought him to the club for. He had been signed to make them more competitive in the league – and achieved that aim. At the end of that loan season, Roma finished third in the table, which would qualify them for the play-off round of the Champions League. So that was mission accomplished.

Mo would wear his favoured Number 11 shirt at the club and made his debut in the season opener at Verona, which would bring a 1–1 draw. He explained why he had chosen the Number 11, pointing out, 'I didn't want to have a crazy number. We don't have a lot of numbers and I didn't want to go with my Egypt number because Number 10 isn't available. I always liked the Number 11. It was available and I did not hesitate to take it.'

Salah settled in quickly and it helped that he had fellow former Premier League stars with him. Arsenal keeper Wojciech Szczęny, Man City striker Edin Džeko and another ex-Arsenal ace Gervinho all featured in the Verona match. Boško Janković opened the scoring in the sixty-first minute but Alessandro Florenzi levelled to earn the point for Roma five minutes later. 'Salah and Džeko need time to settle into the side but they've both done very well today,' coach Rudi Garcia said after the match.

It was a promising start and the potential for a partnership between Džeko and Salah was mouth-watering for the Roma fans. Mo lasted sixty-six minutes on his debut while Džeko played the full ninety. The duo started again in the next fixture, which was a real cracker: champions Juventus at home. Džeko would grab the winner in a fiery contest that saw Juve's Rubinho and Evra shown red cards. Defending champions Juve had lost their opening two Serie A games for the first time ever. The win would spark joyous scenes in the Italian capital and the belief that Roma, with Salah and Džeko, could indeed mount a serious title challenge.

One interesting sidebar to the Juventus match was that Juan Cuadrado had come on as a substitute for Juve with fifteen minutes to go. Interesting, of course, in that he had been the winger Mourinho had so desperately wanted – and signed – in the deal that took Salah to Fiorentina on loan. Now both Salah and Cuadrado were out on loan in Italy from Chelsea. As Sir Alex Ferguson once said, 'Football, eh? Bloody hell!'

Mo netted for the first time for Roma towards the end of September in 2015. Ironically, it was against the same team he had opened his account with for Fiorentina – Sassuolo. The goal came in the Stadio Olimpico and earned his team a point. The other goalscorer for the hosts was the legendary Francesco Totti. Salah was certainly in good company as his Italian odyssey continued and was able to learn a thing or two about attacking play from the Italian master.

Like many of his goals, Mo's first for Roma was a left shot from just outside the box that nestled in the bottom left-hand corner of the net. Mo then netted in his next two games, a 2–1 defeat at Sampdoria and a 5–1 home win over Carpi. It seemed the boy was on fire and at the end of October he made a real statement of intent – and of where his loyalties now lay – as he returned to the Artemi Franchi Stadium, home of Fiorentina.

It would not be the warmest of welcomes for the Egyptian King. When he had played for the Florence club, he had become their idol and they had regularly sung, *Siam venuti fin qua per veder segnare Salah* ('We came here to see

Salah score'). Now he was greeted with some boos and some abuse by fans who believed he had betrayed them not only by leaving, but joining one of their biggest rivals. Mo had not been surprised by the welcome; he had told his manager he knew what to expect and he was OK with it. He was a man who understood human emotions and did not hold a grudge against the fans who had once praised him but now came to jeer him. He understood why they acted like that and later said he still loved them and respected them for the way they had treated him when he was their player.

His generous show of understanding did not extend to events on the pitch. And that grated even more with the hosts, who were yet to drop a point or even concede a goal in their four Serie A games under Paulo Sousa before Mo returned. *The Guardian* summed up best how he wrecked that impressive sequence run and broke his former fans' hearts (again), reporting: 'Of course, it would have to be Salah who put an end to that run. There were not yet six minutes on the clock when he exchanged a one-two with Miralem Pjanić on the right edge of the penalty area before swinging a beautiful shot between two defenders and into the far corner of the net. His celebration was muted, Salah raising his hands to the sky and saying a prayer as he does after every goal but amending his pointed fingers quickly to apologetic open palms.'

Now the jeers became rock-concert loud but Mo stayed cool and calm and again did not celebrate wildly when Gervinho sped in to double the Roma lead.

But maybe the antagonism did get to him as the clock ticked down to the ninety minutes. In an unusual, and totally out-of-character, act he was sent off on eighty-seven minutes. He had already received a yellow card following a tussle with Facundo Roncaglia, and was then immediately shown a second after showing dissent with a gesture towards the referee. Khouma Babacar scored a consolation goal in the fourth minute of stoppage time. The one comfort was the result: it meant Roma took Fiorentina's place at the top of Serie A with twenty points, two clear of nearest challengers Napoli. Juventus were twelfth, eight points behind Salah and Co. But Salah's place at the top would not last. From that lowly twelfth spot, Juventus went on a run of twenty-five matches in which they took seventy-three points out of a possible seventy-five, and secured the title.

At least that season Mo had enjoyed another stab at Champions League glory. He had loved playing in the tournament while at Basel and upon joining Roma had admitted the fact that knowing the club would be playing in the Champions League had been a major part of the reason he had joined. 'This is one of the reasons I chose Roma,' he explained. 'I like to play in the Champions League.'

And it was a fairly successful campaign. The club managed to get out of Group E – no mean achievement as it contained Barcelona and Bayer Leverkusen, plus Belarusian underdogs BATE Borisov. Roma drew with Barca at home, drew in Leverkusen and beat the Germans at home. Mo scored in the win over Leverkusen and the only low point was a 6–1 thrashing in Barcelona. His Champions League dream ended in the Round of 16 when they drew Real Madrid, the Spaniards won 2–0 in each leg for a 4–0 aggregate.

His final goal for the club that season came in a 3–1 win in Milan. That was a happy conclusion to the campaign. He was voted Man of the Match after he destroyed the hosts with his rampaging runs down the right. Afterwards he said, 'I'm delighted at the Giallorossi. I feel at ease with all of my teammates and I love the city.'

More accolades followed. Salah won Roma's Player of the Month in May 2016 and followed it up with their Player of the Season gong. But the fact was that the club had dropped a place, from second to third, in the table from the previous campaign. Mo assessed the season on a personal and club level in this way: 'I think it was good but we did not win any titles and this is a problem.' And despite his thrilling debut campaign he was not going to go easy on himself: he said he still had work to do on his game, adding, 'I want to improve my shooting from outside the box, use my right foot more, use my head more and play with more speed.'

Roma's official website described Mo's May Player of the Month award: 'Roma's leading scorer for the 2015–2016 season capped off an impressive first campaign with the Giallorossi with three goals in the team's final four matches. His strikes against Genoa, AC Milan and Al Ahly were enough to earn him 81% of the fan vote, coming in ahead of Francesco Totti, Radja Nainggolan and Stephan El Shaarawy.' He beat Totti by 8 per cent in the vote, which showed just how far he had come at the club.

To then go on and win the Player of the Season in his first campaign in the Eternal City was a still more outstanding achievement – especially when you consider the candidates he was up against for the honour. Over 210,000 votes were cast and attacking players dominated the shortlist – hardly surprising given that the team had finished the season as the top goalscorers in Serie A, with a total of eighty-three. Miralem Pjanić, who had finished second to Mo in the goals chart with ten, Alessandro Florenzi, who was joint fourth top scorer with seven, and Radja Nainggolan, who netted six, were also on the list.

When the Player of the Season results were revealed, Mo had won, Radja was runner-up, Francesco third and Miralem fourth. The club praised all four players but had a special tribute for Salah, as follows:

> Revealed as the fans' signing of the season earlier in the week, a fine first campaign in the Italian capital for Mohamed Salah is capped off by the forward being named the club's Player of the Year. The supporters evidently took to the Egypt international during 2015–16, as he finished as the club's top goalscorer with 15 goals in all competitions (14 in Serie A). A further six assists made the 24-year-old the club's most devastating attacking outlet, in a squad that was hardly lacking in that regard.
>
> With pace, power and an eye for goal, Salah's presence caused no end of problems for opposition defenders throughout the campaign, becoming a player that could not be left unguarded under any circumstances. Across the campaign he showcased his ability to be just as devastating from long range (witness his first ever goal for the club, a volley against

Sassuolo) as in one-on-one situations (like his last goal of the season, against Milan), and almost all positions in between. Despite changing managers midway through the season, Salah continued to thrive – and fans will be excited to see what he can continue to achieve next season under Luciano Spalletti, as the Italian makes him a cornerstone of his fluid attacking strategy.

That change of manager halfway through the campaign had certainly paid dividends as Roma consolidated their position as one of Italy's top clubs. And Mo enjoyed working with the excitable and enthusiastic Spalletti. As a reward for his consistency and goals, Roma took up the option on the loan deal with Mo to make it a permanent one. They paid Chelsea the fee of 15 million euros (£13 million) that had been agreed twelve months previously.

Roma had got a bargain and they knew it: Chelsea had dropped an almighty clanger, selling a player who would soon be termed world-class for relative peanuts. 'Mohamed Salah has completed a permanent transfer to Italian club Roma,' Chelsea confirmed in a statement. 'The Egyptian winger spent last season on loan at the Serie A side and impressed as they finished third. Salah signed for Chelsea from Basel in January 2014 and made his debut in a home game against Newcastle. His first goal for the Blues came in our memorable 6–0 win over Arsenal when he completed the scoring, racing on to a Nemanja Matić pass and finishing well. After spending the second part of the 2014/15 campaign on loan at Fiorentina, he remained in Italy with Roma the following year. Chelsea Football Club thanks Mohamed for his service and wishes him well for the future.'

Salah's talents had been lost to England because of Chelsea's folly – and it would be a year before we would see them again up close at Liverpool. And so to Salah's final season in Rome, and his final season as a wanderer, before he would find a home for good at Anfield.

The 2016–17 campaign was a mixed bag affair for Mo. He helped the club regain that second place spot in Serie A and contributed with a commendable fifteen goals in thirty-one league appearances. It was even more commendable when you factor in that he was also spending more time assisting Džeko to double that number of goals. That season it would be Džeko who led the Roma goals chart, with twenty-nine in the league and thirty-nine overall in all competitions. It was also Totti's final season at the club he had graced all his professional footballing life. So while hardly taking a backseat, Salah was not the main man in the limelight in his second season at the club.

The season got off to a disappointing start when Roma exited the Champions League in the playoff round. Roma had been favourites after securing a 1–1 draw in Portugal but crashed 3–0 away when Daniele De Rossi and Emerson Palmieri were both sent off with the game only fifty minutes old. Porto, who had been leading 1–0, then scored twice to kill off Roma hopes. This was a setback for Salah, who had admitted one of the reasons for his joining the club had been to play in the Champions League. He had played in both legs of the tie and trooped off disconsolately at the end of the match in Rome.

RENAISSANCE MAN

Mo grabbed his first goal of the season in the 4–0 home win over Udinese but his best performance up to Christmas came when he hit a hat-trick in the 3–0 defeat of Bologna at the Olimpico. The tributes flooded in and the club's website picked out a few reviews from the Italian media to highlight what Salah had achieved in arguably his finest moment at the club. Below are some of the accounts from various newspapers:

Corriere dello Sport:
A helping hand from Adam Masina on the opener, wrong-footing the opposition keeper. He did it all himself on the second, however, before making history with his third, tapping in with his right foot! That's now eight league goals (plus five assists).

La Gazzetta dello Sport:
He struck his first hat-trick in Roma colours, before failing to add a fourth through a combination of unselfishness and bad luck. He heads to the African Cup of Nations in January and his absence will be keenly felt.

Il Messaggero:
At the heart of everything good, he set the tempo on the counter. He laid on a couple of juicy potential assists and scored three himself (taking his tally to eight in the league). The AFCON is still some way off, thankfully for Roma. At times it's like he's got an engine beneath his feet. A souped-up one at that.

Il resto del Carlino:

He's a player that makes your eyes light up. The wide forward hit a treble and racked up kilometres at the pace of a 100m sprinter. A real thorn in the side of the Rossoblu defence.

Leggo:

They even themselves up in the end. He struck the woodwork three times against Bologna last season. Yesterday, meanwhile, he scored three (the first with a bit of help from Masina) for his first hat-trick in Italy. The Egyptian might even have added a fourth or set up one of his teammates there were that many chances.

Il Tempo:

Aided by Masina's crucial deflection, he struck the opener on a night where he scored the first hat-trick of his career. The Egyptian was always in the right place at the right time.

Tuttosport:

He broke the deadlock with a far from unstoppable finish, before taking a while to wrap up the points but he was always on hand and scored his first hat-trick.

It had been interesting to note how the press pack also picked up on how Roma would miss Salah while on African Nations Cup duty. He was away from the start of January until 5 February, the day he played for Egypt in the final of that tournament (which they lost 2–1 to Cameroon). His return saw him hit another ten goals for the club and help them to that runners-up spot in the league. Disappointment came in the Europa League and the Coppa Italia: Salah and his teammates would lose in the Round of 16 to Lyon in the former and Lazio in the semi-final in the latter.

But it had been a successful period spent in the Italian capital and would climax as Mo grabbed his final two goals for the club in a brilliant 5–3 win at Chievo on the penultimate weekend of the Serie A season. It was *arrivederci* – but not goodbye. Mo was finally on his way to Liverpool, but would return to see his former teammates and fans soon enough. His work in Italy was done.

CHAPTER FOUR

NEW KID ON
THE KOP

Mo arrived on Merseyside in a deal concluded on Thursday 22 June 2017. The fee was £36.9 million but I was told that this could rise by a further £7 million to £43.9 million, due to conditional clauses relating to add-ons dependent upon games played and success. Some sources claim the initial and overall figures were less, but that is not my information. Liverpool had to meet Roma's demands for the player. The Romans would not budge when £31 million was offered – they wanted close to the £37 million achieved, plus the anticipation of the extra £7 million should he reach the heights they fully believed he was capable of. They had nurtured Salah and knew just how good he was and could be – hence their demands for top dollar.

Salah would be rewarded with his move from Rome to Liverpool with a much-improved contract, said to be worth £90,000 a week (which would be doubled a year later).

I'll be honest. Many Fleet Street hacks shook their heads in surprise at how much it had cost to bring the player back to England. And few anticipated that the fee would rise to that massive £43.9 million. OK, Salah had done well in Rome but most pundits – and indeed fans of Liverpool and generally those closely involved in the game – believed he wouldn't have a major impact. How wrong they were. And I must admit that I was guilty of being in agreement with them too.

The general feeling on that Thursday in June was that Salah could bring speed with his runs down the wing; however, none of us had the vision to see him as a player who could also hold his own when he slalomed into the centre of the attacking third. Nor did we realise that he had the low centre of gravity, allied with physical strength and an incredible knack for scoring goals from the wing and in the centre-forward role, that would take him to the top of the scoring charts in the Premier League. Yes, even above Harry Kane, the man who had appeared to have that niche sewn up for years to come.

So there was a mooted nodding of heads on that memorable day. All agreed that Klopp had bought a man who could do a job down the right wing, but no one predicted he would be the best player in England, and arguably Europe, in his first season back in the Prem. Even Klopp would admit his surprise at the level of impact Salah had demonstrated when the season concluded the following May.

He said how 'excited' he was at signing him when Salah was unveiled, and that he believed the player would add pace to an attack that was already full of it, with Mané and Firmino. And he had no qualms about the size of the fee, which was a new record for Liverpool, eclipsing the £35 million Kenny Dalglish paid to Newcastle for Andy Carroll in the January transfer window of 2011. Klopp added that as Salah was only twenty-five, Liverpool were buying him in his peak years and that he would only get better as the season progressed. He was certainly spot on with that observation.

Ironically, given that Mo would take that most expensive mantle from Carroll, it was later claimed that he almost joined Newcastle when he was eighteen. The *Newcastle Chronicle* reported that:

> The Egyptian – who was recently named PFA Player of the Season – could have been playing in the black-and-white stripes of the Magpies. Back in 2011 the club were in negotiations to sign the winger, initially on loan, with the player himself even quoted as describing it as a 'dream move'. At the time an 18-year-old Salah was still in his home country playing for El Mokawloon, but even at such a young age he'd already made his national team debut. Somebody from the Magpies scouting team had spotted his potential and Alan Pardew was ready to swoop.

Mo told the Egyptian newspaper *Al-Ahram*: 'Newcastle will soon make an official offer to sign me for one season. I don't think my team officials will refuse to let me play in the English Premier League. It's a dream for any player to play in one of the strongest league competitions in the world.'

It is believed the deal did not go through because the Toon refused to pay a loan fee of around £500,000 to secure the player. If that is the case, it is one of the biggest ever clangers dropped in English football, given that Mo is probably now worth £200 million. Two years later Salah was to sign for Chelsea and they have never lived down selling the player to Roma – and that was for £16 million, which gave the Blues a £5-million profit on their investment. No doubt Mike Ashley would have had his helicopter ready to fly Mo in if he had had any notion of the sort of profit he could have made on the boy – or the effect he could have had on the team.

Klopp said that Mo would wear the Number 11 shirt at Liverpool and added that:

Mohamed has the perfect mix of experience and potential – this is a really exciting signing for us. He knows the Premier League, he has pedigree in the Champions League and he is one of the most important players for his country.

His record in Italy has been outstanding and he possesses qualities that will enhance our team and squad. His pace is incredible, he gives us more attacking threat and we are already strong in this area. Most important, though, for us, is that he is hungry, willing and eager to be even better and improve further. He believes in what we are trying to do here at Liverpool and is extremely keen to be part of it.

He is very excited about performing for our wonderful supporters. He is an ambitious player who wants to win and win at the highest level and he knows he can fulfil those ambitions with Liverpool.

Salah said he was similarly excited and that he was looking forward to playing his part in the Klopp revolution. He had learned much from his time in Italy and was confident he would show that his time at Chelsea was merely a blip on his record. He believed he had not been given a fair crack of the whip by Mourinho while in West London, but acknowledged that he was raw and young back then. It had also been difficult to demand regular starts, given that the Blues had the likes of Hazard and Willian vying for extended runs down the wing.

This time Mo would show Liverpool, and the country, that he was a more rounded player; that Chelsea could still have had a world-class star on their books if they had shown more patience with his development.

Upon his arrival, he told *Liverpoolfc.com*: 'I'm very excited to be here. I'm very happy. I will give 100 per cent and give everything for the club. I really want to win something for this club. We have a great team and very good players. I was watching the games last year and everyone was giving 100 per cent to win something. Everyone can see the coach gives everything. I hope to see that together we can give everything to win something for the club, for the supporters and for us.'

Those opening words were manna from heaven to his new manager. Klopp's basic working mantra is that you must give everything – leave 'nothing in the tank' – if you want to be the best. Half measures would get you nowhere. Success wasn't a given; it was the result of hard graft and total commitment. God-given talent was certainly a key element, but natural-born ability without sweat was not enough. And here was his new boy backing up that belief several times in his first public utterances. Phrases such as '100 per cent' and 'giving everything for the cause' were sweet music to Klopp's ears.

He knew for sure now that the boy was definitely on the same wavelength as he was, that he wanted success but at the same time was aware that it was very much a team game and that he had a role within that framework if he worked hard.

Mo also explained how he thought his game had come on since he had left Chelsea, and how the Italian sojourn had helped him develop from that raw youngster at Chelsea into a player with experience and whose talent had blossomed. He put it like this: 'Everything has improved. Even my personality was different, I was a kid – I was twenty or twenty-one at Chelsea. Now I'm four years older, everything is different. I have lots of experience in three clubs: I was at Chelsea, then Fiorentina and then Roma. I have good experience.'

With the benefit of hindsight, we doubters should have realised that Salah could surprise us with his goals' tally. He had, after all, hit twenty-nine in sixty-five appearances for Roma, a return of almost one every two games. If he were to repeat that total in the Premier League he would be heading towards twenty goals for the coming campaign. But no one expected him to crash beyond that level with such elegant ease and yet with such crushing resolve. This was the dichotomy that fuelled the genius of the man. He moved with agility and speed, yet his end product was the opposite: goals that gave the keeper no chance, such was their power. As Muhammad Ali might have put it, 'Salah floats like a butterfly, but stings like a bee.'

Of course, given his exploits, or lack of them, at Chelsea most Liverpool fans were unsure of the calibre of the player the club was splashing out so much money on. Social media and the websites were full of comments on the signing, many sounding a tad perplexed, others giving it a total thumbs-up. One Koppite said: 'Good signing, I am looking forward to seeing him in action.' But another added: 'We are coming to the era where if you don't spend at least a hundred million then forget the title you have little chance of getting in to the top four. This signing should be just the start, I am expecting at least a couple of £30-plus million players to come in to the squad. Hopefully one that is double that price. That would really be a statement of intent.' And another chipped in: 'Salah is an excellent signing and I wouldn't fancy coming up against Liverpool with him and Mané on the wings.'

One Liverpool fan believed Klopp had brought Salah in merely to cover for Mané, when the latter headed off to the African Nations Cup in the winter. How far off-track that assessment would turn out to be: Salah would become the main man, hardly an adjunct to Mané. Plus, of course, as an Egyptian, Mo himself could be called up to play in the ANC which would, however, become a summer tournament from 2019.

Liverpool fan Chris would come closer than most to seeing what the future would bring with Salah in tow, saying: 'I think it's a great signing by Liverpool and in this day and age for a very good price. I love a fast, pacey winger and he is just that. But with a phenomenal goal return too. And only twenty-five. A front five of Coutinho, Mané, Lallana and Firmino along with this addition is a great front five. Bettered only by city [Manchester] probably in the league. There's goals, pace and passing and they will interchange so easily.'

That summed up the deal, really. A fee that would prove a real bargain come the end of the season as Salah ran riot with goals galore, and an addition who, along with the pace of his fellow strikers, would make Liverpool almost impossible to defend against. The trio of Salah, Mané and Firmino would prove to be arguably the best in Europe, certainly giving Man City a run for their money. Barcelona remained top-class with Messi in tow, but Suárez was not as effective that season and their new boy, Ousmane Dembélé, did not deliver.

Football fans generally appeared bemused by the deal. Chelsea fans, in particular, were keen to have their voices heard. Inevitably, they were mostly unimpressed, judging Salah from his difficult spell at their club, rather than as the impressive forward he had become at Fiorentina and Roma. This in fact was the dominant view across the wider footballing spectrum. One fan commented: 'Let's not get carried away here. It was in the Italian League. Week in/week out there seems to be teams conceding five goals a game. A few crunching tackles in the first few weeks shall determine if he's worth his while. Just remember when Cuadrado came from Fiorentina to play for Chelsea.' Another added: 'Thirty odd million for an average player, money has destroyed football. Liverpool will have to sell more tickets to tourists and go on even more money-making tours to Australia and Asia to keep paying these obscene prices.'

In the event, of course, the fee would prove entirely reasonable, a bargain even. It would be at the middle end of the scale, since prices for top-class stars edged higher and higher that summer of 2017, culminating in that remarkable world-record fee of £200 million for Brazilian genius Neymar. His move from Barcelona to Paris St Germain would put the deals for the likes of Salah into a new perspective. The move smashed the previous transfer record that had seen Paul Pogba move from Juventus to Man United for £89 million. It also brought a fresh, exaggerated recalculation of fees, even if these were only temporarily the norm, such as Kyle Walker's £50-million move to Man City – costing almost £11 million more than Salah, and for a full-back at that. Manchester United manager José Mourinho summed up the warped nature of the market, but served up with a slice of his usual controversy, saying: 'Expensive are the ones who get into a certain level without a certain quality. For £200m, I don't think Neymar is expensive. I think he's expensive in the fact that now you are going to have more players at £100m, you are going have more players at £80m and more players at £60m. And I think that's the problem. So I think the problem is not Neymar, I think the problem is the consequences of Neymar.'

Klopp felt the fee reflected an abuse of the transfer system, pointing out: 'I thought Fair Play was made so that situations like that can't happen. That's more of a suggestion than a real rule.'

And Arsenal manager Arsène Wenger hit out at the Neymar transfer cash as 'irrational' – and you could see his point, given that Mo Salah had cost a fifth of that money. Wenger railed on that it represented everything bad about the way that football was heading in the twenty-first century, adding that:

For me it is the consequence of the ownerships that has changed completely the whole landscape of football in the last fifteen years. Once a country owns a club everything is possible. It becomes very difficult to respect Financial Fair Play because you have different interest from a country to have such a big player to represent that country. I always did plead for football living within its own resources. We are not in a period anymore where you think 'I invest that, I will get that back'. We are beyond that.

The fee today involves passion, pride, public interest and you cannot rationalise that anymore. On the other hand inflation is increasing – we were at £100 million last year and only one year later we are at the £200-million line. If you think Trevor Francis was the first guy for £1 million in 1979 and it looked unreasonable, it shows you how far football has come, beyond calculation and rationality. We still live with rationality and we are not the only ones – 99 per cent of clubs do that – but of course we cannot compete with that.

Ironically, ten months on from Neymar's transfer, it would be widely reported that Real Madrid were also willing to pay £200 million for a striker...Mo Salah! Not that Liverpool would entertain such a deal. No, they had sold Philippe Coutinho to Barcelona for £146 million and had no plans to cash in on Salah as well. The club did not need the money and Klopp was planning to build a dynasty, not keep dismantling it every time a Spanish club came in for his best player. Indeed, the Coutinho transfer was only sanctioned because of the determination of the player to join the Catalans.

He was perfectly happy to remain on Merseyside and be part of the Klopp project. Liverpool were ready to double his money and he knew he could achieve greatness if he stayed. The Kop adored him, he was their new idol, and he could fulfil his ambitions without moving. Liverpool were on the brink of an era of massive success with Klopp, and Salah was an integral cog in the machine.

One fan who clearly did not support Liverpool suggested that the fact Salah 'only' cost £36.9 million showed that both he and the club were 'not in the big league'. The fan crowed: 'Imagine Real Madrid or Bayern Munich going through their entire history and ending up today with Salah as their all-time record buy. And with Andy Carroll as their second most expensive player ever. Hilarious! That's how serious Liverpool is about winning trophies. As serious as Salah!'

That opinion was mischievous and plain daft, as events would prove as the season progressed. Real Madrid would have loved to have signed Salah as part of their inevitable rebuilding plans. Their team was ageing and the management knew the likes of Modrić and even Ronaldo would need replacing sooner rather than later. Salah would bring pace and relative youth and would definitely improve Real Madrid, but he would not be leaving any time soon.

Salah's 'failure' at Chelsea seemed to have put some fans off and played a part in the partially downbeat analysis of his arrival on Merseyside. But you didn't need to be a genius to see that his Chelsea struggle followed a certain pattern – yes, this was what we could call the 'Mourinho effect'. The Portuguese manager preferred to buy big-name, big-money, established world stage stars, and investing in potential rather than ready-made, off-the-shelf players requires patience. So Mo's career at Chelsea had gone the way of others – namely the brilliant Kevin De Bruyne, Man City's midfield genius, and his Belgian teammate, Romelu Lukaku. The latter would see Mourinho rectifying the mistake of flogging him to Everton while he was Chelsea boss. It would cost him £75 million to bring Lukaku to Man United at the same time as Salah was signing for Liverpool.

Mourinho would also claim that he was blameless in the Salah sale, telling ESPN that the club sold the player over his head. He said:

People say that I was the one that sold Salah and it is the opposite. I bought Salah. When they say that I was the one that sold him it is a lie. Chelsea decided to sell him, OK? I was the one that told Chelsea to buy Salah. It was with me in charge that Salah came to Chelsea. But he came as a young kid, physically he was not ready, mentally he was not ready, socially and culturally he was lost and everything was tough for him.

We decided to put him on loan and he asked for that as well. He wanted to play more minutes, to mature, he wanted to go and we sent him on loan to Fiorentina, and at Fiorentina he started to mature. I agreed to send him on loan, I thought it was necessary, I thought that Chelsea had wingers...Some of them are still there like Willian, Hazard and all those players already in a different level.

So the decision to send him on loan was a decision we made collectively, but after that, the decision to sell him and to use that money to buy another player wasn't mine. But even if it was, in football we make mistakes a lot of times, so many times some players develop in ways we were not expecting, some others don't reach another level like we thought they would, so I don't even think this is a mistake, it is just part of the job.

But effectively I did buy Salah, I didn't sell Salah, but it doesn't matter. What matters is that he is a fantastic player, and I am really happy for everything that is happening for him and especially because he scores against everyone and he didn't score against us in two games. He is a great player that has reached the peak of maturity, he has already lived several other experiences and now has fitted perfectly into the style of play of the team, of the coach and of the club as well. So it doesn't surprise me that much.

It was seen as classic Mourinho by many pundits. However, the power of his words emphasises just how good Salah had become in that first season at Anfield. The player was world-class and Mourinho knew it. As yet another football fan pointed out on the day of the Salah signing, 'I'm not a Liverpool supporter but Mané on one wing and Salah on the other adds frightening pace, goals and assists. They still need a couple of defenders and an out-and-out-striker but this is looking good for the Scousers.'

Little did that fan, or come to that most fans generally, know that Mo would become the striker as well as the winger that Liverpool needed to take them to the next level. He was a real two-in-one buy for half the price of Gareth Bale and Luis Suárez.

Although Mo's deal was all sorted by 22 June, he would not officially join Liverpool until 1 July, the day the transfer window officially opened. Not only was he the club's record transfer buy, he was also the first Egyptian to play for Liverpool FC. It was then revealed that he would take Firmino's Number 11 shirt after the Brazilian opted to take Number 9.

Then it was off to training at Melwood under the watchful eye of Klopp, as he and the squad were put through their paces. Always with a smile on his face, Mo quickly fitted into the group and became an instant favourite precisely because of his happy demeanour and his obvious silky skills and talent. The squad were preparing for a busy pre-season that included not only trips to Hong Kong and Germany but also local matches against Tranmere and Wigan. Mo was looking forward to them all. Whether he was picked for the games pitting them against their local rivals, or the more glamorous-looking matches abroad mattered little to him. He just wanted to make his debut for Liverpool FC and then play in as many matches as he could. He hadn't come to Anfield to sit on the sidelines: he was here to make an impact, to show that not only did he justify his fee but that he excelled it. That he was one of the best players in the world. And he would soon get the chance to prove just that.

CHAPTER FIVE

ON A WING AND A DARE

He would go on to become the complete striker during his first season at Liverpool, but would begin as a traditional wing man in his debut. For a player who would be touted as a £200-million target for Real Madrid by May 2018, Mo Salah would begin his Liverpool journey in much more humble surroundings, namely the DW Stadium, home of Wigan Athletic. That came on 14 July 2017, and the fans who made the short journey to Wigan were rewarded with his first goal for the club, on his debut. OK, it was only a pre-season friendly, but it was also a taster of things to come. Mo was on hand to grab the equaliser in a 1–1 draw, nipping in to prod the ball home after Firmino set him up. He declared himself happy with the outcome and his own performance and promised the fans that there was much more to come from both himself and the team.

Mo Salah had shown that he was willing to work hard for his teammates and that he embraced the team spirit with his regular running back to reclaim the ball, putting in tackles and making chances for the likes of Firmino. This was no player out for solo glory; despite his amazing goal figures at the end of the season there was not one Liverpool player who would privately criticise him as being selfish. They all appreciated the job he did for the team and how he was willing to sacrifice himself for their sake, unlike, for instance, some of the other great names of football. Indeed, this altruistic style of play made those goal figures all the more remarkable.

Dejan Lovren had no doubts that Salah was going to be a terrific addition to the team. After the Wigan win, he said,'Sadio Mané was injured and we missed him. But we saw what Salah can give us and we will see more of his qualities. He needs more time as he's only had six days with us and everything is completely new but I think he will be perfect in this system.'

The Croatian defender believed that Mo and fellow newcomer Solanke would add even more quality and depth to the squad. He added, 'I think they have their qualities and Jürgen knows what he needs and what the team needs to improve. I think he made a good choice. These guys work really hard on the pitch and in training so it is always good to welcome such players like these. Quality players are always welcome.'

The draw with their League One neighbours followed on from a 4–0 rout of non-League Tranmere and Mo and the boys were now looking forward to taking on Crystal Palace in Hong Kong, as part of the Premier League Asia Trophy, and then playing some games in their manager's native Germany.

Five days after the win at Wigan the team had touched down in Hong Kong and prepared for the game against Palace. Keeper Simon Mignolet summed up how important the games in the competition could be. He said, 'We'll be playing against Premier League teams and there is no better way to prepare for the Premier League than to play against teams that are featuring in it. This will give us a good base to start the new season in a good way.'

Liverpool beat Palace in a comfortable 2–0 stroll as the opposition struggled under new boss Frank de Boer. The goals came from Dominic Solanke and Divock Origi. Salah may not have got on the scoresheet but he shone as the team reached the final of the Premier League Asia trophy. *The Independent* called his performance 'electric', adding, 'Perhaps some of the Palace players were just feeling their way back to match sharpness but Mo Salah was lively on the ball and caused problems whenever he had the chance to run at defenders. In one notable passage of play, he knocked the ball past Damien Delaney and left the Irishman in his wake, as if running backwards. Salah's dribbling at speed has got to be faster than almost any other player in the world. The pace and verve and dynamism he injects into any attack is frightening and he will do some exciting things in a Liverpool shirt.' The team Klopp put out against Palace read like this: Mignolet; Alexander-Arnold, Matip, Gomez, Moreno, Henderson, Lallana, Woodburn, Salah, Firmino, Sturridge. Subs: Karius, Lovren, Klavan,

Flanagan, Milner, Grujić, Wijnaldum, Coutinho, Solanke, Kent, Origi.

On Saturday 22 July Salah won the first of what he hoped would be many trophies at Anfield as the club lifted the Premier League Asia crown by defeating Leicester City 2–1. He even scored Pool's opening goal, heading home after the Foxes had gone ahead through Islam Slimani. It was his second goal for the club in just his third game. Coutinho grabbed the winner in a well-deserved triumph. Liverpool joined Chelsea (x2), Bolton, Portsmouth, Spurs, Man City and Arsenal in winning the biennial tournament. Georginio Wijnaldum spoke for the team when he summed up the belief within the camp. He said that Mo Salah was settling in well and proving what a brilliant buy he was. Also, the team's performance in the final made him believe that Liverpool could mount a serious challenge for honours when the Premier League season finally got underway. The Dutchman said, 'We came pre-season to do good things and you've got to be happy if everything goes well.

'We didn't see much of Hong Kong because we were training and after training we went back to the hotel to rest. But we visited the city centre and saw a lot of fans. The people are happy that we are here and you can see how many fans at the stadium attended the game.'

Hong Kong had brought success but not much sightseeing. Then again, that was the Klopp way. Down time was down time and match time was serious business, with intense training schedules and a determination to win. After the successful visit to the former British colony, it was on to Germany and a welcome return to his homeland for the manager. Three matches awaited and each would represent a different test. But Klopp was determined to enjoy each. He had been looking forward to taking on his homeland rivals.

The first game at the end of July meant a date in Berlin with Hertha at the sprawling Olympic Stadium. Both clubs were marking their 125th anniversary and the match was played under the banner, 'Celebrating Football since 1892'. It was Liverpool's fourth friendly meeting with the club and the visitors ran out 3–0 winners. Salah was again on target, this time claiming the final goal after he was set up by Coutinho, coolly lifting the ball over the keeper. Klopp was full of praise for both men, commenting on their quality that, 'Players like this understand each other. It's a good thing with having players of this quality. The pass from Phil was very nice and the finish from Salah was not too bad also. We need all these different options.' One fan was perhaps a little carried away by it all – these games were, after all, only friendlies – although he did have a point about the potential of Salah and Mané as a double act, saying: 'Man Utd, City & Chelsea fans are petrified. They know Liverpool are bang in form and have an easy start. Could be 10 points ahead by Xmas. Salah & Mané are as good as Messi and Neymar. They are absolutely world-class.'

The win was another positive step for Salah as he integrated with his new teammates and it wasn't a bad way to show how the team was progressing in front of principal owner John W. Henry. The American was seen applauding wildly at the end of the game.

Next up on the Germany mini tour was an encounter

with the mighty Bayern Munich, the nation's top club side. The teams would meet at Bayern's home, the Allianz Arena, in the Audi Cup, and it was a tournament that also featured Spain's Atletico Madrid and Italy's Napoli. Klopp stressed the importance of this fixture and the one that would follow soon after, saying, 'The tournament is thirteen days before the start of the season and so it is very relevant. We will have been in training for more than a month and this gives us the chance to learn where we stand by playing against top teams.'

In another terrific team display – and another personal one from Salah – Liverpool notched up another 3–0 win over Bayern Munich in their own stadium. This was a result that had people sitting up and taking notice. It was one thing winning the pre-season games they had chalked up already, but quite another to register such an emphatic triumph over the German champions in their own arena. Mo grabbed the second goal, ten minutes before the interval after Mané had put the boys ahead. Sturridge completed the rout seven minutes from time. It seemed Salah couldn't stop scoring and maybe his pre-season burst of goals should have led to the general footballing public – and us red-faced pundits – seeing the writing on the wall. This was suggesting that Mo could be about to shock us all with goals galore in the forthcoming Prem and Champions League campaigns. But his exploits barely registered on the Richter scale and if anyone did happen to notice, the comments were dismissed with the putdown that it 'was only a pre-season high'.

It was the debut pairing of Salah and Mané, and it whetted the appetite for what might be happening soon. They looked like dynamite and were seemingly electric as they sped away from defenders and found each other with fine passes. Their understanding was impressive and suggested good things to come, especially given their link-ups with the third member of what would become a brilliant trio, the irrepressible Roberto Firmino. The only disappointment for the club was that Sturridge, inevitably, left the field injured, this time suffering from a thigh strain.

Salah declared himself happy with his own showing and the fact that he had claimed yet another goal but was far from complacent, saying he still had it all to do and he wasn't at peak fitness yet. He was now looking forward to a day off and then the final of the Audi Cup, which would see him and Liverpool face Atlético Madrid, who were once again in the Allianz.

Klopp was also not as ecstatic as you might have expected about the win over Bayern. He said, 'We won 3–0 but I don't like running around saying, "How good was this?" because it was not. In a few parts of course it was good, in a few other parts everyone saw that Bayern had the ball too often and it was too easy to play through our lines. I cannot ignore this on a day like today. I have to speak about things that are not good because I see it. It is not that I am trying to make the league afraid, "Oh my god Liverpool beat Bayern 3–0 and they can do better." We have to do better and that is what we are working on.'

But the boss did accept that Sadio and Mo had looked a good fit and that, along with Roberto and Coutinho, they offered a mouth-watering line of attacking menace. Klopp added, 'Yes it looks good but they need to get fit and stay fit and hard and resistant because the season will be difficult. That is what we are preparing. You saw that Sadio is not where he can be so he needs playing time, playing time and playing time. Yes, of course, they are both good but they don't need to know it all the time when they play together – and, Oh my God, with Phil Coutinho behind as well to play all the passes for them to run in behind.'

Liverpool lost the final 6–5 on penalties to Atlético but Klopp was more pleased with the performance and less worried about the result. The *Daily Mail* summed up the outcome, saying: 'Jordan Henderson's spot-kick down the middle cost Liverpool a second pre-season trophy, but you can be sure that the Reds will put this set-back behind them soon enough. Jürgen Klopp's side battled well enough and will have learned a lot from playing against a very defensive minded team such as Atlético.'

And Klopp added, 'We lost the shoot-out but I'm not down and out about it. You couldn't have a more difficult job than against a team like Atlético who get results, results, results. If you get to a penalty shoot-out you want to win it, but the boys played really well and it was very good in our preparations. It's important you're prepared for games and have the right state of mind, but we played against Bayern and were very tired today. You want to make life as difficult as possible for opponents; we just conceded a goal today, but had twenty chances – you have to do something out of that, but Atlético are a very strong team.'

It had been a lesson well learnt. Atlético Madrid were a team strong in defence, a team managed by arch dark arts merchant Diego Simeone who believed, as José Mourinho did, in defence first, attack second. Trying to breach Atlético's ultra-defensive team could only prove beneficial for a Liverpool that was being gently welded together by Klopp. He now had the three key components that would propel them to unexpected heights in the season that would follow: the attacking triumvirate of Mané, Salah and Firmino. All pace and silky skills, allied with goals aplenty. Klopp believed that the trio would help push the team up a level during the season. He added, 'It's easy for next season – we want to be as good as possible and better than last year, which isn't easy. We don't set limits to ourselves, some opponents might but we don't. The boys have been great. They've done everything expected of them, they had a very intensive programme and I'm very happy with it. We've got to get the freshness we didn't have today, but there's still one-and-a-half weeks to go and still time to prepare.'

There was also one final pre-season friendly to go. This time the team would have less travel time as they went from Liverpool to Ireland to play Athletic Club in Dublin. The match was played at the Aviva Stadium in front of a strong crowd and the atmosphere was electric as Liverpool stormed to yet another pre-season 3–0 victory. This one saw Salah start the match with Firmino, with Mané on the bench. Mo failed to make the scoresheet but contributed to an entertaining victory before being subbed at the interval (along with nine others, only Mignolet kept his position!). Klopp was yet again cautious in his post-match interview, stressing that it was easy to get too carried away with pre-season successes that brought you down with a bump when the real stuff got underway.

He said, 'Perfection in pre-season is the biggest mistake you can make because it always leads to the wrong decisions. In the second half we had a young side and struggled a bit at first, but after that it got better and I'm happy.'

But he admitted he was 'touched' by the reception he had got on his first visit to Dublin. He said he had heard that it was a Liverpool FC-mad city – and now he certainly knew that to be true! He was asked if he was excited about the imminent start of the Premier League season and how he felt the squad would cope with the demands of the league and the Champions League. Jürgen said, 'The squad is big and I thought I saw today that a few boys really showed up. We can manage it. We will rotate, that's clear, that's not my problem at the moment, I'll prepare for the Watford game from tomorrow on and then the next game, and then the next game, and then I'll think about how we can do this.'

It had proved an ideal preparation period for Mo Salah; the matches on tour had helped him bond with his teammates and have valuable time forging partnerships on the field with Firmino and Mané. Mo said he was grateful in particular for the welcome he had received from the management and the playing staff. He singled out Jordan Henderson for particular praise, saying the Liverpool skipper had been unstinting in his care and his efforts to help him feel at home. Jordan was becoming a fine captain of the club, not just on the field but off it as well. As Jürgen's right-hand man on the playing side it was his job to ensure there was no friction or feelings of resentment that could lead to cliques forming amongst the players. He made sure Mo did not feel left out and took time out to talk with him and encourage him. Not that Mo was the sort to sit alone and brood; his natural demeanour was that of a cheery guy, who was always smiling and eternally optimistic. This mind-set was formed partly as a result of his tough upbringing in Egypt and his determination to make it to the top despite this. He never forgot where he had come from, and how hard life had been for his family, contrasting that with where he was now: his gratitude for his good fortune shone through, and made him one of the most likeable, endearing players I have ever known in the Premier League.

Mo was as far removed from the archetypal spoilt brat, selfish, egotistical footballer as you could imagine. This was a genuinely good-hearted guy whose smile lit up the room when he walked in, whom you would like to call a friend because you knew instinctively he would be a good one. The boy was a winner in every department. And now he was looking forward to his league debut for the club. The experiments and bonding sessions of pre-season were finally over – it was time to get down to the real business of the Premier League. Starting with the opener against Watford away at Vicarage Road on 12 August 2017.

CHAPTER SIX

INTO THE HORNETS' NEST

His Liverpool career would begin in earnest at Vicarage Road, Watford, as the Reds began their 2017–18 Premier League campaign at the start of August. Mo had been keen to get going; he had enjoyed the pre-season matches and getting to know the lads but he – and they – knew that the real business started at Watford. Yet again, following on from his pre-season exploits, Mo was on the scoresheet. But he was unhappy to head back home with just a point after some poor defending cost Liverpool in a 3–3 draw. Miguel Britos earned the hosts a share of the spoils with an injury-time equaliser when the Reds had looked home and dry.

It was a disappointing conclusion to a match they could – and should – have won. And Mo showed his dismay early on in the game after Stefano Okaka met José Holebas's in-swinging corner to put Watford 1–0 up. Klopp had been going over set-piece routines with his backline at Melwood and here they were, blowing it on the very first one of the campaign. It was demoralising after all the work the backroom staff had put in and was an early indication of where money still urgently needed to be spent if they were to launch a credible title challenge.

They were starting the season with an attack that few could match and that would go on to be as prolific as any in Europe. But the team would be like Brazil – brilliant going forward, troubled at the back – and how many times could they score more goals than they conceded?

Here, in their Prem opener, those failings were laid bare – much to Salah, and Klopp's, dismay.

Mo reacted angrily at that opener from Okaka. The defending was poor and he could be seen angrily waving his arms above his head in dismay. He also shouted at the hapless backline, whose poor marking had allowed the goal. After his time at Roma, where he had seen at first hand the brilliance of Italian defending, this was unacceptable in his eyes. Italy's national game had been built on the art of world-class defending and to see the contrast here was a sickener for the new boy. It simply would not have happened in Italy; the defence would have been in the right place, with all parts of the jigsaw spot on, and the ball would have been cleared by a dominant centre-back.

Here, laid bare in the opening game of a new season, the opening game of his new career at his new club, was his new team's Achilles heel. I am told that during half-time and after the game, Mo was not shy in explaining why he had been unhappy, and neither was Klopp. Both men were on a mission to bring back the glory years – primarily the league title – to Liverpool, and this way forward would not end in that achievement. A source said: 'Mo is no shrinking violet when he thinks something is wrong. He may seem a lovely guy who is always smiling – and he is – but when something is not right he will always speak up. It is the perfectionist in him; he is not in the game to be second best. Runner-up may be fine for some players but not Mo Salah. He wants to be the best player in the world and he wants to play for the best club side in the world.'

So something, clearly, would have to change if Mo was to stay long-term at Liverpool. It would, but not for a time. If both Mo and Klopp were perfectionists, the manager also possessed a stubbornness that would see him stand by footballers who most Liverpool fans, and general observers of the game, would say were not good enough for a club aiming for the very top. In this category I would include Alberto Moreno and Dejan Lovren, both of whom Klopp insisted on keeping and slotting into the first eleven whenever he thought he could get away with it. It was not until the arrival of Virgil van Dijk the following January that the club finally acquired a central defender of the calibre you would expect and, even then, Klopp would persevere with the error-prone Lovren alongside him. Moreno would also survive but would be pushed to the sidelines by Andy Robertson, the young left-back signed pre-season from Hull City for £8 million. There had initially been disgruntlement at his purchase, because some fans compared the deal with Manchester City's £50-million outlay on Benjamin Mendy from Monaco at the same time. It was said that it showed the difference between City and Liverpool: that City would spend more than Liverpool's record outlay on a full-back, while the Merseysiders splashed 'just' £8 million on a relatively unproven player, with 'potential' being the key word, for someone playing in the same position.

Well, it didn't quite work out like that in the 2017–18 season, did it? Mendy, for all the cash splashed out on him, got injured early on and spent the season on the sidelines while Robertson slowly but surely worked on his game, arrived in the team, stayed there and played a key role – especially with his attacking forages – in the club's wonderful run to the Champions League final in Kiev.

But he wasn't part of Klopp's plans in that defensive blunder show when the season kicked off at Watford. No, the backline then was Mignolet in goal with Lovren and Joël Matip as central defenders and Moreno as left-back. The only other bright spot in that defence was at right-back, where Trent Alexander-Arnold started. Like Robertson, he would come on in leaps and bounds during the season and even push for a place in England's World Cup squad for Russia.

Okaka had put Watford in the bright August sunshine at Vicarage Road but Liverpool came back to lead 3–2 with goals from Mané, Firmino and Salah. But that defensive frailty kicked in again as the hosts claimed a point with a goal three minutes into injury time from Miguel Britos. It was Klopp's hundredth competitive game in charge of the club and it did not have the most auspicious of endings.

Salah's goal showed his ability to be in the right place at the right time, as he was perfectly placed to score from a pass by Firmino. It should have been a win on his competitive debut but those defensive failings – in particular at set pieces – were once again apparent as they failed to clear from another corner, allowing Britos in for the 3–3 equaliser. It was a sickener and Klopp hit out at the ref for not spotting that Britos was offside – although, to be fair, the Liverpool boss was also quick to criticise his defenders for their travails during the game. He said, 'It was an obvious offside that the linesman should have spotted. But I cannot change it. We would have had defensive areas we need to work on if we'd won 3–2. We were the better team, we should have won. The first half I wasn't too happy with. We passed but couldn't see what we actually wanted. The second half was a lot better. But we forgot to close the game. We defended a little deep. We have to push up. Both teams struggled with ninety minutes, it's the first game. That's normal.'

But what about those defensive failings from set pieces, so apparent even in this opening Prem match? Klopp pulled no punches, opining: 'I'm not fed up talking about set pieces, I have to talk about it. We defended most of them really well, but at the end is it enough if we concede one goal? No. We have to work on it but there are a lot of things to work on. No direction in the first half. Much better in the second half, playing football but it leads to nothing.'

Klopp did say he was pleased with Mo's first competitive game in a Liverpool shirt and that the way he took his goal 'showed what he can do for us'. Mo was also happy to have opened his goals' account but still disappointed to have dropped two points he believed the team should have had, but for those defensive black spots. He felt his fitness was improving after a solid pre-season and said he was 'feeling at home at Liverpool' and that 'all the boys had been great' in welcoming him and helping him settle in easily.

As far as stats go, it also emerged that Mo had become the twelfth player to score on his Premier League debut for Liverpool. When told, he said he was just glad he wasn't the thirteenth, which could have been seen as an unlucky omen!

For many pundits, Mo was man of the match, including for Sky Sports' Andy Hinchcliffe, who was impressed by the player's ability to spark something from nothing, especially in the absence of the injured Coutinho, whom Liverpool usually looked to for inspiration. Andy said, 'Liverpool needed to turn things around drastically at half-time and the player that did that for them in the second half was Salah. With no Coutinho, Liverpool were looking to Salah to be this inspiration, this creative spark, and his pace and his movement off the ball is absolutely superb. He got his goal, which was not the most glamorous he'll ever score but his second-half performance, including winning the penalty, was outstanding.' The penalty referred to was the one that Firmino would convert for Liverpool's second goal of the afternoon.

The Sun newspaper was also impressed with Salah's standout contribution, with my friend Charlie Wyett saying, 'Mohamed Salah almost enjoyed the perfect return to the Premier League when he turned the game around in the space of two minutes as Liverpool were trailing and playing badly. Salah, whose previous Premier League game came for Chelsea in their 5–3 loss to Spurs on January 1

2015, had the simplest of finishes after a terrific lob from Roberto Firmino.' Charlie added, 'He was on fire in pre-season scoring four goals. He bagged himself a starting role in Klopp's side but he didn't always have his shooting boots on today. He had a great chance in the first half but scooped it over the bar. But the rapid Egyptian came out a new man in the second half and completely turned the game on its head. He won Liverpool a penalty with his pace before latching onto Roberto Firmino's lob to put his side ahead.'

The fans were also generally happy on the message boards and social media with Salah's opening gambit but wary of going over the top in predicting big success for the season, given the state of the defence. One Irish Kop fan said: 'A century of games for Jürgen Klopp with Liverpool and no ninety minutes could better sum up his Anfield career thus far. Great entertainment with some pace, intent and class. However, severely lacking in guile, steel and defensive competence. Two more points tossed away.'

And a Liverpool fan in Sweden added: 'Whatever Mamadou Sakho did to Klopp must simply be forgiven and he be allowed back into the squad. He's clearly their best centre-half. Lovren, Matip and Klavan – are they better than Sakho? On the positive side, Mané and Salah are exciting and if Coutinho can stay, Liverpool may have a devastating attack that any club would be afraid of. But my God, that defence is too leaky.'

While another was also full of praise for Mo's debut and his impact on the result, but once again mighty anxious over the defence, saying: 'Salah was magnificent ' along with Firmino and Mané they were so unlucky not to win. Salah not only changed the game getting a penalty for Firmino to tuck away, he got the third goal which should have been the winner, but for the shambles of the back five.'

There were also some calls for Klopp to be given the sack and for perennial Liverpool favourite Rafa Benítez to be brought in as his replacement from Newcastle. Some fans felt Klopp did not deserve the praise he got from the press box precisely because he had not sorted out the defence. On the other hand, the view from Fleet Street was that he should be applauded and kept on even though he seemed to be designing his team from front to back (attack to defence, à la Pep Guardiola), rather than the more traditional back to front (defence to attack, à la José Mourinho). With the new attacking trio of Mané, Salah and Firmino, and an eventual midfield that would include the impressive Naby Keïta backed up by workhouse Jordan Henderson, plus either Alex Oxlade-Chamberlain or Adam Lallana, there was massive intent. And Klopp then planned to sort out the defence, work which would start with the blooding of Alexander-Arnold and Robertson and continue with the record signing purchase of Van Dijk. Those fans on the Kop with the banner that said 'In Klopp we trust' were surely on to something; those calling for his head after the 3–3 draw at Watford had definitely reacted in haste.

Klopp had a masterplan and he simply needed time to enact it. By the end of the season he would be arguably 85 per cent there, with just a top-class keeper and another centre-half to complete the picture.

After the draw at Watford, the manager and his team had to turn their attentions immediately to the Champions

League and a qualifier in Germany. The match at Hoffenheim couldn't come around quickly enough for Salah. These were the games he had signed for Liverpool to play in – the big games in the club world's biggest tournament. High pressure in high-profile clashes that were broadcast around the world. He had tasted the excitement of the tournament at Roma during the 15/16 campaign and enjoyed their run that had only ended in defeat to Real Madrid in the knockout stages. His aim with Liverpool was to progress beyond that level – to prove that he WAS up there with the likes of Messi and Ronaldo. So victory in the two-legged qualifier against the German team was vital – Mo and Liverpool desperately needed to reach the Champions League proper and were desperate to do so.

So a 2–1 win at Hoffenheim in the first leg was just the ticket. Mo didn't get on the scoresheet but he knew that the team was the key in Klopp's world and so it proved as he played his part in a victory that got their European campaign off on the right note. Mo did have a clear-cut chance in the first half but shot wide, which just goes to show even the best people can have off moments. There was talk that Liverpool should shut up shop in the return at Anfield a week later, but if you know Klopp you know that is not how he works. As keeper Mignolet pointed out before the game, Liverpool's strength was in attack – and he expected Salah, Mané and Firmino to pose a huge threat to the visitors. He told a press conference:

We can only play one way and that is forward. To score two goals away from home, if we score one at Anfield it will be very difficult for them. We knew that we can always score. We have so much style up front.

We have the qualities and our natural game will be attacking, and we know we have to fill that in with a really defensive spirit. We know that is where we have to improve. We are not blind. Everybody knows it in the dressing room, but there is no point throwing everything away. A natural footballing side that goes forward, you cannot change that but we know we have to mix that in with a good defensive, aggressive spirit to make sure they don't score the goals. We know we have so much talent in the squad that we have to use it. I just try and improve and help the team out where I can.

Salah was on top form in the return, grabbing his second competitive goal and helping the team to a 4–2 win, and 6–3 on aggregate. That sealed their entry into the Champions League proper. It would still be a long trek from qualification to the final in Kiev, but Manchester United also started off as qualifiers in 1998, and won it in the 1999 final, so there was a precedent and an incentive if ever Liverpool needed it (although I know they would be loath to use bitter rivals Utd as an ideal to aim for). Mo's goal came on eighteen minutes and was his first for the club at Anfield. It came after an effort by Georginio Wijnaldum hit the post. Mo was first to react with the rebound, bundling the ball into the net. His display was part of a brilliant attacking statement by the hosts, undone again by defensive instability, although they got away with it because of the four goals scored.

As mentioned earlier, skipper Jordan Henderson had

been spending a lot of time with Salah after he arrived at Anfield, helping him settle and encouraging him. He said he believed Mo had all it took to be a world superstar and that his encouraging performances, and goals, so far only backed up that belief. Jordan added that all the boys were celebrating in the dressing room as the win – and playing further in the Champions League – meant so much to them. He said, 'Brilliant night, the start we set with the tempo, we scored some good goals early on.

'We can improve on the goals we conceded but we're delighted to be back where we belong. Everything we worked for last season we'll continue to work on. We need to make sure in the Champions League we do ourselves justice. I'm delighted for the lads and the fans as well. We proved we can play against big teams and do well. We'll play whoever we're up against.'

Klopp also had a big smile and said, 'There's not enough words for it. It's amazing. Fourteen months, the hardest work, it feels absolutely amazing. It's fantastic, a big compliment to my team. In the group stage we are excited about whoever we get. Thank you for everyone who was responsible for this atmosphere. In this moment, have a party...in your head!'

While the fans' joy was summed up by one loyal Koppite, who said he paid tribute to 'Super Salah', commenting that his arrival even meant they no longer needed Coutinho, going on to say: 'Simply brilliant from Liverpool. Emre Can best player on the pitch while the new man, Super Salah, what a signing! They don't need Coutinho they play better without him. Firmino and Mané fantastic, too.'

SALAH – KING OF EUROPE

Salah had certainly made his mark in his debut Prem and Champions League games for Liverpool. But he was to get much better – much, much better – and both him and the club would profit in a way they could not have expected from a debut season. The boy's journey to superstardom had begun.

CHAPTER SEVEN

THE KING OF EGYPT

When I mentioned the name Héctor Cúper to a Fleet Street colleague he said, 'What, you mean that bloke from *Breaking Bad*?' In looks, I suppose there is a vague similarity between Cúper, the manager of Egypt, and the film character of Hector Salamanca, although the latter is much more grizzled and has a demented aura. Plus Cúper is hardly the monster that the multi-murderer Salamanca is. No, Cúper is much more in the image of Manuel Pellegrini, the suave former Man City manager, and appears as calm and in control as the figurehead City fans dubbed, 'This Charming Man'. Cúper has the looks of an intellectual and is as far away both emotionally and altruistically from Salamanca as is possible. When asked how he sees his role as manager of Egypt, and that of his players, too, Héctor replied, 'I repeatedly tell my players that we can make people happy. Many people are suffering from the problems of everyday life. Some are poor, some are unemployed. For those people, football might be their ultimate source of joy.'

So how does all this relate to Mohamed Salah? Well, Mo is a player and a man who agrees with that basic philosophy outlined by Cúper. He likes to work with a manager who has passion in his heart, but one who also spends time with his players and is more willing to put an arm around their shoulder and encourage them, even in darker times, than to bollock them in public. So Cúper is more like Mo's club boss Jürgen Klopp than, say, José Mourinho.

It is difficult to envisage Mo working for a man like Mourinho, but characters such as Cúper and Klopp are vital to Salah's cause because they bring out the best in this wonderful footballer. Look how Salah developed as a ruthless goalscorer at Liverpool: it is no coincidence that this 'miracle' happened under Klopp's watch. Similarly, the upturn in Egypt's fortunes – which would see them qualify for the World Cup finals in Russia in 2018, for the first time since 1990 – came about during the partnership of Salah and Cúper.

The Egypt manager helped make Salah a hero in his country of origin by encouraging him to play his natural game and demanding that he should make the difference in a team that had too many times ended up as runners-up or losers. He became Egypt boss in March 2015, and said at the time that his aim was to turn the nation's football team into winners. The reporters made clear the team's huge aims when interviewing him and that fact, rather than scaring him off, actually impressed him. He said he was a man who worked best under pressure and when asked how the interview went, replied at the time, 'The only question I had when I came here was: what do Egyptians exactly want me to achieve? They had a big target which was to reach the World Cup and to win the Nations Cup after some disappointments. This will not be easy and will need time and hard work, and we will be under pressure to deliver, but I believe we can do these things. Otherwise I would not have accepted the offer in the first place.'

A year after his appointment he spoke of his belief that the team was developing with the right mix of youth and experience – with the likes of Salah, then at Roma, and Mohamed Elneny of Arsenal at its base – to achieve those aims. He told *fifa.com*, 'We have the right balance between young and experienced players, some of whom play in top European leagues. I haven't faced any problems since I came here. I adapted very well to everything and the people have warmly welcomed me. Here, there is the kind of football passion that any manager would like to see. You can smell this in the air.'

Those words summed up Cúper, who is an intriguing mix of the intellectual, à la Cantona, and the realist – like any manager trying to hold on to his job. His record in his three-years-plus in the Egypt hot seat stands up to scrutiny. He led them to the African Cup of Nations final in 2017, which they lost 2–1 to Cameroon, and masterminded their progress to the World Cup in Russia. Probably his biggest disappointment was that the team led against Cameroon but could not hold on to that lead. Winning the AFCON, as it is known, would have secured his place in sporting folklore in Egypt; as it was some commentators remained unconvinced by the man, even when he followed it up with the World Cup progression.

Columnist Alaa Abdel-Ghani, writing in *Al-Ahram Weekly* newspaper, was one of his critics, saying he was wasting valuable game time before the World Cup by meddling with the team instead of sticking to a settled one. It was a fair argument, although Cúper's decision to try out new players in pre-World Cup friendlies, rather than bed in his first-choicers in those games, would only prove to have been a success or a failure when results in Russia were analysed. Alaa Abdel-Ghani had summed up what he saw as Cúper's folly like this, saying: 'The present management is calling these debut appearances a surprise and "a good opportunity to try new faces". Good management, though, would consider it the height of folly. This will be only Egypt's third World Cup appearance, the first in 28 years. The country is eyeing a spot in the second round. Failing that, the least the players can do is play decent football on the world's biggest soccer stage. But they can't do that if they don't know who's on their own team.'

Cúper had become known as a 'nearly man' during his travels as a manager. He could have won the league in Argentina with the club Huracán, but fell at the final hurdle. He took Spanish side Valencia to two European finals – and lost them both – and lost a European final and a Spanish Cup final with Mallorca. And, of course, he had lost that AFCON final with Egypt. That defeat prompted him to tell reporters that he sometimes wondered if he had been born unlucky. And he would add, 'The sadness I have is not because I lost another final. It's because there was so much hope especially among the people in Egypt and I am sorry for the players who put in so much effort.'

Be that as it may, he would surely need a welcome slice of good luck, and good management, if he was not to be catching an early flight home from Russia. What also could not be denied was that Cúper would rely massively on having Salah onside with him. The player was his country's only world-class star, make that superstar, and any success in Russia would be in a large part down to him.

And Cúper knew the score: a happy Salah would be an unplayable Salah and that could be the difference between joy and misery. Salah on form would be the deciding factor between the manager most likely losing his job and him being kept in the hot seat for another tournament. Luckily, Mo liked Héctor and believed he was doing a good job. In one press conference it was put to him that many pundits criticise Cúper. But Mo said, 'Our results answer anyone who has a go at him. We nearly won the African Cup of Nations and qualified for the World Cup. His results speak for him.' It was suggested to Mo that facts and figures were OK, but people liked to watch goals and skill, too. He said, 'When you play, do you want to win? Or enjoy? Previous national teams played well but they did not reach the World Cup.'

It was a persuasive argument and one that helped explain the mutual respect Héctor and Mo had for each other. In fact, Héctor liked Mo so much that at every opportunity he would 'big him up' to the press corps, not that he needed such praise any more. In a press conference in Cairo in mid-May, just a month before Russia 2018, Cúper even felt able to claim some of the credit for Salah's extraordinary development. Héctor said, 'We will take advantage of Mohamed Salah's attacking development at Liverpool, just as we have been doing until this moment. I believe we took advantage (of Salah's talents) really well and we were able to get the best out of him. He might have scored more goals in the English Premier League, but that is because there are many more matches to be played there than with the national team. But if you ask me about the change in the tactics and techniques, I believe that he was a very important player in the system that we had set up, and I hope that he can continue in the same way with us moving forward.'

Héctor also made it clear how highly he rates Mo, telling reporters another time, 'I think Salah is one of the best players in the world right now and I don't know if he can be the best player in the world but what he's doing now is really important. I always say that behind a great player there has to be a great team. I don't know if we are a great team, but we cover what Salah gives us, we try to give as much security as we can as a team and until now we have been able to achieve things. We know that as we raise the bar we have to raise the level up.'

Cúper was no fool. He also realised from years of experience that any national team that had dreams of glory had at least one world superstar in its ranks. For Portugal, it would be Ronaldo, for Argentina Messi, and for his side it was Salah. He was an incredibly lucky manager in that respect: he had a player that England, for instance, would kill for. A true game changer; a man who could win a game with a moment of magic. No wonder the manager pampered his star man. Héctor had once surprised journalists by describing Salah as 'just another player'. It was only when put in context that you realised the esteem he held him in, as he explained:

What's most notable about the role of Mohamed Salah is that he was just another player. What do I mean by that? Well, he scored the majority of the goals but worked and ran just like everyone else. For him it's always been about the group and he gets no special privileges. That might seem like a small detail but it's a very significant one. He's an enormously talented yet very modest player. People often say the national team is 'Salah and ten others' to which I reply, 'maybe that's true as he's someone who can win a match for you, but also because he just sees himself as another player.' That's something both him and his teammates understand very well. There have been no ego problems whatsoever.

Salah had been largely responsible for getting his nation to Russia. It had been his efforts – and his drive – that had helped drag Egypt to that first World Cup finals in almost thirty years. It is little wonder that he is a national icon in Egypt. After all, it was his ninety-fifth-minute penalty against Congo that made it 2–1 and saw the team qualify for the World Cup. The draw would put them in Group A. Cúper's men would open their campaign against two-time winners Uruguay on 15 June, before meeting hosts Russia four days later, and conclude their group stage campaign against the Saudis on 25 June. When the draw was made

Cúper commented that he needed time to work out if it was a kind result or a nightmarish prospect.

But he believed the running order of the games was OK. Cúper said, 'I can't quite say it is an easy or a difficult draw. But the order of the group games is quite good. We have big ambitions in the World Cup.' When asked how he assessed the quality of teams at the tournament, he said, 'We are going to face some very strong teams, and I'm sure we'll perform well. We have a large squad and we're working on minimising our shortcomings. In the World Cup, the smallest mistake could cost you a game, so we'll be trying to keep them to an absolute minimum. That way the public will continue to be happy with us, because we have an incredible relationship with them and we do not want to damage it.'

Of course, Cúper was wary of the Uruguayans, who boasted another of the world's top strikers in their ranks – the fiery Luis Suárez. The latter, a former idol of the Kop himself, would pose a real threat to their aspirations. The hope was that they would manage to contain Suárez and maybe get a draw in that opener. And, if Mo was in the right place at the right time, there was even the dream scenario of a key victory. Cúper said the fans had put the pressure on by letting him know they expected to at least get out of the group! He said, 'The public are thrilled, to the point of getting a little carried away in their enthusiasm. Now they are convinced we will progress from the group phase. I was in a supermarket the other day and someone said to me, "We can win the World Cup." And sure, there's no law to stop us from doing that, so we're going to try. Of course,

I cannot tell people, "No, it's impossible", but anyway, our task will not be easy. We need to know who we are to get that across to the public.'

It would be Egypt's third appearance in the finals – they played in Italy in 1934 and in the same country in 1990. But the team was a much better one that played against England in '90, and lost 3–0. And with Salah they had that obligatory world-class star that was needed to make an impact.

Mo hadn't simply arrived out of the blue to star for his country. He had played at younger levels and worked his way up into the national team. Mo had made eleven appearances for the nation's Under 20 and Under 23 teams and was proud to represent his country in the 2011 Under 20 World Cup. He also appeared in Egypt's team that took part in the 2012 London Olympics. Then, as a young whippersnapper of nineteen and plying his trade for Basel in Switzerland, he had arrived in London as a squad player. But after being brought on in their first match at the Millennium Stadium in Cardiff he went on to score in all three of Egypt's group games – and helped them reach the quarter-finals. It was in that opener that he started to make a name for himself. It couldn't have been a more glittering start because the opponents were no less than Brazil, with Neymar in their team.

Egypt were struggling against the Samba boys when Salah was brought on as a substitute. They were 3–0 down to a Brazil side that also included Marcelo, Oscar, Sandro and Thiago Silva. Egypt head coach Hany Ramzy finally introduced Salah as a second-half substitute for Mohsen and he made the difference, scoring their second goal on seventy-six minutes as they put up a defiant show after the interval, eventually going down 3–2 to the team who would finish the tournament as runners-up.

The Guardian reported how a nervous Mo had initially blown a good chance but how he became more 'clinical' as his nerves settled, saying: 'Now Brazil wobbled. Three minutes later Marcelo did not get enough power on a header back to Neto and Salah was running clear on goal. The substitute took too long to get in his shot, allowing Marcelo to catch up and avert the danger, but he was more clinical with his next effort, a left-foot finish to ensure a nervous finale. Egypt can take dignity in defeat; Brazil were both wonderful and vulnerable.'

Salah then started against New Zealand at Old Trafford – and scored again to earn a 1–1 draw for his team. He played the whole match and received a rousing reception from the many Egyptians in the crowd for his fortieth-minute goal. It was a vital goal as it meant he was in with a chance of progressing in the competition. Defeat would have signalled an early flight home after the final group game. That match was against Belarus at Hampden Park, Glasgow, the home of Scottish football. The pressure was still on because only a win would enable them to reach the last eight. Once again, Salah delivered when it was most needed. This would become a regular part of his role for Egypt; he could always be relied upon to score at a crucial time, for example from this clash with Belarus, right up to that ninety-fifth-minute winner against Congo.

Mo scored the first of Egypt's second-half goals as they progressed to the last eight. His goal was typical of the player and the type of classic strike – from an acute angle – that would define him in later years at Liverpool. As *Goal. com* pointed out:

> With ten minutes gone in the second half, Egypt opened the scoring as Salah got in behind the Belarus defence and managed to stroke the ball beyond the outstretched arms of Gutor to put the Pharaohs not only into the lead in the game, but also in the group. With just over a quarter of an hour left in the game, Egypt doubled their advantage as skipper Aboutrika found Ramadan racing down the left wing and he passed the ball into the box, for Mohsen to stroke the ball into the net.
>
> Minutes later two became three as substitute Omar Gaber crossed from the right hand side of the penalty area for Aboutrika to get his name of the scoresheet and Egypt to secure their place in the last eight of the tournament.

The Pharaohs had leapfrogged Belarus to earn that quarter-final shot. But it would also be a step forward as Salah and Co. came up against a strong, determined Japan. The match once again took them to Old Trafford, Manchester, but they lost 3–0 to the 'Blue Samurai' in front of a crowd of more than 70,000. It didn't help Egypt's cause that defender Saad Samir was sent off just before half-time. Kensuke Nagai, captain Maya Yoshida and Yūki Ōtsu were all on target to take Japan through to a semi-final against Mexico.

Mo had been substituted on the hour mark and trudged

off disappointed. It was suggested that he had been carrying a knock, which prompted the Egyptian press to query why he had been started in the first place. The nation is football crazy and fans across the country were gutted that the team had not made it through. There was a further suggestion that too much pressure had been put on Salah to be the saviour; he was, after all, only nineteen and was still only finding his feet in the big leagues of Europe as a club player. But Mo said he had 'been proud' and 'privileged' to represent his nation in 'such a prestigious' event. He had also enjoyed his time in London and the easy-going vibes the city gave off. Maybe someone from Chelsea had had the nous to note those comments from one of the world's most exciting, and potentially brilliant, young talents?

Salah had actually made his debut for the senior team on 3 September 2011, in Egypt's 2–1 defeat in Sierra Leone. It was an unhappy debut, as the defeat meant Egypt failed to qualify for the 2012 African Cup of Nations. This away loss followed on the back of earlier ones in South Africa and Niger and meant that the Pharaohs had earned just two points from five games. Mo was clearly coming into a side that was short on confidence and the Egyptian FA had responded to the dire campaign by deciding to send out their Under-23 team under the senior umbrella.

The player could hardly have been expected to hit the ground running when he was playing with fellow youngsters against teams with more established, and older, players. But a month later he showed that he was going to quickly become an international striker when he scored in the 3–0 win over Niger. It was really a case of 'look what you could have won' for Mo. He had helped the team to a comfortable victory – and yet it would be Niger who would now qualify for the finals of the African Cup of Nations, despite this defeat in Cairo.

Mo was also on target as he and Egypt attempted to put behind them their Nations Cup disappointment. He netted in Guinea as the Pharaohs won 3–2 in June 2013. He scored with the last kick of the game after escaping on one of the speedy solo runs that would become his trademark over the years, and cleverly planting the ball beyond the keeper. The win at that stage meant that Egypt became only the second African team alongside Tunisia to have registered away wins in 2014 World Cup qualifying.

He then bagged a hat-trick for his country in the 4–2 win in Zimbabwe as Egypt triumphed in their fourth consecutive match in World Cup group qualifiers. He had scored fifteen goals in twenty-one matches for his country and they were now just one win away from the knockout stage of the qualifiers. A week later he was the hero again, scoring the only goal in the match in Mozambique. This win put Egypt into the knockout stage and Salah would late score his sixth goal in the competition to become the joint top scorer among all the African nations in qualification.

But his hopes of competing in the 2014 crashed when Egypt were thrashed 6–1 in Ghana in the first leg of their play-off tie in October 2013. Salah's only consolation came when he was bundled off the ball in the box, thus winning a penalty, which his skipper Aboutrika (capped 101 times by his country) scored, sending the keeper Fatawu Dauda the wrong way. That made it 2–1 and raised the hopes of the

Egyptian faithful. But the team collapsed and Mo's World Cup dream lay in tatters. Defiantly, he claimed it was not all over and that Egypt could pull back the 6–1 deficit in the home leg of the tie. But that proved to be wishful thinking.

They put in a shift in the return but it would not be enough. Mo's consolation this time was that he played a part in a performance that at least restored some pride after that crushing away defeat. As Sky Sports summed it up: 'Egypt had a mountain to climb after they were thrashed 6–1 by Ghana in the first game in Kumasi last month, and although they dominated and made two breakthroughs thanks to Amr Zaki and Mohamed Gedo, it was not enough to change their fortunes. Finding at least five goals at home while keeping a clean sheet was always going to be a tall order, but with nothing to lose, the Pharaohs started off with intent against a Black Stars side who were surprisingly subdued before substitute Kevin-Prince Boateng scored in the 89th minute.' It would be Ghana who would jet off to the World Cup for the third successive time, leaving Mo and his teammates stuck at home watching the action.

Mo did have an effort cleared off the line but it was expecting too much to overturn that massive lead Ghana had from the first leg. However, as FIFA themselves pointed out, some pride had been restored, going on to say:

After the devastating 6–1 defeat in Kumasi, restoring pride was always going to be the most achievable goal for the Pharaohs. But in front of a Cairo crowd who had not seen their national team play in two years, and with an away goal to their name, there is no doubt an optimistic few some inside the 30 June Stadium still held on to the slim hopes that a miracle could come to pass. Aboutrika fired wide as the old master looked to conjure up some hope of a maiden World Cup appearance, but when Zaki exited with an injury the writing looked to be on the wall for all in Cairo. With 15 minutes remaining Gedo forced a save from Douda, before Daniel Opare had to be on hand to clear Mohamed Salah's follow-up off the line.

It was tough on Mo: he was exhausted and 'very low' after the Ghana loss. It was little consolation that he had emerged as the join top scorer among all African teams in the qualification stages.

Elation, and relief, would come, though, as Egypt, now under Cúper's regime, started to make major progress. The team qualified for the finals of the 2017 African Nations Cup and, with Salah on fire, reached the final itself. After the years of learning and disappointment at international level, Mo Salah finally came of age on this stage. On 25 January 2017, he grabbed the decisive goal in Egypt's 1–0 victory over Ghana – which meant he and the team had earned the top spot in Group D. It was sweet revenge for that 6–1 thrashing three-and-a-half years earlier in AFCON qualifying. Finally, Egypt had broken the cycle of failure. Some pundits pointed out that Ghana had already qualified, so were hardly giving their all. But they knew that defeat would put Salah and Co. at the top of the group, rather than them, so there was an incentive. No matter, Egypt still had to come up with a result, and did just that.

Salah, wearing the Number 10 shirt, lashed home a free kick to win the game. Now the fun really started, as he propelled the Pharaohs to a final showdown with Cameroon in Gabon. Mo was really enjoying himself and played well in the final. It was a match that bucked the trend of previous AFCON finals, being entertaining and containing goals. The previous six finals had produced just three goals in total, but this one equalled that miserable record. The two nations had met in 1986 and 2008, with Egypt winning both. But this time they were out of luck. Arsenal midfielder Mohamed Elneny lashed home a shot that gave hope to Egypt and a 1–0 lead, but it wouldn't be enough. Nicolas Nkoulou headed the equaliser and Vincent Aboubakar grabbed the winner with a fine shot. Mo's efforts in the event – two goals and two assists in six games – meant he won a spot in the CAF Team of the Tournament. It was also perhaps telling that Egypt as a team won the CAF Fair Play prize; Mo himself is a model pro and his teammates were clearly of the same mould.

Mo's club side, Roma, put out a statement congratulating him on making the tournament team, and for his overall efforts. It read:

Roma winger Mohamed Salah has been named in the official Africa Cup of Nations Team of the Tournament, after a scintillating individual tournament for runners-up Egypt. Salah scored twice and provided another assist as he helped his country reached the final – where his clever pass for Mohamed Elneny enabled Egypt to open the scoring. Cameroon eventually fought back to win the game 2–1, thanks to Vincent Aboubakar's last-gasp strike, but Salah's individual efforts nevertheless saw him named in the organisers' best XI. The centre forward will return to Rome on Tuesday, and be back at Trigoria to re-join his club teammates on Wednesday. And, for the record, here is the team, **Goalkeeper:** Fabrice Ondoa (Cameroon); **Defenders:** Modou Kara Mbodji (Senegal), Ahmed Hegazy (Egypt), Michael Ngadeu (Cameroon); **Midfielders:** Charles Kaboré (Burkina Faso), Daniel Amartey (Ghana), Bertrand Traoré (Burkina Faso), Christian Atsu (Ghana), Mohamed Salah (Egypt); **Forwards:** Christian Bassogog (Cameroon), Junior Kabananga (DR Congo).

Reaching the final of the tournament in January 2017 was the highlight of Salah's international career so far. But he was still obsessed with getting to the finals of the World Cup. And, after the team's success in AFCON 2017, he felt he finally had a realistic chance of achieving that aim. His single-mindedness and determination would turn that hope into reality.

Nine months after the final in Gabon, Egypt qualified for the 2018 World Cup finals in Russia. And it was Salah's goals that took them there – but boy did he leave it late in the crucial win over Congo that raised the roof in the Borg El Arab Stadium in Alexandria. Mo opened the scoring just after the hour mark when he placed the ball through the keeper's legs – such coolness in such a red-hot atmosphere. But Arnold Bouka Moutou equalised as the end of the ninety minutes loomed, leaving the capacity 80,000 fans shocked and wondering if their dream was over, too. Would this be yet another let-down at the final staging post?

Cometh the hour, cometh the man. Egypt won a penalty with the added injury time all but up and Salah stepped up, cool as cucumber, to restore the lead. The goal sent the fans wild and as the final whistle blew just moments later, Mo slumped to the ground and shook his head. He was on his way to Russia. Egypt had become the second African nation to qualify after Nigeria.

Mo would play one more international before this book went to the publishers and would score yet again in the 2–1 friendly defeat by Portugal, played in Zurich, Switzerland. The European champions had trailed until the last minute but then Cristiano Ronaldo popped up with a brace to win the game and leave Mo scratching his head as if to say, 'What the hell happened there?' Salah had scored just after half-time with an excellent drive but Ronaldo headed home the winner. Again for the record, that cap against Portugal was Salah's fifty-eighth. He had scored thirty-five goals, which gave him a very impressive strike rate of 60 per cent, per match. He had also been a regular in the national team for over six years.

So what realistic hopes could Mo and his nation have as they entered the cauldron in Russia with the eyes of the world's media and fans on them? Well, some pundits quite rightly reckoned they were this year's Belgium: dark horses who might, just might, win it. As *The Sun* pointed out: 'Egypt boast one of the most exciting strikers in world football in Mohamed Salah and the World Cup gods have been favourable to them for the group draw. Unsurprisingly

Salah is the most important cog in the Egypt team but he has shown that he carries the weight of the team on his shoulders with ease. With the pace and trickery that Salah possesses he can create chances out of nothing and will strike fear into the heart of any defence he comes up against. The likes of Russia, Saudi Arabia and Uruguay should all be worried. With Salah in this kind of electric form he can inspire Egypt to serious heroics in Russia.'

That sounded just about right. One thing was for sure, Mo Salah would never let his nation or his adoring fans down. He would give his everything in Russia.

CHAPTER EIGHT

SIX OF THE BEST

Mo had got off to a good start at Anfield and in the space of an early season month would set down a marker as a goal machine. As we have noted, few people imagined that he would score such a remarkable number of goals by the end of the season, but if we had sat up and taken more note of his exploits from 23 August to 23 September 2017, we would have found sure-fire clues of what he was capable of. In that month, he would find the net SIX TIMES. The first of the six came in that Champions League qualifier at Anfield against Hoffenheim, while the last of the six arrived at Leicester. And in those six games in which he scored, he was never on the losing side.

Four days after his goal against the Germans, Salah was on target as Liverpool chalked up another resounding victory: a 4–0 Premier League triumph over Arsenal at Anfield. And Mo's goal was truly something special. It came after Arsenal fluffed a corner and Liverpool counter-attacked. Mo ran sixty yards from his own half to fire the ball home and later said it was 'one of my best ever goals because it was so unusual'. It certainly highlighted his strength, power and stamina as well as that unerring goal poacher's ability to be in the right place at the right time. The *Mail*'s world-class columnist Martin Samuel called Salah's afternoon 'electric' and summed up the brilliance of his goal, saying: 'A Liverpool corner was cleared but fell to Bellerin 25 yards inside the Liverpool half. He mis-controlled and was caught in possession by Salah who then had a run of roughly 65 yards to Arsenal's goal with no other blue shirt to cover. Arsenal were like the Keystone Kops in pursuit, except not quite as well organised. Having been given a rehearsal, Salah knew exactly what to do this time: and then it was three.'

Meanwhile, there was an interesting sidebar to Mo's goal tally for the Anfield giants and as *The Sun* pointed out: 'Mohamed Salah now has as many goals for Liverpool, three, in four matches for the club, as he got for Chelsea. Salah was on the books at the Blues for 29 months, although he spent more time out on loan than he did in West London.' Liverpool skipper Henderson admitted that the result was 'beyond the boys' wildest dreams' and that Mo was already proving a brilliant buy, even a bargain. He had settled in so seamlessly and Henderson said that his constant smile 'lit up the place'. He added, 'I thought we did very well. I always thought we were pretty solid, we defended well as a team, put them in areas we wanted them to be. And we devastated on the break. I felt as though we controlled the game everywhere really, [I was] delighted with the lads, they were brilliant, we worked ever so hard and got our just rewards.'

Klopp was just as delighted, telling BBC Sport, 'After midweek games you have to reach the mountain immediately. You really feel it is intense, we wanted to force ourselves to be strong physically and that is what we were. We were really well organised. If you give Arsenal space and time you lose before the game starts so I don't think they could do a lot of what they wanted, Arsenal, and that is all credit to the boys because they worked really hard.' He said he was excited by the potential of his new three-headed attack of Salah, Firmino and Mané. The speed of the trio would cause big problems for defenders, he predicted, and he was enjoying watching them and urging them on from the touchline.

And now Jürgen was about to learn that he had bought a player who could plug the goals gap that the club had suffered since the end of the Suárez/Sturridge partnership. Sure, he knew Mo could score given half a chance – that much was clear from his record at Roma. But Klopp had imagined him as a speedy winger who could contribute goals at an equal rate, similar to Firmino and Mané. He had never contemplated him as a complete striker in the mould of Suárez: one who would smash goal records and be the most feared goal scorer in England. Yes, he was about to be surprised by Mo Salah, on a massive scale.

The early season goals continued to come as Salah scored against Seville in the Champions League and Burnley and Leicester in the Prem. For good measure, he also netted twice for his country Egypt in the international break, but there will be more details of his national appearances elsewhere in this book.

The match against the Spaniards at Anfield was Liverpool's first in the Champions League for three years. Mo grabbed their second goal with a slight rebound off a defender. Lucky maybe, but Mo was still claiming it! Yet again defensive weaknesses cost Liverpool dearly and it didn't help that Klopp had decided to play Karius in goal for the European matches instead of Mignolet. That contributed to the unease that had become a constant problem for Liverpool. The eventual 2–2 draw was not the end of the world but it put undue pressure on the team as they had lost two valuable points. And yet again Klopp seemed oblivious to the defensive problems, saying, 'It was pretty much a winning performance for eighty-five minutes and the team played well against a side who play well. We had answers for everything apart from the goals. I have to see them again. That is not the good thing. It was an exciting game from my side, everyone saw our desire and passion but we got a point.

'We know we have to improve but there is so much potential and we can work with this. It is a draw – it does not feel too good but I am fine with big parts of the performance.'

The fans were not as easy-going about the rocky backline; many voiced their displeasure that the back four were shipping goals that could cost the team dear if the fault was not remedied. Henderson was a mite more realistic and honest in his assessment. He made the point that the result was a good one after the 5–0 thrashing at Manchester City a few days earlier. He told the press, 'We could have taken the three points with the chances we created in both halves but they got us on the counter-attack. We are disappointed not to take the points but the lads reacted well to the weekend after the defeat at City. We looked exciting and could have scored a few more goals. We wanted to win the ball back quickly and get the crowd behind us. The lads reacted brilliantly to going behind and there are positives from the game.'

The Times's reporter Henry Winter was less lenient, highlighting the errors that Liverpool continued to make. Under a headline the next day that read 'Defensive weakness proves Liverpool's downfall again', he wrote: 'Attack against defence in training at Melwood must be an absolute goal-fest. Liverpool continue to delight with their exhilarating forward movement, and continue to cause palpitations with their inability, individually and collectively, to resist opposition surges.'

The *Daily Telegraph*'s Paul Hayward said that Liverpool were 'a crimson tide going forward, but a red warning light at the back', while the newspaper's chief football writer Sam Wallace was struck by the emerging wonderful partnership between Mané and Salah, explaining: 'In the first half, Sadio Mané and Mohamed Salah, scorer of Liverpool's second, looked like one of Europe's great emerging attacking forces and the futile attempts of Nicolás Pareja in conceding a penalty before the break showcased it perfectly.'

Mo himself said he was glad to be back in the Champions League, after spending a season out of it with Roma. He too was disappointed the team could not register a win but was happy with his own performance and that he had his wits about him to rifle home that rebound. 'I love scoring goals,' he said. 'But the main thing is always the team and hopefully my goals will help the team win more than we lose. I feel honoured to play for this club and will give my all. I love the fans and the way they cheer us on and sing about me. I am so happy here.'

Those words would be music to Klopp's ears, and to the Kop's too, no doubt. The little man was unstoppable as he drove in from the wing and scored goals from all angles and in all sizes, easy ones and magical ones.

Mo proved just what the Champions League meant to him when Liverpool next played in the competition. On target yet again, with a brace, he helped Liverpool win 7–0 at NK Maribor. OK, the Greek minnows were hardly Barcelona or Real Madrid, but you can only deal with what is in front of you and Mo put in a man-of-the-match showing to get Liverpool's Champions League campaign right back on track. The fans were ecstatic about Salah and it showed on the message boards as they commented that 'Mo Salah owned that game' and 'I love Salah'.

The feeling was mutual: Mo loved the fans and when asked about them always commented on their sheer enthusiasm and encouragement. He knew they helped pay his wages and considered that, after the manager, it was the fans he answered to. Mo was a hard worker and never shirked his responsibilities to the team. He scored a pile of goals that season, but also was a creator. He would work back to win the ball, head forwards with it and pick out a teammate in a good position. The match against Maribor highlighted just that as he grafted, edged forward on the right wing and set up Firmino for the first goal.

The result was a real boon after the crushing defeat at Man City, but then again the defence had hardly been pushed to the limit against the minnows. A bigger test would surely come against Tottenham in the Prem at Wembley five days later. And it did with, unfortunately, predictable results as the backline crumbled yet again under pressure. Mo scored again but the defence let him down (again). It couldn't continue, could it? If Klopp truly was aiming for the stars – as in the Prem title and the Champions League – he would surely need to upgrade his side's weak links? If not, why would Mo Salah stay long-term at a club that could not compete for the biggest honours in the game because it was trying to do so with one hand tied behind its back?

On paper, it looked a no-brainer and many on the Kop were wondering why Klopp wasn't sorting the mess out. In truth, he was – and he had tried to – with the signing of the first piece of that upgrade we were all expecting. But Virgil van Dijk's arrival would take time after Southampton took umbrage at his and Liverpool's attempts to force through a deal in the summer of 2017. Klopp believed the player would come to Anfield but there was little he could do about it after the summer transfer window closed. In fact, there was little he could do about upgrades in any of his defensive slots until January, or more likely the following summer, unless he could come up with some genius, but unlikely, loan deals. I was told that at the same time as Klopp plotted to sign Van Dijk he also wanted to bring in goalkeeper Butland from Stoke, but decided he couldn't deal with two sets of aggravation from rival clubs at once! Maybe with Stoke's relegation, Jack Butland will be the next arrival to plug that porous defence after Klopp did eventually secure Virgil?

At Wembley, Liverpool's defence without the not-yet-signed Van Dijk shipped another four goals. The match featured the two top strikers in the country: Mo for Liverpool and Harry Kane for Spurs. The duo would battle all season for the golden boot and their displays at Wembley in October 2017 showed exactly why they were head and shoulders above their rivals in the goals department. Kane won this battle, with his brace to Mo's single strike, but Mo would have the last laugh at the end of the campaign. The match showed Liverpool's pulling power as it was played out in front of a record Premier League crowd of 80,827.

The contrast in the style of the goals showed how Salah is perhaps a more inspirational striker than Kane. Harry's goals were typical of him in that they bore all the hallmarks of a goal poacher. His first came when he rounded Mignolet and slotted the ball home from ten yards, his second when he netted from a rebound. In contrast, Mo got on the scoresheet with an individualist goal that had considerable skill and pace to it. Mo collected a pass from Henderson and sped past the Spurs backline before threading the ball home from a delicate angle. It had echoes of his strike against Arsenal earlier in the season when he scored after a sixty-yard solo effort. It was hard to imagine Kane scoring such a goal; he did not have the turn of speed or stamina of Salah but, of course, he was a master in the six-yard box. Each player had his own strengths and deserved the acclaim that was coming their way.

But while the win left Kane on a high, the defeat, and the severity of it, had Mo shaking his head again as he left the pitch. This was not what he had signed up for: it was not how Klopp had sold the deal to him. But he knew it was early days and knew the manager was ambitious as he was. He also saw how Klopp was a manager who was keen to get the best out of his attack with a high-pressing style. And that suited Mo's game. He was already finding he could play with Firmino, and Klopp had privately dangled the prospect of the duo also teaming up with Mané as a front three. That really appealed to Mo – being part of a trio who had the speed and skill to take on all comers. It was a tantalising prospect, with Coutinho pulling the strings behind them. As it transpired, of course, the Brazilian playmaker would eventually move on to Barcelona, leaving a void, but the attacking trident would become reality. Mo was a patient guy and he believed in the Klopp project, so as painful as the heavy defeats to Man City and Spurs were, he would continue to believe in Klopp and the Anfield project under him.

Salah's goal was his fifth in his first nine Prem appearances for Liverpool and his prolific talent could be gauged by the fact that only Robbie Fowler had scored more goals (with six) in that many Prem games for the club. To be hot on the heels of such a master marksman showed just how far Mo had come – and how quickly – since his transfer. And the real shock of it all was that this would only be the start of the fairy tale – by the end of the season everyone in world football would know how deadly Mo Salah was in front of goal. At the other end of the pitch, the dire defending meant that Liverpool had conceded more goals than any other team in Prem games, shipping a shocking total of fifteen. The overall total of sixteen in the league was their worst after nine games since the 1964–65 season, fifty-three years. It was Dr Jekyll and Mr Hyde stuff and would cost Liverpool dearly unless Klopp could eliminate the 'Mr Hyde' defects of his team. It was telling where Klopp must have known a good deal of the blame for his team's faults lay, as he took off the error-ridden Lovren after just half-an-hour, replacing him with Alex Oxlade-Chamberlain.

Afterwards Klopp told the press that he took full responsibility for the defeat. He said, 'We had it felt like 60, 70 per cent possession, but after 2–0, you saw the goals, what we did around the goals – should have been easy to defend. We have defended situations like this all season. We had our chances, scored one, and the game was on the table. Being down one goal at Tottenham, you can fix it. The third is down to completely not concentrating off the ball. Four mistakes from us. It is my responsibility. I don't coach the type of defending for the first throw-in. The second goal, we miss the ball and then Son is quicker. We put it on a plate. It's not about confidence. It's just about being 100 per cent spot on. It was a really average day for us today.'

His skipper Jordan Henderson tried to cushion what had been an embarrassing early bath for Lovren, claiming joint culpability for the defeat. The boy was growing into the captain's role as he attempted to deflect the flak from the defender, who had been left, I am told, 'pretty distressed and low' by the substitution. Henderson explained, 'I know Dejan came off but it could have been any of us. We got back into it but then we conceded a sloppy goal that killed us. It was a disappointing and frustrating day but we will go back to the training ground, work hard and take it from there.'

Klopp must have had a magic potion at Melwood on those training days, for after the loss at Tottenham Salah would be part of a team that would now go on a magical, unexpected sixteen-game unbeaten run that would last from Saturday 28 October 2017 to Monday 22 January 2018. That sequence would include highlights such as a 4–1 win at West Ham, a 7–0 thrashing of Spartak Moscow at Anfield, a 4–0 win at Bournemouth and, best of all, a 4–3 victory over the best team in the country that season, Manchester City. In the same sixteen-game sequence, Mo would hit the back of the net fifteen times – almost a ratio of a goal every game. It seemed that he was lifting the team to new heights during that unbeaten streak; that as he scored, so they would win or draw. They were starting to believe they could achieve something big with such a world-class player in tow.

For Liverpool fans, and indeed footie fans everywhere, Salah's metamorphosis from speedy winger to world-class striker was something to behold. It was happening before our very eyes and was something extraordinary. Probably the best similar example of such a remarkable transformation would be to compare Salah's rise to that of Leicester when they won the Premier League. One minute they were a good team, enjoyable to watch and could beat the very best on their day, but not a team you would ever have put money on to win the title. But they did and it shocked and delighted everyone when they did so.

Similarly, Mo Salah had arrived at Liverpool as a player we knew was good, hence his record transfer fee, but we never foresaw his amazing goals tally or that he would, like Leicester, earn the plaudits and trophies to prove that, yes, he was the best in the league. This had been a player who had been average at Chelsea and had to resurrect his career in Italy, so had fallen off the scale as far as fans in England were concerned. Yet here he was, outscoring Harry Kane and becoming the main man at Liverpool, a club with other world-class stars like (for half a season at least) Coutinho, Mané and Firmino.

The utterly unexpected nature of Salah's rise from nowhere was part of our unadulterated joy in witnessing it. Even fans of other clubs applauded Mo and loved watching him as he weaved his magic that season. He brought a zest to the Premier League and his obvious elevation to the level of Ronaldo and Messi during the campaign made us proud to have him in the Prem. His talent reflected well on the league itself – it proved that the Prem could still attract the world's best. That it could match Real Madrid and Barcelona in that department.

For Liverpool, Salah's rise meant they became a club that was now expected to make the top four and to go far in the Champions League. He was their talisman and was taking them on to a higher ground. Now they had to reward him by building a team around him, which Klopp intended to do bit by bit.

In November 2017, Mo scored EIGHT goals for Liverpool,

starting with a goal in the 3–0 win over Maribor at Anfield in the Champions League and concluding with a brace in the 3–0 victory at Stoke in the Prem. He also grabbed two-goal hauls in the 4–1 win at West Ham and the 3–0 win over Southampton at Anfield, both in the Prem. Salah also netted Liverpool's goal in the 1–1 draw with Chelsea at Anfield.

That goal against the Blues meant a lot to Mo, given that he had played for the Stamford Bridge club in his first spell in England and was allowed to leave without any fuss. To score against them was yet another kick in the teeth for them after they let him go. OK, Mo said he had nothing to prove and that he had no big resentments against Chelsea for that failed spell early in his career. But he wouldn't have been human if he hadn't felt elated at putting one over on them with his goal for Liverpool. He didn't celebrate the strike because that is just how he is: a humble guy who doesn't like outward shows of defiance and arrogance. But a Liverpool source said that Mo had certainly enjoyed the goal and that it DID mean a lot to him in private.

Indeed, the following May, when he had secured a raft of Player of the Year awards, he admitted he had felt he had something to prove after leaving Chelsea and that he was enjoying proving them wrong. He said, 'I was here like four years ago and a lot of people said he couldn't have success, that he could not play in the Premier League, that it was very difficult for him. So it was always in my mind to come back. From the first day I left Chelsea, it was always in my mind to make [prove] them wrong. I made [proved] them wrong.'

In an interview with CNN's *Inside the Middle East*, Mo

elaborated upon his desire to show Chelsea just what they were missing: 'I didn't have my chance there, so I had to leave. In my mind, I didn't want to be someone sitting on the bench, waiting to be Number four or five and play two minutes yet saying he's still in the big club. It doesn't work. I went to Fiorentina, then I went to Rome. I had two-and-a-half seasons in both clubs. I did very good there. When I had a chance to come back, I said, "Yeah, it's time to come back to England."'

It later emerged that he also felt that celebrating the goal against Chelsea – indeed, against any team – would have been inappropriate at that particular time. This was because some of his fellow Egyptians had lost their lives in a terror attack. More than 300 people died in the attack on a mosque. The goal was his fifteenth of the season, which meant he had become the first to score that many for Liverpool since Suárez (31) and Sturridge (24) in 2013–14. Mo opened the scoring just before the hour with a strike from close range. It was also his tenth in thirteen Prem fixtures for the club. Mo was chosen as Man of the Match, another highlight against his former club and of a season that was becoming full of them.

If only Willian hadn't equalised five minutes from time Mo's day would have been complete. Klopp was furious that he hadn't been allowed to make a vital substitution before that equaliser; he believed it had robbed him of two points. The manager went on to say, 'I was angry because we wanted to change the system but the referee didn't give us the opportunity. I don't know what he thought in this moment, he told me something about taking too long, I don't understand it. How can we take too long? We didn't want to time waste, we wanted to change the system and that's why I was angry.'

Chelsea boss Antonio Conte was generous in his praise of Salah, conceding that this was a different player than the one who had been at Stamford Bridge. As an Italian, and observer of Serie A in his time as Italy boss, Conte had seen at first hand how Salah was developing. He said Salah had improved season by season to the extent that he was now undoubtedly in the top echelon of players worldwide. He could see similarities in the style of play and determination to win between Salah and his own superman, Eden Hazard. Both were impossible to push off the ball, both could leave you dazed with their dribbling and both were lethal in front of goal. To be compared with Hazard, who was arguably just below Ronaldo, Messi and Neymar in terms of quality, was a further indicator of just how far Mo Salah had come. 'He caused us problems,' Conte admitted, 'and took his goal well. He is a very good player.'

Given Mo's display, Conte was just relieved to be heading back to London with a point, rather than a drubbing. He added, 'I think we must be pleased. Both teams played with a great intensity from the start to the end. It was very difficult to play this game after a long travel and no rest for my players, and also because when you play at Anfield it is not simple. In our best moment we conceded the goal and were unlucky. But at the same time I was very happy to see a great reaction from my players, with the way they fought and didn't accept a bad result at Liverpool.'

Liverpool fans were cheered by Salah's ever-increasing

pack of goals and his obvious commitment to the cause. But they were disappointed to have thrown away two points. One fan said, 'We are great going forward and Salah is already the best buy of the season, a bargain at what we paid for him. He just can't stop scoring! I knew he was good but I never knew he was this good! If we could just tighten up at the back we'd be flying. It's a sickener that we can't keep more clean sheets.' Liverpool had, in fact, kept three clean sheets in the previous month, but the problem was more about when the defence went missing at key moments in key games.

Most home fans agreed on the message boards about the worrying defensive lapses, picked Mo as their Man of the Match and could see progress in midfield and attack. One summed it up this way: 'It was a fair result in the end although we threw away two points really. Hazard, Azpili and Alonso all played well and Willian took his chance for the equaliser. Courtois saved some decent shots from us too. Salah our best player today, Oxlade, Couts and Milner not bad either and Lallana looked decent on his first game in months, even if it was only a few minutes. Thought our subs were made a bit late though.'

Chelsea fans were more peeved that Salah had been one who got away, along with Kevin de Bruyne and Romelu Lukaku. They imagined just how their team would be with those three in the line-up...imagined and mourned their loss. One fan said he had a bad feeling that Salah would come back to haunt his former club, adding that, 'I told my friend yesterday that Salah was gonna score against us [Chelsea] and I was spot on. He has been scoring against Chelsea since when he was playing for Basel. Thanks Mourinho for selling another talent, Salah, De Bruyne, Lukaku and the list goes on.' It shows how informed footie fans are that they keep tabs on their former players – this fan was referring to that cracker of a goal Mo netted against Chelsea in the Champions League group stage back in November 2013. The difference being that that night Mo's goal won the game (1–0); this time his goal had been cancelled out for a 1–1 draw.

Even a Man United fan joined in the praise for Salah while, at the same time, lambasting his teammate Jordan Henderson and Utd's Jesse Lingard's qualities. 'I am a United fan but I admit Salah is a great player. But I feel sorry for him having to play with Jordan the Clown – a player like our version of Lingard. Salah is brilliant but those two players don't bring anything to the game, they're useless.'

It was a top description of Mo but harsh on Jesse and Jordan, in my opinion. I'll admit I too doubted Henderson and Lingard's right to play for their club's first eleven, let alone England. But those doubts evaporated the more I watched the pair over that season. Sure, they aren't individual world-class talents like Salah and De Bruyne and Hazard. But their influence on games and their teams should not be underestimated. Henderson grew during the campaign as a solid, reliable starter in midfield and as an inspirational skipper at Anfield and for England. And I can't think of a footballer who more consistently delivers vital goals in big games than Lingard. He is also under-rated given his work rate, dribbling and vision to see the bigger picture in games.

Salah's two goals at West Ham the day before Bonfire Night helped Liverpool to a 4–1 victory – and also led to the sacking of Hammers boss Slaven Bilić two days later. *The Telegraph* felt that win was all down to Mo's influence and made the point that he was proving a bargain buy, even as Liverpool's record acquisition. The report went on to say: 'Liverpool won their third consecutive game, a feat they have not managed since August and much of it was down to Salah who now has 12 goals this season and resumed his partnership with Mané in a fine breakaway goal for Liverpool's first. Salah came to the club in the summer, Klopp said, as the unanimous pick of the scouting department and the coaching staff, a £34-million acquisition from Roma who already looks value for money.'

When Klopp spoke to the media after the win, he was almost purring with delight about his main man, saying, 'We watched him so often and the scouting department wanted to do it even earlier so no one else can jump in, but we had a lot of different options. He was the decision of all of us. When you find a situation when everybody doing the job agrees on one player you can be sure it will work. It is really nice to have him in the team. He is a real goal threat; he is an offensive midfield player who is more a striker. He needed to adapt to the different style.'

Interesting how Klopp admitted that he didn't rush straight in for his man: how he and his team did thorough due diligence despite the player's obvious talent. Also that Klopp himself had initially seen him as a winger/ midfielder and then recognised he had a man on the books who could not only dazzle with his dribbling but also score goals at will. That the winger/midfielder could become the complete striker he was at the end of the season. Salah's transformation was a sign of how football generally was changing.

He wasn't the only winger who could also play in the middle to such devastating effect. Cristiano Ronaldo is probably the best example: he started out at Man United on the right wing in the Number 7 shirt and ended up often scoring from what would have been the centre-forward's role when playing for Real Madrid six or seven years later. His powerful build and physique meant he had no difficulty adapting to a central striker's role. Similarly, Raheem Sterling (who remains a hate figure on Merseyside to many Kop-pites because they believe his transfer to Manchester City was all about money rather than ambition) has played centrally for Pep Guardiola rather than simply as a straight wingman. So, given Salah's low centre of gravity and goal threat, it is perhaps no surprise that he has been such a success in front of goal when he has drifted into the centre. Sergio Agüero, after all, is of a similar build, and look at the goals he has scored as a central striker for Manchester City.

Most media organisations were by now united in their acclaim for Salah, and their belief that the player was the star of the season so far, and definitely the bargain buy of the summer. As BBC Sport pointed out about his contribution to the West Ham win: 'The opener was Salah's fifth goal in as many games for the club and the winger is proving to be worth every penny of the £34m Liverpool paid Roma for his services in the summer. The Egypt international's second of the game, a neat drive across Hart into the far corner, means he has now had a hand in fifteen goals in all competitions this season, more than any other Liverpool player. The win marked the first time since August that Liverpool had recorded back-to-back wins and maintaining that sort of consistency will be crucial to their hopes of finishing in the top four.'

So, of course, would be their keeping Salah fit for the rest of the season. With Mané back in the team as well as Firmino, Salah was part of a triple attack that would take some stopping, both at home and in Europe. Mo's worth to the team was highlighted by the fact that, after the West Ham match, no player had scored more goals after eleven Premier League games for Liverpool than he had. He was joint top with Sturridge on seven. And when it came to goals and assists, he was on nine in his first eleven Premier League games (seven goals, two assists) for Liverpool. Only Sturridge could better that after eleven games for the club, with his total of ten.

Salah was continually delivering the goods and threatening to rip up the record books in his first season at Liverpool. He was clearly made for the club, and the club was made for him. They were a perfect fit and could only get better and better. Mo had taken next to no time to settle in and his goal record was extraordinary. Could the magic continue, or would he fade as the season moved towards Christmas of 2017 and the New Year? Well, he would have the chance to show he was no flash in the pan at the start of December, with a key fixture against Liverpool's bitter local rivals, Everton. Yes, his first Merseyside derby awaited him.

CHAPTER NINE

KING OF THE KOP

Mo continued his goals glut into December 2017 with a crucial strike in the Merseyside derby. Any Liverpool player who scores against their fierce local rivals Everton is guaranteed an automatic place in the hearts of the Kop. In Mo's case, he had already done that with his performances and stats in the first four months of the season, so this goal only served to strengthen that bond. The fans had waited since July 2014 for a new hero – that being the date when Luis Suárez quit the club for Barcelona. Now the waiting was finally over. After three long years Mo Salah had arrived on the scene and was acclaimed King of the Kop by the faithful. Just as they adored him, so the feeling was mutual. He would often raise his fist in delight towards the fans after scoring yet another goal; they would always be the most important thing in the game to him.

His goal against Everton came a couple of minutes

before half-time at Anfield and, boy, was it a cracker. Mo dribbled past Everton defenders and then superbly curled the ball past Jordan Pickford into the opposite top corner of the net. This was footballing artistry at its most sublime; a gem of a goal by one of the game's most gifted performers. It was a goal worthy of Goal of the Season and it had Liverpool fans off their seats, jumping for joy. But the joy turned to despair ten minutes from time when Wayne Rooney converted a dubious penalty, awarded after Dominic Calvert-Lewin was deemed to have been pushed by Dejan Lovren. Jürgen Klopp would later say he thought Mo's strike was 'wonderful' but he was too het up to comment on it immediately after the game. The penalty had left him furious and he ranted on SkySports, saying, 'Calvert-Lewin is smart and takes a step but even then it's nothing. The referees don't understand that the player is doing that. I cannot believe in a game like this when only one team is trying to win it and the other team were never in our box, and then you give it, you open the door for them like this. In my understanding, it's not a penalty.'

Klopp's Everton counterpart Sam Allardyce, inevitably, had a different take on the award, stating, 'He can moan all he wants but it's a penalty. It's an extremely brave decision and I think he got the decision right.' Big Sam would rub salt into the wound by saying that for him it was simply a case of mission accomplished, and that, 'The object of the exercise was to frustrate the opposition. Clear-cut chances for Liverpool were very few and far between for such a talented team. When I arrived at Everton we'd conceded thirteen goals in the past four games. We've conceded one goal in four games since. Our platform for success is being built from the foundations and that's extremely important if we are to move up the league.'

The goal was Mo's nineteenth in twenty-four appearances for Liverpool in all competitions in the season thus far, and he had been directly involved in twenty-three goals in all competitions of this season, two more than any other player in the top-flight. His influence on the team could be seen in that his goals had helped them to fourth place in the Prem table – but it could have been so much better had the defence not kept letting them down.

The next match was a let-down, a 0–0 draw at home to West Brom but Mo ensured it was a happy Christmas at Anfield as he got back on the goal trail with one in the 4–0 win at Bournemouth and another in a 3–3 draw at Arsenal. That massive result down on the south coast took Mo's tally for the season to twenty goals and *The Telegraph* summed up the nature of the achievement, pointing out: 'From Robbie Fowler to Michael Owen, and then Fernando Torres to Luis Suárez, Liverpool have had some great goalscorers over the past thirty years, but still no one who has begun a season quite like Mohamed Salah. An emphatic 4–0 win here might have been most inspired by another attacking masterclass from Philippe Coutinho, but he was still ultimately overshadowed by Salah, who would join only Ian Rush and Roger Hunt – the two most prolific strikers in the club's history – by reaching twenty goals before Christmas. You have to go back all the way to 1895 to find a player, George Allan, who reached that landmark quicker for Liverpool than the twenty-six games Salah has now played.'

And the *Daily Mail* said: 'Mohamed Salah has made a brilliant start to his Liverpool career after joining the club in the summer and continued his hot streak on Sunday. The Egyptian scored his team's third goal with a fine left-footed finish after beating two defenders with mesmerising close control. The strike was a landmark one for the forward as he became the first Liverpool player to net 20 goals in a season before Christmas since Ian Rush in the 1986–87 campaign. He is also the first Premier League player to reach the milestone in all competitions this season.'

Mo scored his team's third goal of the day – and it was yet another classic. A brilliant left-foot finish after he left two defenders for dead with immaculate close control of the ball. A display that even had teammate Alex Oxlade-Chamberlain shaking his head as if in disbelief. The former Arsenal midfielder had seen many quality goals in his time at the Emirates but few of that extra-special calibre. The Ox knew class when he saw it and he knew that this man was a genius. I am told he shook Mo's hand afterwards and demanded a selfie with 'the best player in the world!'

And even the much-criticised Dejan Lovren got on to the scoresheet while helping the Pool keep a clean sheet! Klopp was pleased with the result but urged his men to become more consistent if they wanted to win trophies rather than mere garlands. He said:

It was a very important win as we had two draws in the last two games and both of those games we should have won. We need to be really consistent, on track and show all the time who we are and that we are all together. I'm really pleased about pretty much everything because the start was serious like it should be. We really deserved it and I enjoyed the performance.

We were disciplined, I like how we defended different situations, and our tactical discipline was good. You can't score all the time, all the games are hard. It was a fantastic first goal, and the third was world class. We could have scored more, but we didn't really give a lot away so it was well deserved and I enjoyed the performances.

It was telling that the Liverpool boss called Mo's goal 'world class'. He didn't like to single out individuals but it was becoming increasingly hard not to as Salah continued his brilliant form. The man wasn't carrying the team – the likes of Coutinho, Mané and Firmino were also major contributors – but he was proving to be by far their best player. And that was quite something, considering how the spotlight had shone so vividly on Coutinho and his on/off transfer to Barcelona. It's not pushing it too far to say that Mo's form had taken the spotlight off the Brazilian and on to him. It was he, rather than Philippe, who was leading the team to glory. It was Salah, not Coutinho, who was the star man and the idol of the Kop. The situation also made many pundits on Fleet Street question just how much Salah would be worth by the end of the season if he maintained his incredible goal rush. If Coutinho was worth £146 million to Barcelona, then it was not inconceivable that Mo could fetch the best part of £200 million from Real Madrid.

Not that Klopp would even consider selling his star man. It would be bad enough when Coutinho eventually left in the following month's transfer window. No way would the Liverpool boss countenance the sale of his other key player. And Mo had no intention of leaving, either. He had found his home at Anfield; he loved the city, the fans, the football club and the manager. Klopp had made him feel wanted and his particular brand of 'arm around the shoulder' management had helped Salah settle in quickly.

The key was that Klopp believed in him, totally. The boss had known that Mo was good but not this good. As soon as he twigged just what a superstar his new man could be, he decided he would build his team around him. Hence, there was no longer a need to bring in another expensive striker. Klopp wasn't convinced by Sturridge – that much was clear by the way he rarely started Daniel when he was fit. But Mo's emergence as a prolific goalscorer meant there was no urgency to find someone to replace Daniel: he now had the very man to do the job on his own doorstep.

Mo's emergence was a blessing for Klopp in another way: it meant he could now concentrate his funds on sorting out the defensive woes that continued to blight the team's progress. He would be able to splash £75 million on Van Dijk in January and still had the money from the sale of Coutinho in the same month to invest in more defensive recruits come the summer.

In the 3–3 draw at Arsenal that followed directly on from the win at Bournemouth, Mo grabbed Liverpool's second goal. The match had been a thriller three days before Christmas and meant the team stayed fourth in the table, a point clear of Arsenal who would have overtaken them if they had won. The scene was set for a Boxing Day encounter with bottom placed Swansea and a final game of the year against Leicester. Hopes were high as both matches were at Anfield. Liverpool would crush the Swans 5–0 and perhaps the most remarkable aspect of the win was that Mo did not get on to the scoresheet!

No matter, he made up for it by hitting both goals as they beat Leicester 2–1 in the final match of 2017. The halfway mark in the season had seen him reach twenty-three goals, with seventeen in the league. That tally of twenty-three meant he had equalled the mark set by the legendary Roger Hunt in the 1962–63 season. It was the perfect end to a perfect 2017 for Mo Salah. As his manager said afterwards, 'On perfect days we win football games.' He might have added that it helped having a perfect striker. And he did go some way to voicing that opinion, saying, 'Mo was fantastic with his dribbling and his vision. I couldn't ask more from him. Staying in the game is the real deal of football in this league – but I am happy for Mo, I am happy for the team, because this group is a fantastic group of players. It's a good team performance and a well-deserved win.'

What would 2018 hold for Mo? He couldn't continue his goal run, could he? He couldn't get any better, surely? We were about to find out.

CHAPTER TEN

SLICKER THAN CITY

The New Year of 2018 began with pundits and fans now openly discussing the phenomenon that was Mo Salah. To some, it seemed he had come from nowhere, as if the years of learning and toil at Chelsea and in Italy had not existed. As if it was a miracle that he was scoring so many goals at such a fast rate. As if the many goals he had hit at Roma in his final season before coming to Liverpool had not provided at least a clue, an inkling, that this footballer could be a goal king in the Premier League. Obviously, many fans had been unaware of his exploits as a Roma player, so their amazement was understandable. But we pundits should have known better of course; we should have nodded sagely and said, 'Well, look at his record in Italy'. But we mainly said nothing because we couldn't have imagined that he would have SUCH an impact.

By the start of 2018 everyone within the game was

talking about Salah. Some still questioned whether he could maintain his form – the answer would not take long in coming. On the fourteenth of January he propelled Liverpool to a Premier League win that showed he could do just that, but also signalled that he and the team were now worthy rivals to the best team in the country: Pep Guardiola's Manchester City. City's local rivals, United, would end the campaign as Premier League runners-up but most everyone in the game ended up agreeing that it would be Salah and Liverpool who were best equipped to run closest to Guardiola's team over the next eighteen months. United would grind out results by practising a largely mundane style of football under the arch pragmatist José Mourinho, while Klopp's boys – spearheaded by Salah – began to march to glory with a high-pressing, wonderfully entertaining, easy-flowing system. And it was that game against City at the start of the year that confirmed Liverpool as Pep's main threat to his team's continued hegemony.

City arrived at Anfield as the players that every other team wanted to beat because they were so good. But also because, as amazing as it was, they arrived at Anfield unbeaten in the Premier League. City had gone twenty-two league games without defeat and were being tipped to become the first team to threaten the remarkable record of Arsenal's so-called 'Invincibles'. The Gunners chalked up a record forty-nine consecutive top-flight league games unbeaten from May 2003 to October 2004, breaking Nottingham Forest's previous record of forty-two, set between November 1977 and November 1978. Their run ended at Old Trafford as in a 2–0 defeat to Manchester United in October 2004. That run also included an unbeaten top-flight league season, only equalled by Preston North End, who did not lose in 1988–89. But Preston had played just twenty-two league games that season against Arsenal's thirty-eight.

Modern-day City had beaten Manchester United, Chelsea, Tottenham and Arsenal to go fifteen points clear at the top of the table. And Jürgen Klopp's side was thrashed 5–0 at the Etihad Stadium the previous September, although the dismissal of Sadio Mané on thirty-seven minutes contributed massively to that loss.

Guardiola had played down the chances of doing an 'Invincibles', but I was told he privately harboured such a dream. So avoiding defeat at Anfield was a key stepping stone to achieving that ambition. It would also have shown just how good his side were as he considered Liverpool, along with United, to be the main threat to his plans for domestic domination over the next couple of seasons. It was therefore all the more admirable, if not to say significant, that Salah and Co. thwarted them. Liverpool ran out 4–3 winners in a thriller of a match and, yes, Mo was, inevitably, on the scoresheet. Additional goals from Alex Oxlade-Chamberlain, Roberto Firmino and Mané helped Liverpool go 4–1 ahead. The visitors threatened a comeback with late goals from Bernardo Silva and İlkay Gündoğan but to no avail. And how Liverpool celebrated, having halted City's brilliant run.

City, however, who had not won at Anfield in the Premier League since 2003, remained massive favourites for the title with that fifteen-point lead still intact. It didn't matter, for Salah and his teammates had put down a marker: next season might be a different story altogether, as Klopp added final pieces to the jigsaw. If he could just strengthen that ever-creaking defence the Reds would surely be up there with City. Like City, their attacking play was sublime and arguably a match for the team who would go on to win the league. It showed in the way that Salah, Mané and Firmino destroyed City. And Klopp later told pals how chuffed he was to be the only manager to beat Guardiola five times!

Guardiola conceded that his defence had been unable to cope with Liverpool's mercurial attacking trident, but he also paid respect to the Anfield supporters, whom he said contributed to the downfall. Pep said they made the atmosphere at Anfield 'one of the best in the world of football' and added, 'We tried to play but made mistakes and sometimes that happens – but always I give credit to the opponent. We have in many positions a young team. We played good until the goal from Firmino and after that we lost a little bit of our control. We were involved in the environment of Anfield for many, many reasons. You have to try to be stable. We lost that a little bit, but we were still fighting and we found two goals. It is our first defeat. You need to live those situations to realise what we have done. Football is unpredictable. You lose today against a fantastic team.'

While Klopp added, 'You can watch it as a manager or as a football fan and I prefer to do that – wow! What a game. Two teams, full throttle. This was a historic game you will talk about in twenty years because it looks like City will not lose another one this year. People watched this game all over the world and this is why – take your heart, throw it on the pitch and play like this, both teams. I was not scared at the end, not that I didn't think we could concede a fourth, I have known my boys long enough now, it was so intense. If you combine quality with attitude you see a game like this. I really loved it. You will find someone who wants to talk about defending, no clean sheet, but he can blow up my boots.'

That last comment about 'blowing up my boots' sums up Klopp perfectly. He is a modern-era manager, like Guardiola, who wears his heart on his sleeve and is interested primarily in providing attacking, entertaining football that is also winning football. He is the antithesis of José Mourinho, who also loves to win, but who does not mind boring his fans to death to do so. One manager advocated freedom and spontaneity, the other favoured defensive discipline and pragmatism. Was it any wonder that Salah saw his future as being intertwined with his German boss? The move from Roma could not have turned out any better for him: here he was, top of the goals chart in England, and being backed, nay encouraged, by his manager to simply be himself.

While Mourinho warned his forwards that they would not be in the team if they did not do their share of defensive work, Klopp simply told Mo to be himself, to get the goals that took Liverpool higher. Mo being Mo, he also put in a shift helping out the midfield and contesting every loose ball, as did Firmino in particular. They shared common ground with Mourinho's January signing that season: Alexis Sanchez. The Chile forward also covered every blade of grass in the opponent's half of the pitch, tackling back and hunting down the ball. Salah had now scored twenty-four goals and assisted another seven in thirty appearances for Liverpool in all competitions during the season, so he was clearly delivering the goods at both ends of the pitch for his new club. It was also Liverpool's first match since Philippe Coutinho's £142-million transfer to Barcelona.

There was a school of thought, which strengthened as the second half of the season progressed, that the Brazilian's controversial move to Spain actually IMPROVED the team. In one sense this was true, because it hurried along the incoming transfer that same month of £75-million central defender Virgil van Dijk from Southampton. That brought a much-needed anchor to a defence, which was at best described as rocky, while also bringing in a level of leadership that had been missing. But Coutinho's departure in another sense allowed Salah to thrive still more and become the team's new superstar. Mo had already played a crucial role in Liverpool's season but had been overshadowed by the Brazilian and the constant debate over whether he would stay or go. Now he was thrust into the central limelight and was the main story on the back pages every week. Consequently everyone could see just what a magnificent player he was and how Liverpool's success was irrevocably linked to his exploits in front of goal. When Philippe left, Mo the superstar emerged in full view.

Sean Cole, of *thesportsman.com*, backed up that idea, saying:

They [Liverpool] are the only team to have beaten City in the league, inflicting an eventful 4–3 defeat at Anfield in the first game after Coutinho's move to Barcelona was confirmed. Liverpool seemed in no way negatively affected by the loss of the Brazilian international, who many regarded as the club's star man. They attacked with verve and relentless intensity, as Firmino, Salah and Mané all found their way onto the scoresheet. It was a sign of things to come. The trio have blossomed in Coutinho's absence, scoring 28 goals between them in the 13 games since he left. It's an exceptional record, demonstrating the fluid and incisive nature of their football, as well as the way their individual skillsets complement each other. They have a great understanding, and although Salah has undoubtedly earned most of the plaudits, Firmino and Mané have more than shared the burden.

A couple of months after the significant win over City, Klopp would also concede that far from destabilising Liverpool, Coutinho's move had in some ways been the making of the team he was trying to create. He told a press conference, 'Phil Coutinho was a very dominant player in our game and when we were not at our best it was always a good idea to give him the ball. Maybe he has an idea. But it was always clear when Phil didn't play we had to do the job differently, to put responsibility on different shoulders and spread it between the players. You can never be sure it will work but now it is a few weeks ago and I am really happy with the reaction of the boys. They stepped up. It makes us a little bit more unpredictable on the pitch. Of course we were fighting for Phil, we wanted to keep him here and in the end he decided differently. I am happy it has worked so far pretty well.'

Former Liverpool defender Phil Babb had proved to be a bit of a Mystic Meg even before Coutinho left, telling SkySports News that Salah, through his goals and presence, had already shown he was now Liverpool's most important player – and that he could only get better. Phil said, 'Mo Salah, what he's added is a surprise element. His pace has been electric, he's starting to convert more chances. He gets three or four a game but he's putting them away, shown composure, matured and now he's Liverpool's greatest asset at the moment.'

Salah's performance against City in January 2018, had shown that Babb had been spot on with his analysis. With Coutinho now gone, no one would disagree with Babb that Mo had become the Reds' most important player. And the final months of the Premier League season would only cement that position.

CHAPTER ELEVEN

LOVE & EIGHT

That momentous win over Man City seemed to take a lot out of Salah and his teammates. The next two matches saw them come up against teams struggling at the bottom of the Premier League table – and they lost both of them. The first saw them crash at Swansea, with local lad Alfie Mawson scoring the only goal. It ended Liverpool's eighteen-match unbeaten run and proved a disastrous first run-out for £75-million defender Virgil van Dijk as he headed the ball down to set up Mawson for the winning goal. The closest Liverpool came was when keeper Łukasz Fabiański tipped an excellent free kick from Salah over the bar. Mo trudged off the field dejectedly at full-time in South Wales. He never suffered defeat lightly and he was upset that the team had lost their unbeaten record which he had been so proud of. It also irked him that he had not scored. 'Mo's a great guy but gets down when he's on the losing side,' I was told. 'But the thing is with him, he's always dead keen to get back on the training pitch to put things right. The next match can't come soon enough to erase the bad result from memory.'

Maybe so, but the next game brought no soothing balm. West Brom, under new manager Alan Pardew, parked up at Anfield and somehow contrived to leave with a 3–2 victory in the fourth round of the FA Cup. The only consolation was that Mo was back in the goals, grabbing Liverpool's second one in the net, twelve minutes from time. But it was only a consolation as they were 3–1 down before he slammed the ball home. It was the team's first defeat at Anfield since the previous April. Salah again trudged sadly off the field but Klopp told him and the rest of the team to put the two losses behind them. The boss urged them to forget them, as if they had not happened, and to get their focus back in training at Melwood so that they would be ready for the away game at Huddersfield a few days later.

It was good advice and, if Mo had been a psychic, he would have realised that there was a silver lining to the black cloud that had descended with the defeats to the two sets of strugglers. For, including the goal against West Brom, he would have netted a total of EIGHT times in SEVEN matches from Saturday 27 January 2018, to Saturday 3 March. This was a remarkable run of goals in consecutive games from a player who was tearing away in the chase for the Golden Boot and who would also be tearing away with all the major personal awards come the end of the season. As Liverpool profited from his goals and efforts, so they would be rewarded by his fellow pros, pro writers and the fans come May time.

Mo Salah would become the king of all he surveyed –

and he deserved every accolade that came his way during this exceptional debut season at his new club.

The first of those eight goals on the trot came in the perfunctory 3–0 win at Premier League strugglers Huddersfield, but it was his brace in the next match which was much more vital to Liverpool's season. For it came at home against Tottenham, who would be their main rivals in the fight for third and fourth place in the league. Man City looked sure to win the league and their neighbours United were odds-on to nick the runners-up spot. So a good result against Spurs was key if Liverpool were to finish at least in the top four (with Chelsea also in the background) and, hopefully, third.

The BBC had Mo as their Man of the Match and that was justified given his two goals meant that they earned a point and deprived their rivals of what would have been an undeserved two. Salah struck very early and very late in the game. His opener came on just three minutes in, while what looked like his winner arrived in injury time. The first was a relatively straightforward goal as Mo zoomed in and planted the ball home with ease after a blunder by Eric Dier gave it to him on a plate. But the second was a Salah classic. He got the ball and slalomed between the Spurs defence before lifting the leather over a despairing Hugo Lloris in the visitors' goal. Mo scored many wonderful goals that season, but this was one of the best. The way he beat the backline and carefully lifted the ball over the keeper brought to mind Messi at his immaculate finest. It was similar to how you just know with Messi that he will score in certain, sometimes even apparently impossible, situations – from angles that are beyond the normal footballer's capabilities. So it was that Salah was now hitting that level of genius.

This factor should have been the difference between the two teams. It certainly deserved to be, if only to make it the main talking point of the day. But the craft of the goal was lost in the slipstream of a controversial penalty. Referee Jon Moss decided that Van Dijk had fouled Érik Lamela in the box and Harry Kane, who had already missed one penalty, scored from the spot for his hundredth league goal. The result left the Reds in third place in the table on fifty-one points, Chelsea fourth on fifty, and Spurs fifth on forty-nine.

It also left Salah feeling that he had been robbed. His two goals, and that wonder strike especially, were worthy of winning any match. He told pals it was a result that was hard to swallow and that he did not believe it was a penalty. After watching the replays, I think he was right, and the alleged incident was no more than a coming together, and I certainly didn't see that Van Dijk had fouled Lamela.

Klopp had set off on a run down the touchline after Salah's goal, believing that the points were in the bag. That helped explain his dismay, and anger, when Kane equalised from the spot. After the game Klopp told reporters:

There were so many situations to talk about but the ref's decisions decided the game so I can't help but talk about them. I don't understand either of the penalty situations. The first one was offside and the second, I know already what the ref and his assistant will say. There was a touch, a little touch. But Lamela has jumped into him and wanted the touch and to go down. If the ref kept playing at that level then fine, but in the first half he wasn't giving fouls. Then for the softest touch of the whole game he decides it is a foul.

In the second half we had to defend like crazy, they had to chase the game. We had counter-attacks, the high pressure was good and we put in some super crosses. We were a bit unlucky here and there but we had enough chances to win the game. And we would have if it wasn't for those decisions.

For his part, Kane admitted he had felt nerves as the Kop cranked up the pressure on him. He said, 'I was nervous before the second penalty. It was a big moment, with a lot of pressure, but I stuck to the routine. There was a lot of pressure, in front of the Kop. The first one, I did everything I wanted to and the keeper made the save. You've got to take the chances. I thought the second one was a penalty; the defender took out Lamela.'

BBC Sport provided a series of stats to show Salah's influence on Liverpool in the season – and how he had made inroads into some records from previous seasons. Some of them make interesting reading here. For instance, at this stage of the campaign, Mo had netted twenty-one goals in twenty-five games in the league – achieved in the least number of appearances by any Liverpool player to reach twenty goals in the competition. He had been directly involved in twenty-seven goals in the league, the joint most of any player in their first twenty-five appearances for a club in the competition. He was also only the second Liverpool player to score twenty or more goals for the club in his debut Premier League campaign, after Fernando Torres in 2007–08 (who scored twenty-four).

Finally – as if the other achievements weren't enough to be going on with! – his opening goal after just two-minutes sixteen-seconds against Tottenham was Liverpool's quickest strike in the Premier League since April 2016, when Daniel Sturridge scored against Newcastle in one minute seven seconds. *The Independent* summed up the magic of Salah that day – and what it meant to the player and Liverpool, reporting: 'The Egyptian has slotted in seamlessly at Anfield and perhaps that is because he feels as close as possible to a physical representation of Jürgen Klopp's thrillingly aggressive – if frequently profligate – side. He was once again Liverpool's best player, responsible for both of their goals, and has now notched up twenty-two in just twenty-five Premier League games.'

And all this was being done in the player's first season at a new club while playing in a more advanced role than he had been used to at his previous clubs. It was a footballing achievement as remarkable as the team success that had seen Leicester City shock the world when they won the Premier League in 2016. Back then, no one had expected or envisaged that miracle: just as no one had foreseen Mo Salah's elevation to world-class forward status.

Mo's goals now sent the team on to win the next four games and then he and the Reds hit a blank in a disappointing Champions League last Round of 16 with a 0–0 draw at Anfield against Porto. Having said that, a fortnight earlier Mo had netted in the 5–0 away win at Porto in the reverse fixture. But he wasn't the hero that night. No, it was fellow musketeer Sadio Mané who earned all the acclaim with a brilliant hat-trick that left the Portuguese side in bits and took Liverpool a massive step towards the quarter-finals. Something that the 0–0 draw at Anfield would only serve to confirm. But there'll be more of Salah's Champions League exploits in another chapter.

Salah also played a key role in the Premier League demolition of Southampton (2–0 at St Mary's) and West Ham (4–1 at Anfield) and Newcastle (2–0 at Anfield), grabbing a goal in each of the three games. The defeat of West Ham saw the Reds temporarily climb to second in the league table, overtaking Man United. This would be their high point of the season in terms of position; they would eventually drop down to fourth. This was still Champions League territory but it meant a qualification round unless, of course, they won the tournament – in which case they would qualify automatically as champions. West Ham boss David Moyes admitted after the game that he had anticipated a torrid afternoon with Salah, Mané and Firmino attacking his team. He said, 'We knew how hard it would be. The quality of their forward line is tremendous. If it's not Salah coming at you, it's Mané or Firmino, and we couldn't quite cope. But I thought we played well in the first half.'

Mo Salah was, yet again, voted Man of the Match and took his goal with aplomb, finding the back of the net with a shot that Adrian in the Hammers' goal had no chance of getting to. Mo's fellow strikers, Mané and Firmino, were also on target and Klopp gave the three of them a little treat towards the end of the match by subbing them all within a five-minute spell from the eighty-second minute.

That allowed them all to accept the crowd's acclaim. Mo's goal led to yet another entry into the record books for the season – it meant he had scored twenty goals with his left foot in the Premier League, the most scored by a player in a single season in the tournament's history. After the match, when told of his latest achievement, he smiled, laughed and said he would 'have to start learning how to score with his right foot!'

The win made it sixteen home games in the league unbeaten for the Reds and Klopp shook his head when asked to comment on Salah's display, as if to say, 'What more can I say that's not already been said?' However he told the BBC, 'We defended well and attacked well. Our counter-attacking was outstanding, the work-rate was outstanding and the attitude was fantastic.'

Disappointment would come as March 2018, kicked in, when the Reds went down 2–1 at Man United on the tenth of the month. For the second successive match, Mo failed to get on the scoresheet. He seemed a little weary; maybe fatigue had finally caught up with him after the goals he had scored and the effort he had put in for the club during the previous seven weeks.

United wing-back Ashley Young had arguably his finest game for his club, constantly shadowing Mo and sniffing out any danger. United fans delighted in Salah's relatively miserable afternoon, tweeting about his 'non-showing' and claiming that Young 'had Salah in his pocket all day'. But it would be Mo who enjoyed the last laugh on United and their fans after the game, tweeting: 'The UCL draw can't come soon enough' – accompanied by a knowing emoji of a laughing face. It was a clear reference to Liverpool being through to the last eight of the Champions League along with Man City, Juventus, Real Madrid, Roma and Seville. United, of course, had crashed out to Seville after a poor performance at home, losing 2–1 with a brace from Ben Yedder, who had come off the bench. His goals made Romelu Lukaku's late goal irrelevant and it was the Spaniards who progressed from the last-16, much to José Mourinho's fury.

Mo had got his own back on United in a most humorous way. But was he about to hit a drought? If so, that would be no laughing matter for him or his club as the business end of the season loomed. It would mess up his bid for the Golden Boot and could hit Liverpool's Champions League ambitions and even their hopes of finishing in the top four. But we needn't have worried; in fact, during the very next game, just seven days after the lows of Old Trafford, Salah showed he was the man to drag his team out of a temporary depression, back into the light, by scoring FOUR times as Liverpool crushed Watford 5–0 at Anfield. As a statement of intent by the player and the team, it was pretty impressive. And Salah would later say that this was the highlight of his season – apart from the Champions League semi-final and final – as he felt it was his best performance of the season in the Premier League.

The four goals took his total for the season to thirty-six in all competitions. Mo scored twice in each half and even had time to provide an assist to set up Roberto Firmino for the fifth goal of the day. Stats anoraks also noted that Mo had became the first player to score four goals from four shots in a Premier League game since Andrey Arshavin had done so for Arsenal at Liverpool in April 2009. After the game Salah told BT Sport he owed a debt of gratitude to his teammates, who had helped him reach the total of thirty-six goals. In typically humble style, he said, 'I have to thank everyone, without my teammates I couldn't reach these numbers. Each game the three points is the most important. During the game I want to score and help the team. I think we showed a good reaction after the last game and that was most important for us. We had a good result, clean sheet and three points which was most important.'

Probably more important for Liverpool and their loyal army of fans was Mo's statement of intent a couple of days after his wonder show against the Hornets. He made it clear that he loved Liverpool Football Club and the Premier League and had no intention of leaving. He told ESPN Brasil, 'In Chelsea I didn't play, so I didn't have my chances. I said to all my friends, I think I said it on many interviews as well, that I wanted to come back. I like the Premier League a lot. I feel it has my style of football. I like to play in the Premier League. If you look at me now and five years ago, everything has changed – mentally, physically, everything. Klopp changed something in me. Now I play closer to the goal than in any club before.'

He also admitted that his dream was to win the Premier League – and that he wanted to do so with Liverpool, adding that, 'If you see my goals and everything I did in my last four or five years, every year is better than the year before. It's a dream to win the Premier League here after a long time. A club that hasn't won it for a long time, it's my dream. Honestly. I want to win it with this club.'

Mo's pal at Anfield, left-back Andy Robertson, whose crosses had helped the Egyptian in his constant hunt for goals, said he believed the player could become the new Messi. He told reporters, 'Messi has been doing it for years. Mo has had a great career but I think now he is really hitting his peak and he has still got youth on his side. Hopefully if he can keep doing it he will be in that bracket but I don't think you can argue that there probably isn't anyone better in the world than him just now.'

Robertson added that Mo's display against Watford had shown just how good he was – and how difficult he was to stop when goal-bound, explaining that:

He's easier to play with than against – that's for sure! In training, everyone dreads playing against him. I think he's one of the best in the business and nobody can deny that. I thought [against Watford] he was unplayable. I thought he was unbelievable and I think that could have arguably have been his best game so far.

To top it off with four goals was just ridiculous but it all comes from all of us working so hard. Mo gets in those positions all the time and just now he's putting everything away. He's not missing any chances and that's a good thing for us. Hopefully that continues because we've got a big run-in until the end of the season and if the front three can keep scoring the goals then hopefully that can be enough for us to reach our objectives.

Mo's comments about being happy at Liverpool – and wanting to stay to achieve his ambition of winning the

Premier League – were received with joy by Liverpool FC and the fans. They did not want to lose their new idol. It still hurt that Luis Suárez and Philippe Coutinho had left for warmer shores, with both of them dropping anchor at Barcelona for combined fees of around £226 million. If Mo also was to go to Spain, Liverpool could get upwards of £200 million, but what would be the point of selling their best player yet again? Both Suárez and Coutinho had demanded that they be allowed to leave for Barca and it made sense to let them go rather than have two unhappy players in the dressing room. But it would make no sense to sell Salah, however much money it brought in, when the player was loving his time on Merseyside. Any sale just to cash in by the board – i.e. John W. Henry – would be met with rebellion on the terraces and, no doubt, in the manager's office, too.

The third goal, in particular, was truly worthy of Lionel Messi, as Salah jinked his way past defenders and then buried a shot beyond them and in the opposite side of the net away from the keeper. It was wondrous to behold how he bamboozled so many defenders and still had the temerity, and genius, to get that ball past them into an angle to goal that looked impossible. It was pure magic, or pure genius was what the army of Liverpool fans in Ireland were saying that night, as they toasted their hero with pints of Guinness.

Liverpool fans across the world were queuing up to pay homage to the man they had dubbed 'The King of Egypt' on message boards and social media. One said: 'I'm not saying he's as good as him, but in terms of style of play Salah is the closest thing to Messi right now.' Another added: 'He is our real Egyptian King. We thank the lord for sending him to Anfield. And I believe he will stay with us for many years to come.' While a self-confessed 'older man' said: 'The fans composed a special song for him. Time to build a sphinx with his bust at the gates of Anfield. Long may he stay at LFC. Where else would he enjoy this kind of support from teammates and adoring fans. And be part of the most formidable front three on the planet. I don't remember being this excited watching the game for over fifty years. It has been a privilege. Thank you LFC. Thank you Mr Klopp.'

On Twitter, Empire of the Kop said: 'LFC need to give Salah the biggest contract in club's history. Van Dijk is on double what he is!' LFC Fans Corner tweeted: 'Mad how Salah is the best player in the world.' A Liverpool fan tweeted: 'In terms of great Egyptians he's gotta be right up there Salah with Tutankhamun.' And even club owner Henry's wife Linda got in on the act, tweeting: 'Brace for two...hat-trick for three. What is the word for four?' adding to her tweet the hashtags #LFC and #MoSalah.

Yes, the boy was all the rage after his four-goal demolition of Watford. Everyone wanted a piece of him; everyone wanted to acclaim him as football's new superstar.

There were also suggestions after the Watford wonder show that Salah was more in the mould of Suárez than Messi. Both were natural goalscorers, both were deadly in the box and both had played for Liverpool. My own feeling is that Mo is a more intelligent all-round footballer than Luis; that is why the Messi comparison feels more appropriate.

Liverpool skipper Jordan Henderson was also unsure about the comparison with Suárez when asked about it at a press conference. His opinion was:

They are both fantastic players in their own right and you can't compare them. They are different players. I know they score a lot of goals and both work hard off the ball but it is very difficult to make that comparison. Luis moved on to Barcelona and is doing fantastically well. He is a fantastic player who I was privileged to play with. But Mo this season has been unbelievable. Absolutely unbelievable. He is doing it every week without fail. You have someone like Mo who does the hardest part of the game, which is putting the ball in the back of the net. Then, as a team, if we work as hard as we possibly can, Mo – or even Sadio and Roberto – are going to finish it in the final third. We had that with Luis. You know when you are walking out there are so many goals out there for you.

You'd think that after that four-goal haul Mo Salah might take a game or two to draw breath. Or maybe to help Mané or Firmino to take centre stage by playing a more supporting role. That he might step out of the limelight for a few minutes. After all, it was hard work playing the lead role in every performance. But if we'd tricked ourselves into thinking that, we didn't know how the boy worked. For he followed up the four goals in one match with a further SEVEN in the next SIX games.

The goal machine was showing absolutely no signs of letting up. In fact, as we turned into the business end of the campaign, Mo Salah appeared determined to speed forwards in an even higher gear. It was as if he was being egged on by a personal desire to keep Harry Kane from winning the Golden

Boot for a third consecutive year, at his expense. It was no coincidence that the seven goals saw the team go unbeaten in the six matches (plus the seventh, of course, the previous match against Watford). It had generally been the case that season that when Salah scored, Liverpool tended not to lose.

And there were some pretty important matches in that fresh unbeaten run. The two most important came against Man City in the Champions League (full details in another chapter) with Liverpool winning both and Mo grabbing a goal in each game. Pep Guardiola was heartily sick of the sight of Salah and Liverpool by the middle of April 2018. Sure, City had won the first of the four meetings that season – and won it with a drubbing – but Liverpool had triumphed in the latter three when the trio upfront had fully bedded in (and Mané managed not to get sent off in any of the three, after his red card in the 5–0 earlier defeat).

For all the brilliance and the largely unbeaten run, City just couldn't seem to get to grips with Salah and Co. They couldn't fathom a way to keep them in check, much to Pep's private fury, I was told. He had tried every formation and every attacking trick he had up his sleeve, but still the great Man City kept losing to Liverpool. It was this situation that had many pundits, and fans, believing that it would be the Reds and not the Red Devils (Man Utd) who would be the biggest threat to City retaining their Premier League crown the next season.

Mo also netted in key results against three Prem strugglers who had hit some consistency of form as the season end loomed: Crystal Palace, Bournemouth and West Brom. The 2–1 win at Palace was an especially fine result in the light of their surge from bottom of the table to mid-table safety. It was also a fine result in the sense that it wasn't one of Liverpool's better displays of the season. If they were slightly lucky to come away with a crucial win, they were even luckier that Salah was in their ranks. Even when Liverpool's performance is slightly under par you can rely on their Egyptian superstar to save the day like some footballing Superman. Or as *The Telegraph* described the phenomenon: 'To be clear, this was a long way from vintage Liverpool, who found the going tough against a Crystal Palace brimming with energy and speed. But with Salah finishing like this, Jürgen Klopp's side hardly need to play well to win. Anfield's "Egyptian King", as ever, needed just one clear opening to make the difference. It arrived with the score in the balance, six minutes remaining. He took one touch to kill the ball, and another to kill the game.'

Klopp was almost purring when asked of his latest debt to his best player. 'That is what makes him a proper striker,' the manager announced. 'If you only score when you have a perfect day, you can't score in all the games he has. Outstanding.'

The stats showed just how outstanding the player had been thus far in the season: the goal was his thirty-seventh of the season and his twenty-ninth in the Prem. It was also the twenty-first league game in which he had netted, which equalled the record for an entire season that was previously shared between the illustrious talents of Cristiano Ronaldo and Robin van Persie. Or as *The Mail on Sunday*'s brilliant reporter Oliver Holt put it: 'Man City may be unstoppable, but they do not have a player like Mo Salah!' Olly went on to say: 'Liverpool are on a roll and even if City are uncatchable in the league, they do not have Mohamed Salah. Salah is simply unstoppable and he was unstoppable again in south London. With the scores level and the game in its closing stages, it was, inevitably, the prolific Egyptian who appeared in the box to rifle home Liverpool's winner...City, in their current exalted state, do not fear many players but they will fear him.'

The Champions League success seemed to cast a shadow over Mo and the boys in their final three league matches of the season – a shadow that almost cost them fourth place, and with it that final Champions League spot for the following season. Did they become obsessed with the European Cup at the expense of their domestic challenge? Very probably. You'd have to be superhuman not to let your mind wander as the biggest club match of any footballer's career looms ever closer.

The penultimate couple of Prem games saw Liverpool draw 0–0 at home with doomed Stoke and, more dangerously, lose 1–0 at Chelsea. As Chelsea had now become their main rivals for that final Champions League slot, the defeat was extra damaging as it meant they would now have to secure victory in their final league match to avoid the chance of the Blues nicking fourth place. Salah's main claim to fame in the matches with Stoke and Chelsea was, unfortunately, not one he would have wanted, namely, no goals and one yellow card earned in West London for diving. To be fair, it was his first caution of a long season and that record of just one card is a credit to him; it shows that he is generally an honest player who plays it by the book. It reflects his nature: a genuine, nice guy who always has a smile and a kind word for everyone.

Mo received a rare rebuke from his manager for the dive. Klopp said, 'I don't want to see that. Yes, I think it was a dive. Or he waited for the contact. I am not sure. That is not what he wants to do. But obviously it happened.' The Liverpool manager told the press he believed it had something to do with Salah facing a former club. He said, 'He has now played twice against former teammates. Roma played against him and were very friendly before the game, hug here and there, then in the game, bang. Today it was the same with Antonio Rüdiger. You have to deal with that. He has to be much better.' Mo apologised later to Klopp, saying he had been caught up in the emotion of wanting to win against his former club.

It was a rare aberration from a great player and he made up for it in the final game of the season, scoring against Brighton in a 4–0 victory at Anfield. It was the victory that confirmed Liverpool finishing fourth in the league and guaranteed them one foot in the Champions League – via a qualifier – even if they failed to beat Real Madrid in Kiev. Mo scored a record-breaking thirty-second league goal to win the Golden Boot. There will be more of that and his other honours in what had been a magnificent first season at Anfield elsewhere in this book. Suffice it to say here that, with that goal against Brighton, Salah had also notched forty-four goals in a total of fifty-one matches. No wonder they called him the King of Egypt...no doubt that honour will be extended to include 'King of Liverpool', too, some time soon. He was certainly King of the Premier League in the 2017–18 season.

CHAPTER TWELVE

THE ROAD TO KIEV

The road to Kiev and the Champions League final would certainly be long – and winding, to quote the lyrics of Liverpool's favourite musical sons, The Beatles. Before that classic final on 26 May 2018 in the Ukraine, Mo Salah would travel far and wide as he and Klopp's men attempted to bring the trophy known as 'Big Ears' back to Anfield for a sixth time. Liverpool drew Hoffenheim in the play-off qualifiers, which meant a return to Germany for Klopp. This round had become increasingly more dangerous for English teams over the years as big clubs from the main European leagues now competed. No longer was it a case of expecting a walk in the park against minnows from Switzerland, Denmark or the like. This particular season the playoffs contained – as well as the potentially tough Hoffenheim – Ajax Amsterdam, Sporting Lisbon, Sevilla, Napoli and CSKA Moscow. So you could certainly say that

Salah and Co. had dodged a bullet in not drawing Napoli or Sevilla, both of whom had the potential to cause major problems for any team in Europe.

It would be the first time Klopp had faced a German team in a competitive match and it would be a return to his former club for Firmino, so spice and intrigue there aplenty. Klopp told Liverpool's official website the tie was 'very interesting' and added, 'Actually, it was exactly what I expected when I had a look – if there's a choice we always seem to take the German team! Sorry! It was clear from the first moment when we knew who we could face that there would be no easy game. It's Hoffenheim and that's for sure not an easy game. But we should always not forget what they thought in the moment they saw the draw – it's not the best thing they could get. They have a very young manager, just thirty years old, a very talented man. That's a real challenge but I'm looking forward to it. It's really exciting.'

Klopp was right in two of his comments. It wouldn't be a stroll, and the Germans' manager was indeed 'a very talented man'. Indeed, at the end of the season, there would even be speculation that Julian Nagelsmann was in the running for the Arsenal manager's job, after Arsène Wenger's departure from the Gunners.

But the precocious Nagelsmann was powerless to halt the Klopp juggernaut as Liverpool progressed into the Champions League proper, with a 6–3 aggregate win. The first leg had seen the Reds win 2–1 in Germany, the second 4–2. Salah scored in both legs – even at this infant stage of the season he was hitting the back of the net regularly. And let's not forget this was BEFORE Klopp realised how golden a goal mine he had on his hands. At this stage, Mo was being kept on the right, with no thoughts of him operating as a flexible striker. Even playing him on the right of Liverpool's attack rather than the left would, in retrospect, be viewed as an early misdemeanour of Klopp's. The player was left footed and had always thrived on the left, so why start him on the right?

Certainly he wasn't as comfortable there and Reds fans were unconvinced by his performances – even with those two goals against Hoffenheim. After the second leg, some even took to Twitter to express their worries, with one fan labelling him a potential 'Egyptian Theo Walcott'. Another supporter said: 'Salah should work on his finishing', while another added: 'Think Salah is a dangerous player but has a bit of the Raheem Sterling about him when it comes to being clinical. Hope that improves.' I won't name the fans, but no doubt they are now hanging their heads in shame! It just goes to show how swiftly opinions can change in the always emotionally charged world of Premier League football.

And to be fair to those pessimistic fans, there was a certain anxiety in Mo's play when he was stuck out on the right, even though he had started to hit the back of the net. It would only be as the cascade of goals continued, and Klopp moved him to the left, that the manager realised more precisely what his record buy was capable of, and the damage he could inflict upon opponents. Mo then started to instinctively drift more and more into the centre and it all clicked into place in Klopp's head. The manager then decided to let him roam free, with a left-side starting point.

He now set upon becoming Liverpool's Messi, in terms of that free-to-roam licence and the inordinate number of goals he scored.

So Hoffenheim home and away, allied with the goal he had scored in the Premier League opener against Watford, was a good introduction, and a mighty strong nudge, to his manager about Salah the goal machine. This was the beginning of an idea that gently fermented in Klopp's mind about Salah's ability and would, eventually, lead to the German building his team around the Egyptian's mercurial talents.

Both Klopp and Salah breathed a sigh of relief that the playoff was done and dusted and that the team was now in the Champions League proper. Klopp liked fantasy in his team – hence his reasoning for sorting Liverpool's attack before focusing on defence – but he also had an ingrained realism. He knew it would take something of a miracle for him to win the Premier League that season; in essence, he knew his team was still a work in progress and that the backline required further investment. In his mind, he envisaged a real League push the following season.

For now, given that situation, he believed winning a knockout tournament, one of the cups, was more of an achievable ambition. Even then, the Champions League was more of a pipe dream than a defined target. Liverpool had only arrived in it via a qualifier and the final seemed a long, long way off as Klopp sat in his office at Melwood that August. Possibly the League Cup or the FA Cup might be secured if they had the luck of the draw and stayed relatively injury-free.

So the Champions League, in the group stage at least, was a chance to enjoy the fantasy and excitement it brought, without an overt pressure, or expectation, that Salah and his teammates would win it. It was a marathon event, spread over the season, and at this juncture Klopp told his men to simply go out and enjoy the experience. Enjoy it, do your best and let's see where we stand in December, after all the group games. That freedom to express themselves was evident in Liverpool's first match in the group – the home tie against Sevilla. The Spanish team had themselves evidenced a free-flowing, dynamic football over the past few seasons in Europe – freedom that also brought success as they became the first team to win the Europa League three seasons on the trot. They would come to Anfield to play; theirs was not the sort of Mourinho-style football that demanded you regularly lift the handbrake. In that sense they were viewed by many pundits as a Spanish Liverpool: constructed with the same attacking focus and high-pressing game. It made for a potentially mouth-watering clash – and so it proved.

This was the type of night Mo Salah loved: it was why he had come to Liverpool. He believed in Klopp and had faith in the German when he told him he was joining a team that would soon challenge for the Champions League and the Premier League. That was how Klopp sold him the Liverpool dream; the boy hadn't come just for the increase in wages. He was ambitious, he wanted to be the best player in the world and he wanted a manager who believed in him – and a manager who believed that together they could be the best in the world. Salah had been sold on Klopp and his enthusiasm, determination and generosity of spirit. A cliché maybe, but Klopp was the sort of manager who could inspire such loyalty in players that they would run through brick walls for him.

And on 13 September 2017, Salah showed how much he wanted to win the Champions League and repay Klopp as he helped Liverpool to a 2–2 draw by scoring his team's second goal. As would be the case for much of the season, the rocky defence let him down, conceding twice when Liverpool should have sealed all three points. They had to settle for one, which wasn't the worst start to their group campaign, but it could, and should, have been three. Wissam Ben Yedder had fired the visitors ahead but Firmino equalised. Salah then stepped up to the plate, slotting the ball home, although it did take a deflection, to put Liverpool ahead. The Reds then allowed Joaquin Correa to equalise and thus ensure Sevilla took a point back home to Spain.

It was a disappointing outcome and was made worse by Joe Gomez's sending off in added time. Klopp refused to be downcast, pointing out it was only the start of what he hoped would be a long journey in the competition. He also declared himself 'very, very pleased' by Mo's performance and the way he dovetailed with Mané and Firmino up front. There were definite signs of a 'lethal understanding' between the trio and that could only improve the more they played together.

Klopp told the press, 'It was pretty much a winning performance for eighty-five to eighty-six minutes and the team played well against a side who also play well. We had answers for everything apart from the goals. It was an exciting game from my side; everyone saw our desire and passion but we got a point. We know we have to improve but there is so much potential and we can work with this.'

Salah was voted UEFA's 'Player of the Match' and said he was happy with his performance and his goal and that he would now 'work hard to improve in every match'. He was settling in well at Anfield and enjoying training and making new friends.

Sevilla's Correa admitted that his team were delighted to have achieved a point – and praised Salah. He said, 'This is a really good point. We had to overturn the form of the game to get it. Liverpool are full of quality, extremely fast, with Salah and Mané, and we had to get accustomed to that. My goal was just what we needed. They say, here, that you never walk alone and our travelling fans ensured that that was the case for us too.' His boss, Eduardo Berizzo, agreed that the speed of Salah out wide was a worry all night, adding: 'Even though we went ahead in the first half it was really hard to contain their pace, especially wide, and they play a very vertical style which we couldn't get on top of for a long while.'

The English press were, predictably, critical of Liverpool's defence the following morning. 'Defensive weakness proves Liverpool's downfall again' was the headline in *The Times*. Their chief football writer, Henry Winter, wrote: 'Attack against defence in training at Melwood must be an absolute goal-fest. Liverpool continue to delight with their exhilarating forward movement, and continue to cause palpitations with their inability, individually and collectively, to resist opposition surges.'

But Winter's counterpart at *The Telegraph*, Sam Wallace,

preferred to concentrate purely on the potential of the new strike partnership of Salah and Mané. He wrote: 'In the first half, Sadio Mané and Mohamed Salah, scorer of Liverpool's second, looked like one of Europe's great emerging attacking forces and the futile attempts of Nicolás Pareja in conceding a penalty before the break showcased it perfectly.'

A fortnight later and Mo was packing his suitcase for a trip to Moscow and a tough-looking encounter with local heroes, Spartak. This time he drew a blank in his goals chase but a 1–1 draw meant that Liverpool were still in with a fighting chance in the group. It also meant, of course, that they had now dropped four points in two games. So it really was all about how you viewed the two draws. Was it two points gained, or four lost? Again, looking on the bright side, the team hadn't lost and the point equalled their total away points in their previous Champions League campaign!

The match also signalled the first time that season that the so-called 'Fab Four' – Salah, Firmino, Mané and Coutinho – had started a competitive game. Coutinho equalised but otherwise it was a fairly quiet night for the four stars of the Liverpool team in the Russian capital. Klopp told reporters, 'I'm more happy with the performance than the result, because part of the performance is creating chances and we created a lot of chances. Every Spartak player had to work really hard to get this point somehow. We were not lucky in a few situations. It was a wonderful free kick, to be honest. Then we equalised and had five 100 per cent chances to score more. But we only got a point, that's how it is. The race is still open, we're only in the middle of the race.'

That just showed how pragmatic Klopp could be; he

wasn't kidding himself. He knew he still had much work to do to turn his team into the finished product. But at least the attack was starting to function – and that would certainly be seen in the next fixture in the group.

Once again, Salah would pack his case as this time Liverpool headed to Maribor in Slovenia. The distance the team were travelling was hardly conducive to good rest and fitness but, as Klopp pointed out – and Salah knew from his experiences at Roma – it would be a lot worse if they finished third in the group and ended up in the Europa League. Then the miles would really add up, with extra games and more trips to the grounds of Eastern European minnows. Maribor was famed for being a wine region but Liverpool hadn't journeyed there as tourists – the closest Klopp would get to tasting the wines would be taking a bottle back home. It was more a case of coming in on a daytime flight and back out the same day – leaving John Lennon Airport early on the day of the match and catching the plane home from Maribor that night.

Even then, it was a tiring adventure. Fortunately, it also proved to be a most beneficial one, as Liverpool strolled to a 7–0 victory. This gave them confidence to move forward in the group and proved a good workout for the team. Salah was on particularly good form, scoring twice in the romp in the nineteenth and fortieth minute. Afterwards he told BT Sport: 'It was a great game. We did very well. It's an important result for us, but we have to keep looking forward and win the next games. It doesn't change anything [who scored the fourth goal], the most important thing is the win. We need to focus on improving our position in the Premier

League now, so we need to keep moving forward. We've created many chances and been unlucky in recent games, but we are in a good position now.'

Just how emphatic the victory was could be gauged by the stats that emerged afterwards. It was Liverpool's biggest away win in Europe and the biggest Champions League away win by an English team. It equalled the biggest Champions League away win. And it was Maribor's heaviest home defeat in Europe and their worst Champions League loss. Klopp was also jubilant, telling the press, 'It's nice to do something for the first time in the rich history of the club. It is quite rare to win 7–0. It's nice to write history. But tonight we did unbelievably well. Maribor were quite confident before the game, and they were optimistic because an English team had yet to win here. It was a challenge and remains a challenge to stay confident. We'll try to use the result now.'

It was a big night – sure, the result had been achieved against a team hardly among the European heavyweights. But it had been emphatic and, as Jürgen pointed out, no other English side had ever won at Maribor. And now, with a home match against the Slovenians up next, Liverpool were in the driving seat in Group E. After the two opening draws, the complexion of their challenge suddenly looked much rosier. All they had to do now was continue the goals rush, and hope that the defence avoided its usual creaks.

A fortnight later, the defence held strong and three more goals were added to the tally. Mo opened the scoring that night and the win propelled the Reds one point clear at the top of the group. The *Daily Mirror* had Salah at the top of their ratings in the match, with an eight out of ten mark, and noted that he was 'always dangerous' and 'provided a deft touch for the opener'. Salah declared himself pleased with his strike and that the Reds were now at the top of the group – a sentiment echoed by his manager, who said: 'We knew Maribor would play like this. That was no great surprise to us. But I'm pleased with our result and our reaction. It was not perfect from us, but we scored three goals, kept a clean sheet and are top of the group – perfect!'

Mo had now been involved in thirteen goals for Liverpool so far in the season – ten scored and three assists. In Group E, he had scored four times in four games and had one assist. He was already becoming Liverpool's main man in the Prem and in the Champions League – and was already paying back chunks of his record transfer fee with his displays.

Into November and what looked like being a crunch match for Liverpool's hopes of progressing to the knockout stage: the away match with Sevilla in Spain. Unbelievably, the Reds were 3–0 up within half-an-hour. I had to double check this news after a colleague in Fleet Street told me. Two goals from the increasingly influential Firmino and one from Mané had set a blistering pace – surely that was it, the Reds were home and dry, weren't they? But that was discounting the spirit of a team seemingly flat-lining – cue Liverpool's wonderful win against AC Milan in Istanbul in 2007 – and the wobbly backline that the Reds had in November 2017 (before Van Dijk's arrival added some much-needed stability). Yes, sure as night follows day, so the dam burst as Liverpool conceded three goals to leave

Spain with just one point. It also denied them immediate qualification into the knockout phase – a scenario that would have eased the pressure for their last game in the group, and allowed Klopp to rest some of his stars. Now that plan was up in smoke.

Predictably, the morning's papers in the UK did not make pretty reading for the back four 'marshalled' by Lovren and also featuring Gomez, Moreno and Klavan, with Karius in goal. *The Guardian* said: 'Liverpool owed Sevilla for defeat in the 2016 Europa League final. Instead, they were transported back to Basel as another astonishing second-half recovery from [Klopp's] Spanish nemesis cancelled out a three-goal interval lead and denied Liverpool qualification for the knockout phase of the Champions League.'

And the *Liverpool Echo* later described the draw as a 'wretched capitulation' and blamed a 'lack of game management, maturity and cool heads'.

ESPN summed up the absurd gap the side had between attacking genius and defensive incompetence, reporting that: 'Roberto Firmino, Sadio Mané, Philippe Coutinho and Mohamed Salah all started against Sevilla and the four of them caused havoc during the first half...Liverpool went in at half-time having scored 10 away goals in 135 minutes of Champions League football, following the 7–0 win against Maribor, and they were playing like a team that could score against any opponent. But then came the second-half wobble...'

So the pressure was on. They now had to avoid defeat against Spartak at home to progress. Now the Fab Four would really come into their own, lashing seven goals between them. Perhaps the only surprise was that Mo was only on the scoresheet the once, his goal being the last of the seven. That sent them through to the knockouts as group winners and meant they had hit a remarkable twenty-three goals in just six games.

Coutinho hit his maiden hat-trick for the club, while for Spartak it was their worst defeat, and the heaviest ever loss by any Russian club in European competition. Klopp was elated but found another angle to mention in his press conference – mentioning how impressive Daniel Sturridge was! He said, 'When our front four play like they did tonight they're a threat to any team, but look at how Daniel Sturridge played tonight! He did brilliantly to set up Sadio Mané's second goal. So it's not all about those four.' And when asked which of his Fab Four he liked the best, he replied, rather brilliantly, 'Paul!'

Salah's goal was almost overlooked in the commotion surrounding the win and the hat-trick by Coutinho, who was also skipper for the night. For the record, it was an excellent goal as Mo lashed the ball into the roof of the net from ten yards out. It was a wonderful climax to a wonderful night on Merseyside. The *Liverpool Echo* rated Salah a nine out of ten and said, 'He was never going to be denied, was he? You can take for granted what a fantastic player he is. Just the one goal!' Those comments highlighted how far Salah had now come – both at Liverpool and back in the Premier League.

It was 6 December 2017, and within four months, Mo Salah had become the most lethal goalscorer in Britain. After arriving as a left-winger he was now viewed as a complete striker by his manager, the club, his rivals, the media and the fans. The transformation had been swift and startling and he would progress and develop still further, even outscoring Harry Kane to lift the coveted Golden Boot for the most goals in the Premier League by the season's end.

For now, the main interest for Salah was who the Reds would draw next in the stage of the tournament, the knockout round, now renamed the Round of 16. Then he, and the club, could forget about it and get on with the business of the Premier League and the FA Cup until mid-February.

The draw took place in Nyon, Switzerland, and it was favourable to Liverpool, or viewing it another way, it could have been much worse, since they avoided the European heavyweights Real Madrid and Juventus. The Reds could have faced either of that duo because they both finished second in their groups. Instead, Porto came out of the hat and that had many in the Anfield delegation breathing a sigh of relief. The Portuguese side had admirers for their attacking strengths but, like the Reds, were not as strong defensively. Plus, if the past was anything to go by, the omens were good. The teams had met four times – with Liverpool winning twice and two draws.

But Klopp killed any sense of complacency around the draw, warning his team that Porto were extremely strong opponents, who had significant Champions League experience over the years. They would be no pushover, he said. Porto had finished in second place, behind Turkish side Besiktas but ahead of Bundesliga outfit RB Leipzig to secure their place in the last-16. However, Klopp's words could not quench the elation among Reds' fans, who believed they now had a straightforward passage to the quarter-finals. Indeed, many of them poured on to social media to thank their former midfielder, Xabi Alonso, who was taking part in the draw, and for doing them a big favour by pulling Porto out of the hat!

In the event, they were spot on. Once again, the Reds delivered when it was most needed. In another goals extravaganza the boys demolished the Portuguese 5–0 in their own backyard in the first leg in February 2018. It was a result no one expected even after they had crushed Spartak and Maribor 7–0 apiece, and taken that stunning 3–0 lead at Sevilla. This was just sensational.

Let's not forget that Porto had won the Champions League under José Mourinho, albeit many years previously, and performed regularly at the top table – as Klopp had pointed out beforehand. Yet here they were, losing by almost a cricket score at home. No prizes for guessing who had scored the five goals – the deadly forward line of Mané, Salah and Firmino again took the honours. Mané was the hat-trick man this time, with Mo on target on the half-hour mark. He was on hand with a poacher's knack to slot home after a James Milner effort rebounded off a post. That goal meant Salah had become the first Liverpool player to net thirty in a season since Suárez in 2013/14. It was as if the front three were involved in a personal battle to see who could grab the most goals in the competition.

After this win, it stood at seven for Firmino, six for Salah and five for Mane, and all three featured in the top five for the tournament so far. Klopp refused to pick out his favourite goal of the five on the night, insisting that 'all were fantastic' and added, 'It was very professional, very mature and, in the right moments, very aggressive. It was not easy – it was hard work – but the boys enjoyed it and that's the most important thing. I saw a lot of fantastic performances tonight, and a result like this is only possible if everyone is really at the top of their game.'

It was no coincidence that the team also looked much more solid at the back, with Van Dijk making his Champions League debut after signing for Liverpool a month earlier for £75 million in the winter transfer window. It finally seemed to be coming together at Anfield and Salah would tell pals he was becoming 'more hopeful and more optimistic' that the team could achieve something special in the Champions League that season. He had become great friends with Dejan Lovren and the two of them would talk about their hopes and dreams when they roomed together on trips. Salah was glad that Van Dijk had arrived to ease the pressure on Dejan – he believed the Croat would now show just how good he was and prove the doubters, including myself, what a defender he was. And what of Mo's Premier League hopes?

When he had come to Liverpool he had said his main aim was to win the league. That it meant everything to him after that turbulent spell at Chelsea. Winning the league would erase the spectre of what some considered his 'failure' (although it was hardly Mo's fault that Mourinho didn't play him). He knew the league would have to wait until next season – it was all over bar the shouting as Man City's triumphant procession continued from Christmas (bar that special defeat at Anfield in January, of course).

And Salah knew better, given his experiences of how football could leave you in the doldrums, than to count his chickens and believe he was a certainty to play in the last eight of the Champions League. There was, after all, the small matter of the Porto return at Anfield still to negotiate. That would prove fairly elementary, if a bit of a damp squib after the fireworks Liverpool exploded over in Portugal. The game on 6 March ended o–o with Klopp so confident of a result that he allowed Salah to have a rest on the subs' bench until seventy-four minutes in, when he clearly felt it was time to inject some urgency into proceedings. It may not have been a goal feast for the home fans to gorge on, but the result did leave both clubs happy.

As for Salah and his cohorts, they had now progressed to the quarter-finals of the Champions League, and for Porto, it was respect salvaged after that first leg savaging. Porto coach Sérgio Conceição was generous in his praise and his predictions. He said with that speedy forward line of Salah, Mané and Firmino, Liverpool could even win the tournament: 'Liverpool are definitely one of the teams who can win the Champions League this year. They might not have been at their best this evening, but they're definitely one of the contenders to win the competition.'

Meanwhile, Klopp added in that typical laid-back way of his, 'Being in the last eight is cool. This year I think we belong at this stage. It should not be a big surprise. The next round will be very difficult, that is clear. There could be four other teams from England in the last eight, but I'm not sure if that makes it any easier for us!'

Klopp explained that he had kept Mo on the bench to ensure he was fresh for the weekend's massive clash with Man United, and added, 'Mo Salah did well when he came on. We didn't really plan on bringing him on at any particular time. But he was lively and had some nice touches.' Mo headed over to hug Iker Casillas at the end of the match. The former Real Madrid keeper had given a good performance and received a rousing reception and send-off from the Kop in what would be his last European match. As Mo and Iker hugged, you got the feeling that as one European legend was leaving the biggest stage, another was about to become a dominant player for years to come. A changing of the guard, perhaps. Mo enjoyed the moment and then admitted he was impatient for the draw for the quarter-finals – and to see who was next in his firing line.

CHAPTER THIRTEEN

PEP TALKS

The draw for the quarter-finals of the Champions League threw up a match that left Mo Salah tingling with anticipation. He and Liverpool had been pulled out of the hat with Man City, the Premier League champions-in-waiting. OK, they could have had an easier draw with Sevilla still in the mix. But Mo and his teammates had no fears about taking on Pep Guardiola's team. City had drawn first blood when they had beaten Liverpool 5–0 early in the season. But that game on 9 September 2017 had hardly been a fair representation of the Merseysiders. Sadio Mané's sending-off on thirty-seven minutes had given City an unfair advantage and the initiative. City were a difficult enough team to beat with eleven men on the pitch, let alone ten. Klopp had also taken Salah off at half-time, sacrificing him at the interval for Alex Oxlade-Chamberlain in an attempt to shore up the midfield. At the time the Liverpool backline was much more feeble than it was now – and the reverse fixture at Anfield in January 2018 had seen Liverpool gain revenge, with Mo netting, in a thrilling 4–3 victory.

So Salah was extremely confident that the Reds could overcome City over two legs and was looking forward to the ties. He had scored in his last seven starts at Anfield – with twelve goals in total in those games – and now had forty-one goals in forty-six matches for his club and country in what was becoming an amazing campaign. Mo was a close follower of the game and would analyse his opponents with staff at Liverpool and on his own. He knew that City's Achilles heel was their defence, but he also realised he could make hay down the left wing, cutting into the centre, as they were particularly vulnerable down that side. Benjamin Mendy and his deputy Fabian Delph were out injured and Guardiola had turned to new signing Aymeric Laporte to fill in at left-back. This was not ideal, as he was a big man and a natural centre-back, not a left-back. Salah looked at how the Frenchman had played against Everton in a previous match and believed that he could expose his lack of mobility.

He reasoned that he could get in behind him and get a shot in or, if his two fellow hitmen were in a better position, get the ball over to them. There was much to be optimistic about for Mo Salah as the first leg at Anfield loomed ever closer.

There was also the fact that Klopp had beaten Guardiola more than he had beaten any other manager. He would be seeking his seventh win in thirteen matches over his Spanish counterpart. Klopp also believed his high-pressing system was the way to beat City, who were otherwise an all-conquering outfit. He said, 'You have no alternative if you want to beat City. You could sit deep in your box and hope nothing happens but we are Liverpool and we should try to win this way.'

And then there was the prediction from the TalkSport 'Supercomputer'. The radio station fed a stack of information into a computer and it then came up with an expected result. This time, it predicted a 4–3 win for Liverpool, which was surely as good an omen as any! The computer reckoned Liverpool would win the first leg 3–1 at Anfield with Guardiola's side unable to overcome the deficit, despite winning 2–1 in the second leg.

But respected journalist Ian Hawkey went the other way on website *The National*, (*www.thenational.ae*), saying, 'City's defeat to Liverpool – 4–3 by the end, but 4–1 at 68 minutes, at Liverpool's peak of swashbuckling command at Anfield – in mid-January is not a game Guardiola would care to replay too often, but it will be dissected again now, for fear of another such blitz. This City seem well armed against misfortune repeating itself so anticipate better mechanisms to cope with Liverpool's trio of speedy sophisticates up front. And also a few pointed reminders of what happened when Liverpool went to City, as they must in the second leg, back in September. That finished 5–0 to Guardiola's men. Prediction: Guardiola and City to prevail.'

But it was clear that Salah, Firmino and Mané had become a nagging worry for the City boss as the day of the first leg arrived. Before the match he admitted their speed of play, which he thought made them 'almost unstoppable'. And maybe he could one day take up a second career as a clairvoyant – or a feeder of information to that Supercomputer at TalkSport – because that was exactly what happened at Anfield on 5 April 2018.

Guardiola's worst nightmare became a grim reality. The three musketeers left his City defenders dazed and confused as the Reds stormed to a brilliant 3–0 win. Salah, Mané and Oxlade-Chamberlain supplied the goals but Firmino also played his part with a series of breathtaking runs and clever passes. Mo started what was nineteen minutes of mayhem with his goal in the twelfth minute, Oxlade-Chamberlain added the second in the twentieth minute and Mané headed the third after thirty-one minutes as City's defence predictably crumbled under the non-stop onslaught.

The only minus point was that Salah limped off with a suspected groin injury on fifty-two minutes – an injury that could have ruled him out of the return leg. A hush descended upon Anfield, and BBC Radio 5 live pundit Robbie Savage said, 'You wonder how bad that groin injury might be for Mo Salah. He has walked off, so it could be precautionary, but potentially a huge blow to Liverpool.' Mo had shown his predatory skills with his goal, being in the right place when Kyle Walker failed to clear his lines.

Those fifty-two minutes earned him the title of 'UEFA Key Player', with the commendation: 'He went off injured shortly after half-time, but Salah's first-half contribution might well have earned his team a place in the last four of the UEFA Champions League. The Egyptian was initially quiet but burst into life on 12 minutes, showing superb composure to open the scoring before delivering a delicious cross for Liverpool's third.'

Mo had now been directly involved in forty-nine goals in forty-two games for the club in all competitions. That level of impact put him right up there with Messi and Ronaldo in the European leagues.

And Klopp suggested afterwards that the injury might not be as bad as first thought – and that he had brought the player off purely as a precautionary measure, explaining that: 'Mo came to the touchline and said, "Sometimes there is something." That was for me enough...after the game I asked him and he said, "I will be fine." Now we have to wait for the real diagnosis.' In typical Klopp style, he played down the result, saying it was all still to play for – and even managed to focus on a couple of negatives, saying, 'We lose one player to injury [Salah] and another – the captain [Henderson] – to a yellow card, so it does not feel good. Mo said he feels good but we'll have to see about that.' Klopp was right about Henderson. That yellow meant he would miss the second leg in Manchester. But Salah would recover from the injury niggle and play.

Klopp would then expound upon the brilliance of his side, with perhaps a little regret that they hadn't shown the same qualities all season because they would then be challenging City for the Premier League title. He said:

The first half was brilliant. It was how football should look. We knew about City's quality but also about our quality as well. If we could control the game better against a team like Man City and not give the ball away we would be closer to them in the league. The result is not what we expected but we needed to play more football in the second half. They did not have a lot of chances but we didn't play much football ourselves. It is only half-time.

Now we're 3–0 up it's better than being 3–0 down, but they want to strike back, they didn't play bad – they didn't create the usual number of chances because we defended a lot of moments outstandingly well.

[Klopp then came up with one of his greatest ever quotes about not celebrating too early in football because it had a habit of then making you look rather foolish if you do]:

Three years ago we played Dortmund against Real Madrid and we lost 2–0 away. Everyone told me it was done and I was really angry with that...*You have to celebrate a party when the party starts, not four weeks before.*

Mo paid tribute to Liverpool fans for their backing, saying they were 'brilliant' and had 'helped the team achieve the win'. Anfield on European nights has a tradition of being remarkable with the noise and support the fans generate – a real footballing wall of sound that lifts and inspires the home team and sucks the confidence out of opponents. Tonight had been no different and Henderson added to Salah's tributes to the fans, saying, 'We knew the atmosphere would be brilliant and it was.'

Meanwhile, Guardiola was under no illusions about the size of the mountain his side would now have to climb if they were to make the semi-finals. He dismissed the Salah goal as being 'a mistake' – although it had still required sufficient speed of thought and action by the player to convert from Walker's error – and added, 'The second time they scored a fantastic goal. In the second half we reacted and we played well. We needed one goal but could not score it. We cannot deny it is tough to win now. But we have ninety minutes more.' He was asked whether he himself had made a mistake by dropping Raheem Sterling for İlkay Gündoğan at the time. He answered, 'We lost three-zero', but then tried to justify why he had taken the decision, saying, 'More passes, more control, Gündoğan is very good at arriving in the second line, we wanted to have more control in midfield.'

The media reaction the following morning told the story of the night before. How Salah and his teammates had attacked City without fear and made Guardiola pay a heavy price of an unusual bout of safety-first tactics. *The Guardian* said, 'City ran into a swarm of red as well as a wall of noise. Some City fans sang about Liverpool "living in the past" but the astonishing first 31 minutes of football signalled that Liverpool's fearless approach was very much the future.' While the *Daily Mirror* opined, 'The history is only half written, but this night will go down in Anfield folklore. Liverpool were too good, too fast, too dangerous. Their famous old stadium came alive to revive memories of past European glories and inspire Jürgen Klopp's new generation of heroes.'

And the *Daily Express* was awestruck by the sheer intensity of Liverpool's attacking play, reporting that: 'When Liverpool work up a head of steam like they did last night they take a lot of stopping. A tremendous night was marred by two concerns – the apparent injury to Mo and Henderson's ban from his yellow card –but it was City who picked up all the bruises to their pride and prestige.'

Mo picked himself up and took it easy for a few days. Salah spent time in a hyperbaric oxygen chamber and was ordered to avoid working out and rest up. Hyperbaric oxygen is widely used in sports science to help with recovery. It helps with the reduction of swelling, facilitates healing and reduces fatigue. The oxygen is dissolved into affected areas and helps the body heal.

The day before the Premier League derby clash against Everton, Klopp insisted he had not completely ruled Salah out of the game. He said, 'Of course we've tried everything to make him available. There's still twenty-four hours to go until we start, let's see what happens. But you cannot push a player through a game, not even our supporters would want that.' The manager was absolutely spot on. Of course the fans would want their star man out on the pitch against their bitter local rivals. But on this occasion local pride took a back seat to a golden opportunity in the Champions League.

Sensibly, Klopp decided he would rest him for the derby. It was a joint decision: both Mo and Klopp knew that their chance of honours this season now rested purely upon Champions League success. Of course, it meant a lot to them – and the fans – that the club get a result in the derby game, but everyone connected with Liverpool understood that the Champions League return tie with City now took precedence.

Klopp also left Firmino out of the starting line-up against

Everton, instead opting for a new-look three-pronged attack of Mané, Dominic Solanke and Danny Ings. Firmino was on the bench but Salah was left out altogether. The match against Everton at Goodison Park ended goalless but the point kept Liverpool third in the league, still on target to qualify for the Champions League should they not win it. So the damage-limitation exercise had been achieved: a point away from home and Salah getting the days off so that he could be fresh and ready for the vital second leg at City a few days later.

Salah headed to the Etihad Stadium on 10 April fit and raring to go. His aim was simple – to destroy City and fire Liverpool into the semi-finals of the Champions League. The plan got off to a bad start when Gabriel Jesus put the Blues ahead after just two minutes. It raised hopes within the home team and geed up their fans. They started to believe that the impossible could yet be possible: that they could overwhelm the visitors' three-goal lead and knock them out.

It was a quiet Liverpool dressing room at half-time with City still leading 1–0, the only sound being Klopp's ever enthusiastic voice telling his players they were still 3–1 ahead on aggregate and that they could even still win the match. He encouraged Salah, Mané and Firmino to continue their runs at the City defence and urged the team to maintain their high-pressing game. 'It's only a matter of time – our chances will come,' he said. 'Get back out there and hit them hard!' With that he grabbed each of his team with a familiar bear-hug as they exited the dressing room and exalted them to 'reach for the stars', his fists pumping, the adrenaline electric.

In this manner, Klopp was proving that Liverpool had been right to hire him; he was showing world-class managerial skills. He knew that his team were now hyped up while City looked deflated and lost five minutes into the half. The reason? Their manager and leader was up in the stands after being sent off just before the interval for rushing on to the pitch to argue with the referee over a goal disallowed for offside. Without Guardiola urging them on from the sidelines, City looked rudderless and lost. While Klopp was showing that he was a world-class football manager, his City counterpart, the so-called 'best manager in the world', had lost his head and been sent away from the front.

The proof of that particular pudding arrived just seven minutes into the half as Salah – who else? – ran free through the City defence and lobbed the ball above keeper Ederson for the equalising goal on the night. It was a masterclass in finishing that City's own goal king, Sergio Agüero, would have been mighty proud of.

Mo was yet again in a season of achievement, the Man of the Match, with the BBC commenting: 'Another game, another goal for Mohamed Salah. His cool equaliser on the night took the wind out of City who had dominated a breathless first half.' After Salah's goal City looked lifeless and Firmino knocked the stuffing out of them completely thirteen minutes from time with Liverpool's winner on the night. That made it 5–1 on aggregate and the tie was over. City, supposedly the best team in England by the proverbial mile, had been crushed.

Klopp had steered Liverpool to their first Champions

League semi in ten years – and Mo Salah to his first. Speaking after the win at City, Salah was typically humble about the impact he had upon that game with that wonder goal equaliser. He said it wasn't all about him scoring; it was about the team winning – that was what mattered most to him. 'The goal was a good time for us because they were pressing very high and had many chances,' Mo told BT Sport. 'But we came back and played hard and the win was deserved. I have said many times I play for the team – to help the team win the games. That is the most important thing for me.'

Young Liverpool full-back Andy Robertson was more on the money about Salah's importance to the win: he made it clear, pointing out that Salah had been the key that locked the door on City, just as the hosts had hoped to go on to make it 2–0. Andy went on to say, 'In the first half we struggled to get Mo, Sadio and Roberto into the game. The manager just changed them around a wee bit and in the second half, they were pressing from the front – and then Mo pops up with a goal.'

Salah and Firmino had now scored more goals in a single Champions League campaign for Liverpool than any other player in the history of the club. Each had netted eight times. And the team had hit thirty-three goals in the Champions League this campaign – the most by any English side in one single tournament.

Klopp was ecstatic and made no attempt to hide his joy. He told reporters, 'We completely deserve to be in the semi-finals. We have scored five goals against Man City and only conceded one. These numbers are usually not possible. The boys are maturing constantly. If we have a good day we can beat anyone, on an average day we concede cheap goals. We're still in a development phase, but we're already a good team. I couldn't believe it when I heard Barcelona were out. Roma lost Mo Salah and are in the semi-finals. That's incredible.' Jürgen was talking, of course, about how Roma had overturned a 4–1 loss at the Camp Nou to beat Barca 3–0 in the second leg to also reach the last four of the tournament.

Guardiola was feeling low but, to give him his due, paid Liverpool huge compliments and congratulated them. He said:

We did absolutely everything in the first half. We created chances, even though it's not easy when they have eleven players at the back. In this competition you don't need to play perfectly for 180 minutes, but you need to play well. We were playing against a very good Liverpool side. Look at Barcelona today! This competition is so special. Liverpool fans believe that the Champions League is their competition. We weren't able to create chances at Anfield but did better in the second half. Same as we were here in the first half. We were up against an exceptional team. It's impossible to maintain the same rhythm and intensity over the course of an entire season. Maybe in the future I will realise how we can be better, but I give my players huge credit for their efforts tonight.

Pep would still have his moment in the sun when City finally clinched that Premier League crown. But in this tournament they were already yesterday's men: the whole of the focus and the limelight was on Salah and his teammates and people were now talking openly, rather than whispering, that Liverpool as a unit, with their attacking trio and a defence bolstered massively by Van Dijk's arrival, could actually win the Champions League. Three teams lay in their path – Bayern Munich, Roma and Real Madrid. After the two thrilling, exhausting quarter-final ties with City, surely the semi-final legs would be less demanding on the old heart? Not a chance...cue Mo Salah's former club, Roma.

CHAPTER FOURTEEN

ROME SWEET ROME

When the draw was made for the semi-finals of the Champions League you got the feeling that fate would send Mo Salah back to Rome. Given the choice between Real Madrid, Bayern Munich and Roma, Liverpool would obviously rather the Romans came out of the hat. They were the least dangerous team on paper. Bayern were European heavyweights who always posed problems at this stage of the competition and they had world-class stars like Franck Ribéry, Arjen Robben and Thomas Müller at their disposal. Like Real Madrid, they knew their way around this stage of the tournament and would present a clear and present danger. Real Madrid...well, they had won the Champions League for the past two seasons and were favourites this time around. With Cristiano Ronaldo, Gareth Bale and Toni Kroos they had the talent to take any team apart. On the downside, both Bayern and Real were ageing teams and Bayern had been hit by a number of cruel injury blows. Yet still, Liverpool would take Roma over the two European heavyweights because it would be a contest of two teams of, again what looked on paper, roughly equal talents and hopes.

For Salah, the tie represented a chance to meet up with old friends and to progress to the final. Without being overconfident, he knew his new team had the firepower and resilience to overcome his old team. He looked forward to the two meetings and also to seeing the fans who had cheered him on while he starred for the Serie A side.

It was little wonder Liverpool had no massive anxiety about facing Roma. The Italians had speed and power in their team but lacked the experience of latter stage Champions League matches, which was often the key at this business end of the competition. Liverpool had won the European Cup five times, so the club was well versed in the particular strengths and experience required to go that final step.

Roma, in comparison, were Champions League novices. True, they had enjoyed some good moments in Europe but had never won the Champions League, or even previously progressed beyond the quarter-finals. Having said that, they had, of course, played in a European Cup (the predecessor to the Champs League) final...against Liverpool in 1984. And lost. The club's official website summed up the aching disappointment Roma felt at the time, particularly as they had expected to win given that the final was in their own stadium, stating: 'With Roma enjoying home advantage at the Stadio Olimpico, victory had been expected. The team coached by Liedholm seemed unstoppable with victories over Göteborg, CSKA Sofia, Dynamo Berlin and Dundee United.'

Liverpool were out to spoil the party and after Pruzzo had cancelled out a much-debated opening goal by Phil Neal – with the Roma players complaining that the goalkeeper had been fouled in the build-up to the goal – the match went to penalties. Liverpool, aided by goalkeeper Bruce Grobbelaar's bizarre behaviour on the goal line, triumphed. It proved a great disappointment for Roma and its fans, who saw this as their biggest chance yet to be crowned the greatest team in Europe.

That win showed just how strong the Liverpool team of the era were, both physically and mentally. Their mental resilience proved to be the key, along with Grobbelaar's goal-line antics which were designed to distract the Roma penalty takers at the death.

Mo Salah and Co. would need to have the same mental fortitude if they were to triumph in the second leg in Rome. The modern-day Roma may not have had the experience of Real Madrid or Bayern Munich but they were a more dangerous team in that their star players were faster and had more hunger than their Madrid or Munich counterparts. Liverpool had drawn what looked to be the easier tie against the Romans but they posed a different sort of threat: they were a younger team and were renowned for their pressing, dynamic football, a sort of Italian version of Liverpool, if you like.

The Liverpool of 1984 that the Liverpool of 2018 would have to emulate had much more experience of winning big games and trophies. They had triumphed in three of the last seven European Cups under the genius who was Bob Paisley, and were top dogs at home too. The league title seemed to be their personal fiefdom and they had won it before they faced Roma in the final. Mark Lawrenson was a key player on that wonderful night in Rome in '84 and he said confidence had been vital: the team had believed they would win and that it was their right to do so. In their minds, they were kings of England and of Europe, so of course they would triumph, even if it meant overcoming Roma in their own ground and in front of their massed fans. 'We were a top side,' Lawrenson said. 'We rarely worried about the opposition. We just went out and played. And if we played, we reckoned nobody would stop us.'

'You're aware you're walking into the lion's den,' he was to tell *Goal.com*. 'When we walked around the pitch about an hour before the game, the Roma fans were already inside. They went nuts!' Lawrenson related the oft-told tale of how the Liverpool lads broke the tension by singing as they waited to come out on to the pitch. It showed their rivals that they were not awed by the occasion or the fact that they were in the proverbial lion's den against the home team. He continued: 'I don't remember who started the song. But it was the Chris Rea song "I Don't Know What it is But I Love It". It was just one of those spontaneous things really. The Roma players must have thought we were off our heads.'

Liverpool's star man of the era would later admit that the singing helped. Kenny Dalglish said, 'The boys were singing their heads off. They [Roma] must have thought we were insane.' But if Mark Lawrenson hardly felt the pressure of the cauldron, his defensive partner Alan Hansen certainly did. 'It was the most intimidating sight I've ever seen in my life,' he has said. 'It frightened me how much those fans wanted Roma to win the match.'

However, Michael Robinson, a sub on the day, sensed Liverpool could pull off the win as he watched Graeme Souness do battle with the opposition, saying, 'There were banners outside specially welcoming the English infidels. But it never crossed my mind that we'd lose. We were brainwashed into believing we'd win. Graeme was a Trojan that night. Every player on the pitch was in awe of him. He was brave and magnificent, and led the team like a warrior. Roma had Falcao and Cerezo – two fantastic Brazilian players in midfield. But I forgot they were playing, because of Graeme's performance.'

Roma's proudest moment apart from reaching that 1984 European Cup final against Liverpool came when they won the Inter-Cities Fairs Cup in 1960–61 – that remained their biggest Euro achievement. They could at least say there was one good omen for their clash with Liverpool from that win, as they beat an English side in the final. It saw them come up against Birmingham City in a two-legged affair. The first leg was at St Andrews in the Midlands, the second back at the Stadio Olimpico in Rome. The first leg ended 2–2 but the Romans triumphed 2–0 in the return to take their one and only European trophy. The aura surrounding the competition in England could be gauged by the fact that only 21,000 people turned up at St Andrew's. Roma took a 2–0 lead but Brum pulled two back for an honourable draw.

A crowd of 60,000 enjoyed the return, also showing that the tournament was rather more well-regarded in

Italy than England, with Roma triumphing by two goals to take the trophy on a 4–2 aggregate scoreline. The trophy was presented to Losi, the Roma captain, by Sir Stanley Rous, England's newly-elected FIFA president. The Italian newspaper *Stampa Sera* described Roma as deserving of their win, saying they were the technically superior side and that they had more possession. The victory was not that much of a surprise. Roma were doing OK in the Italian League while Birmingham were bottom of the old English top-flight, Division One. The paper rather un-sportingly took the mickey out of Brum, saying that they were a team of poor quality whose only reasonably good players were stalwart Trevor Smith and teenager Mike Hellawell.

In 2012, the *Birmingham Mail* did a piece on Birmingham City's European adventures and focused on the final against Roma. Even their analysis did not make brilliant reading for the locals – although the semi-final had brought some joy: 'The home leg, in September 1961, was played just 48 hours after an embarrassing League Cup exit at the hands of Third Division Swindon Town. Fabio Cudicini – Carlo's father – was inspired in goal for Roma. Had it not been for his stunning series of saves, Blues would have had a healthy lead to take to the Italian capital. The semi-final tussles against Internazionale also made major headlines. At the San Siro, Blues and Jimmy Bloomfield in particular were scintillating. He set up Jimmy Harris for the first and an own goal paved the way for a 2–1 success. No British club was to win at the ground for another 42 years, until Arsenal's 5–1 victory there in 2003.'

Roma's own website, *asroma.com*, reveals how that final

win over Brum meant a great deal to the club and their fans after the Second World War left them in disarray and anguished, going on to say:

> The club, more than any other, suffered the consequences of the war and was left penniless with no players. After several seasons of under-performance, Roma suffered relegation during the 1950–51 season – the only relegation in Roma's history. The Giallorossi soon bounced back to Serie A – trained by Gipo Viani – but for 10 years the only success was a second-place finish in 1954–55.

At the beginning of 1960, Roma supporters would recapture their enthusiasm via European competitions. In 1960–61, Roma tasted their first international success when the club reached the Fairs Cup final, beating first Union St. Gilloise (0–0, 4–1), Colon (2–0, 0–2, 4–1) and then Hibernian (2–2, 3–3, 6–0) on the way. The final saw Roma, led by Luis Carniglia, take on English team, Birmingham City. In the first leg, away in England, Roma took a two-goal lead thanks to Pedro Manfredini, only for Birmingham to claw back two goals and level the tie. The return match, played at the Olimpico, went more smoothly – with Roma winning 2–0, thanks to a Birmingham own goal and another scored by Paolo Pestrin. The star of the tournament was undoubtedly the great striker Manfredini, who scored 12 goals.

In the Champions League, when Roma qualified, they were perennial group stage or round-of-sixteen hopefuls. Twice, they had made the quarter-finals, in the consecutive seasons of 2006/07 and 2007/08. And this is where it got hopeful again for Liverpool – because Roma twice lost to an English team at this stage of the tournament. It was their best achievement to reach the last eight, but their worst result ever in Europe in one of the matches. Manchester United, Liverpool's bitterest rivals, were the club who tormented the Romans. That heaviest defeat came in the quarter-final second leg at Old Trafford in April 2007. It was even more of a crushing result in that Roma had won 2–1 in the first leg. I was at the second leg and remember how United fans were initially wary that their team was facing an exit from the competition. They reasoned that given the Italians' usual quality defending it could end in a 0–0 draw. So imagine the shock on all sides when United battered Roma 7–1 to progress to the semis on an 8–3 aggregate. Once again the Roma fans and the team were spitting blood; once again the English enemy had wrecked their dream.

The Italian press bemoaned the lack of fighting spirit and ripped into the Roma team. 'Last night was an epochal beating that Italian football has never previously suffered at the hands of the English,' columnist Candido Cannavò wrote. 'Now I run to father Dante to find out what circle of Hell my beloved Roma has fallen into: maybe that of the proud and vainglorious. Conceding three goals in eight minutes could only have happened to a squad that thought it was divine.'

Writing in the newspaper *Corriere Della Sera*, Mario Sconcerti lamented a 'savaging' and did not hold back in his criticism of the team, saying: 'No technical explanation holds. Roma simply arrived second to every ball and to every English move. Experienced players, of an international class like Chivu, Mexès, Panucci and De Rossi, suddenly became fragile like debutants. They didn't understand Manchester's trajectories; they didn't find the ball. We are among the lauded people, we are among the best teams in the world. We are in a time of theoretical equilibrium in football. A technical savaging like this leaves one genuinely stupefied.'

That phrase 'We are among the lauded people' helps explain the way Roma fans see their team. They believe they are one of the best in the world and so expected to watch a triumph in their two-legged clash with another English team eleven years later. All the anger, all the fury and disappointment in Europe had come at the hands of two English teams for these past thirty-odd years – and now Liverpool were going to pay. It mattered little to them that Mohamed Salah, their former idol, now played for Liverpool. He was now one of the sworn enemy: Salah would not get a hero's welcome on his return to the Olimpico in the second leg of the tie. No, at times he would even be booed. The club's pain from the past at the hands of the English meant that he too had to suffer.

After that humiliation at the hands of United, Roma had an immediate chance to put things right the following year – against the same team at the same stage of the same tournament. But once again the English wrecked their party, with United winning 3–0 on aggregate to progress to the semi-finals of the Champions League.

Liverpool would renew hostilities with Roma in the early 2000s in the Champions League and the UEFA Cup. Yet again, they would triumph. Liverpool took four points off Roma in the group stage of the 2001–02 Champs League and went on to knock Roma out of the UEFA Cup the following season. The constant victories – and, in particular, that defining win in Rome in 1984 – helped to explain why there was such a buzz in the Italian capital when Roma were drawn to face Salah and the boys in the 2018 Champions League semis. Revenge was on the minds of the players and the fans; they wanted to ease the pain of '84 by beating the modern-day Liverpool and reaching the final. It meant everything to them and the heightened emotions emphasised why Klopp, as manager, was taking the two-legged semi extremely seriously.

Roma was like a wounded animal: wounded a generation earlier, but determined to exact revenge on the new generation. It would take a major degree of courage and discipline, as well as talent, if Liverpool were going to progress to the final. There could be no hot-headed outbursts or run-ins with the referee; the last thing Klopp wanted was to be facing his opponents with ten men for varying sections of the two games. He told Salah and his teammates that they would need to keep their heads, because Roma's fans, and the Italian press, would be fuelled by that loss in 1984, and those emotions could transmit to the players. Roma would undoubtedly be fired up and Liverpool would have to keep their cool and meet their aggression with disciplined play, Klopp told his players.

But the boss had no worries at all about how Salah would cope with it all. The player had such a wonderful temperament and he was not the type of character to suffer under stress and pressure. Mo always kept his cool, even when defenders tried to kick him out of the game. He would jump over their crude challenges and just smile. What's more, his cheery disposition and mild-mannered approach was no act: what you saw was what you got. Even when he returned to the cauldron of the Olimpico he refused to rise to the bait when some Roma fans booed him. He just got on with the job of helping to destroy their team and taking Liverpool into the semis.

I can only think of two incidents where Mo is claimed to have acted out of character. In April 2018, he seemed annoyed by the attentions of Stoke City defender Bruno Martins Indi in the 0–0 draw at Anfield, and his hand appeared to connect with his rival's face as they both battled for a high ball. Referee Andre Marriner took no action during the game but the FA could have done so using retrospective action, and levelled the charge of violent conduct against Salah. But my take on it was that Mo was trying to win the ball and his arm accidentally connected with Bruno. That view was backed up by a review of the incident by the FA's three-man panel of former referees. They decided it was not a red-card incident and Mo was cleared to play on, thus avoiding a potential three-game ban.

The other flashpoint incident was also in April 2018 when Mo was upset that the official team plane being used to fly Egypt to the World Cup featured a huge image of him on its side. He was 'insulted' that no one from the Egyptian FA consulted him over whether the design would conflict with any of his personal commercial deals. The plane was paid for by Egypt's official team sponsor, telecommunications company WE, and Salah had his own individual deal with Vodafone. Mo took to Twitter to voice his anger and said: 'Unfortunately, the way this has been dealt with is extremely insulting...I was hoping dealings would be classier than this.' Depicting Salah next to the corporate logo of WE could have potentially cost the Liverpool star millions, as doing so would have breached his contract with Vodafone.

But the row was settled after the Egyptian government ordered FA officials to cave in to all Mo's demands. Youth and Sports Minister Khaled Abdel-Aziz summoned the game's bosses for an urgent meeting to resolve the issue. He then said, 'Consider that all the demands made by them [Salah and his agent] are met.'

After that was settled Mo felt able to concentrate fully on the Champions League. Those meetings with his old team Roma would be eventful and emotional, especially given, as we have noted, how the Romans viewed the two matches with Liverpool.

For Mo, that was all irrelevant. For him all that mattered was ensuring that his new team Liverpool overcame his old team and reached the final. His focus and supreme talent would help him achieve just that and, as we shall see, earn him a new moniker that would delight him but also make him shake his head as if to say, 'No, I'm not at that level. Not yet, anyway.'

It was time for the Red Messi to take the stage.

CHAPTER FIFTEEN

THE RED MESSI

Someone in Fleet Street pointed something out to me a day or two after Mo's new nickname became commonplace in April, 2018. He said, 'If you add two letters to the end of the Red Messi you get another word that many Liverpool fans would use about Salah. To them, he is the Red Messiah as much as anything.' I told him that might come over as a tad blasphemous in terms of Christianity, but he just laughed and said, 'So what? To most Liverpool fans their team is their religion!'

The Oxford Dictionary gives this definition of messiah: 'A leader regarded as the saviour of a particular country, group or cause.' The club's supporters have been tempted to regard him as a messiah rather than a manager.

Change 'manager' to 'player' and I suppose you do have an argument that Mo became Liverpool's messiah in his debut season. Henderson may have been the skipper but Mo was the team's leader in that he dragged them on to greater heights with his goals and assists, plus his unbeatable determination to win. This wasn't a footballer who simply showed his genius with a touch here or there, or a bit of wizardry now and then to get the supporters out of their seats. He was a dogged performer who gave his all for ninety minutes; a grafter who put in a shift for the team as well as earning personal glory with the avalanche of goals that defined him as Liverpool's outstanding player.

So in that sense there IS something to substantiate Salah the messiah.

But it was the other moniker, the Red Messi, that would start to be used as the season progressed. It had been another legend of the game who had first publicly commented on Mo's similarity to Lionel. Former Arsenal star and now TV pundit Ian Wright had said earlier in the season, 'I'm not saying he's as good as who I'm going to say, but he reminds me of Messi, the scampering way he plays. He gives me a Messi vibe. He's short, his style. He's got a Messi vibe.'

A couple of dozen more goals later and the nickname had caught on, and was being openly used as the Reds' two crunch Champions League semi ties with Roma loomed. When the draw was made Roma sent a tweet to Mo. It said: 'We'll be opponents for 180 minutes, but whatever happens we'll be friends for life. Looking forward to seeing you again.' Mo's reply was simple but typical of the man: '100%'. It was clear from those exchanges that Roma and Mo still felt great affection for each other. However, that wasn't the case as far as Roma's fans were concerned: they wanted to beat Liverpool, and Mo as well, so as to dust away the cobwebs of despair that still lingered from those bruising earlier encounters. Indeed, some Roma fans would even boo their former hero during the return leg in the Olimpico.

Mo told cable channel CNN International how the Roma players had said they did not want to draw him or Liverpool in the semis. He commented, 'They've all said: "We don't want to play against Liverpool."' But he was looking forward to taking on his old teammates and said he had no bad feelings whatsoever about the club or the fans. He added, 'It would be nice to go back to Rome, it's my old club. I love the fans there and they love me too. I still talk to most of the players there. We were very close to each other and we are good friends. Of course, I have happy memories. We played together for two years and were fighting together in all the games. We had a good time in the dressing room.'

He was also confident that Liverpool would not only overcome Roma, but would win the final, even if it were against Real Madrid.

Roma's Director of Football, Ramón Rodríguez Verdejo, universally known as Monchi, admitted that the tie made him nervous and said the team would need to repeat their second leg performance against Barcelona in the quarter finals if they were to progress. They beat the Spanish giants 3–0 in Rome after losing the first leg 4–1, a quite remarkable turnaround against the team who were favourites to lift the trophy. Monchi could not help indirectly referencing that 1984 loss when he spoke to the press about the Liverpool ties, saying, 'It feels like a great opportunity to chase the joy that we were not able to experience so many years ago. But of course, it will be difficult because Liverpool are an extremely strong side. We need to think about ourselves, and try to reproduce what we were able to show against Barcelona.'

Monchi held great sway at Roma and was credited with being the mastermind behind their march to the semis. He was responsible for bringing in players at realistic prices and players who still had a hunger to win. Men such as Aleksandar Kolarov, who had seemed washed up at Man City, and influential midfielder Lorenzo Pellegrini, who had lost his way at Sassuolo. Monchi's power base at Roma meant he was THE man whose opinion counted, unlike in England where the head coach (or manager) has the final say. Monchi would guide and work with head coach, Eusebio Di Francesco. The system was paying dividends as Roma headed upwards in Serie A and made the semis of the Champions League.

But Monchi would admit that he 'didn't have the best relationship' with Mo Salah. Could it be because he made a rare transfer market blunder in letting the player leave for a fee that would be around five times less than what he was worth? Monchi, a former goalkeeper with Sevilla, would tell *calciomercato.com*, 'I've never played at Anfield but the last final I won with Sevilla [when he was their director of football] was against Liverpool. It will be a debut for me. Salah? I don't have the best relationship with him, we didn't spend lot of time together and he is very shy. I will be happy to greet him anyway. Our priority is qualify for the Champions League. I would swap the Champions League final with the fifth place only if in the end we win the Champions League.'

All Monchi's efforts would come to nothing as Liverpool ruined his dream and added another level of bitterness to Roma's attitude towards the Merseysiders. The majority of Liverpool fans had been ecstatic that the club had drawn Roma – they believed that it presented the easier route to the final given that the alternative scenarios would have seen their team taking on the might of Real Madrid or Bayern Munich. One fan tweeted: 'Apologies in advance Roma!' while another said: 'That's it then. Liverpool winning their 6th European trophy,' and another added: 'Yessss! Six times!' There was an element of overconfidence in the outpourings of joy but Salah would ensure that they weren't misplaced. After his masterclass in the 5–1 aggregate quarter-final win over Man City he was again the genius who propelled the team on to glory in the first leg against Roma at Anfield. There'll be more of the City masterclass in another chapter.

If his display against City had started the talk of him being the 'Red Messi' this was the performance that truly justified the nickname. He simply tore Roma apart at Anfield. Mo scored twice and left the Italians' defence dazed and dejected. Like Messi, he had that wonderful ability to slalom between defenders and to control the ball majestically even when it looked as if he was off balance. That low centre of gravity that all the modern great forwards share – Messi, Agüero and Paulo Dybala included – meant he was dastardly difficult to knock off the ball. And when he had gone past two or three – usually cutting in from the left wing, or when in the centre – he invariably managed to complete the magic trick by jinking the ball into the back of the net. Or smashing it home or, on occasion, nodding it past the keeper. This was the stuff that greatness was made of it. Roma had known the threat he posed when he had been in their ranks at the Olimpico. But now, unfortunately for them, they saw it from the viewpoint of the vanquished enemy.

The tie appeared over when Liverpool went 5–0 up and Klopp brought Salah off to a standing ovation after his goals on thirty-five and forty-five minutes. The little genius had also made assist for two of the other goals. He had now entered the Liverpool record book for Champions League achievements. He had netted in each of his past five Champions League starts, thus matching the feat of Steven Gerrard from October 2007 to February 2008. And he had hit ten goals in the Champions League in his first season at the club, equalling Roberto Firmino as the most scored by a Liverpool player in a single season in European competition. Plus he had become the first African player in history to score at least nine goals in a single European Cup/ Champions League season.

For all that those record breakers showed just what a player he had become, his seventy-fifth minute substitution felt akin to an actor receiving rapturous acclaim after a brilliant performance at the theatre. But the decision by Klopp to take off his star man backfired. Psychologically, it may have left his team feeling as if the job was done; after all, if you sub your best player you must be pretty darned confident that you believe the night's work is complete. It could have led to those left on the pitch taking their feet off the pedal. Or it could have meant that Liverpool simply weren't as effective without Salah. Or, more likely, it revved up the opposition to believe that they could snatch some consolation – that psychologically, it boosted them.

Whatever, the bad news now would be that Roma would grab two late goals, including a debated penalty that left the final score 5–2. On paper, it still looked as if Liverpool had enough of a cushion to make the return leg in the Olimpico a formality. But no one at Liverpool was thinking that. Indeed, the mood in the dressing room – which you would have imagined would have been celebratory after such a resounding win – was in fact fairly downbeat. There wasn't exactly a sense that Liverpool had blown it – just that they might have made their task that much harder now. That was down to Roma having beaten Barcelona 3–0 at home in the previous round after that first leg 4–1 trouncing at the Camp Nou. It suggested that Roma were a very different animal on their home turf and served as a harsh warning to Liverpool. The goals' difference was the same as Roma had faced with Barca, and a 4–1 win would take them through to the final on away goals.

So there was a tempered joy in the home dressing room at Anfield. It was a fine result in that Klopp would have anticipated it before kick-off but there was a realisation that it could have been so much better, and easier, to take a 5–0 into the second leg. The press take was generally of that view, but that didn't stop the extravagant praise for the 'Red Messi' gushing forth. BBC Sport led the way, commenting: 'Another Mohamed Salah masterclass helped Liverpool take control of their Champions League semi-final – but two late Roma away goals gave the Italian side a glimmer of hope for the second leg. Liverpool, who last reached the final in 2007, repeatedly breached the visitors' naively high defensive line and scored five times in the opening sixty-eight minutes at a raucous Anfield. Salah, who has now scored forty-three goals since his summer move from Roma, scored twice and assisted two other goals.'

The pundits also lined up to pay homage. 'You've got to give him the Ballon d'Or,' former Leicester ace Robbie Savage told Radio 5 Live. 'He is that good. Never mind the PFA Player of the Year, just give him the Ballon d'Or.' Former Liverpool striker Robbie Fowler said, 'The form and confidence he's in at the minute, to have the class and style to score those goals just speaks measures of the man. The man we all talked about before the game – the man for the big occasion. He is a phenomenal player.'

Another ex-Anfield idol, Steve McManaman, also did not hold back in his effusive praise, telling BT Sport, 'It's just like a stroll in the park. I'm amazed by this performance tonight. It's absolutely unbelievable! You just can't believe it!' While former Liverpool and Roma defender John Arne Riise tweeted: 'The work-rate and intensity of the Liverpool team is insane! They just don't stop. The front three are destroying the Roma defence, who can't cope with the pace and movements.' And *Match of the Day* presenter Gary Lineker tweeted: 'Oh Mo. Oh My.'

The boss also got in on the act. Klopp told reporters that his man was world class but cautioned that he would have to produce the goods again and again to be considered the greatest, adding that: 'To be the best in the world maybe you have to do it for a longer period. His first goal is a genius strike; he's scored a couple like that. The second goal was also great play. He is in outstandingly good shape. He is a fantastic player that we are really happy to have. What a player!'

Salah had felt a bit emotional and nostalgic when the draw had been made but Klopp had told him that would change when the action began. And so it proved. Mo may have seemed reluctant to celebrate wildly when he scored but his display proved he emphatically was not affected emotionally. Klopp had told reporters before the match that Mo 'would feel very early in the game that they are not his teammates any more' and that he had encouraged him 'to strike back in a football way'. Well, he had certainly done that – and lived up to the nickname 'The Red Messi'. Now he just had to do it again in the return leg in Rome.

CHAPTER SIXTEEN

ETERNALLY YOURS

Mo hopped on the private jet for the return leg in Rome with a spring in his step. Sure, it was a big game – the biggest of his life – with lots at stake. But he was determined to enjoy himself. Nights in football didn't come much bigger than this, barring the Champions League final, of course. And Salah was returning to Italy, where he had not only repaired his reputation after that disastrous spell at Chelsea but had developed to become a footballer in much demand. His performances at Fiorentina, and in the Italian capital particularly, had led to a host of the biggest clubs in the world knocking on his door. Liverpool had been the most insistent contender and Klopp had offered the most vision to a player who always wanted to be moving upwards. Now he would return to Rome and have a chance to see friends and (the majority) of fans who had adored him would now welcome him back.

You could sense the good feeling emanating from Mo and the crowds who gathered at Rome airport as the Liverpool plane landed. No sooner had he walked down the steps on to the tarmac than he was hugged by a representative from Roma. Then a gaggle of fans – supporters of both Roma and Liverpool – implored him to sign autographs and have a selfie with them before he and his teammates were hustled on to a coach that would transport them to their hotel. Police were on hand – including officers from Liverpool – at Fiumicino Airport as part of the ramped-up security that would accompany the team and their fans throughout their stay, as a result of the violence that left a Liverpool fan fighting for his life in hospital after he was attacked by Roma thugs before the first leg. One security officer stayed close by Mo as he disembarked from the plane, but he wasn't needed. There was no one who wanted to hurt Liverpool's star man; the fans had come to praise Caesar, not to bury him.

One well-known Roma fan explained why Mo could expect a warm welcome on his return. 'We have good memories of Salah. We loved him. Nobody was angry at him when he left,' Daniel Manusia, editor-in-chief of the sports website *L'Ultimo Uomo* (*ultimouomo.com*) told the *Bleacher Report*. 'Normally when an ex-player plays well or scores against you, you are sad and angry. If Pjanić [who quit Roma for detested rivals Juventus], for example, curled two free kicks into the net against Roma and provided two assists, we'd be after his life. But Salah will always be very welcome. He was always a very professional player and he was always very kind towards Roma's supporters.'

And Liverpool boss Klopp had no doubt whatsoever that

Salah would take the return to Rome in his stride. He told reporters before the trip, 'With Mo, everyone likes the hype around him. When we came out for the Champions League training against Manchester City I said to the boys, "We go out naked because no one will notice – they are only here to see if Mo is okay!" The boys are smart enough and Mo is so thankful. Now we go to Rome and I don't think the hype will be a little bit less for him. Everybody knows how big Mo's impact on our season has been – and they've played a season without him. Where would they be if Mo was still there in Rome? It makes it a really interesting thing and for him, it will be 100 per cent special. He is already of interest wherever we go, but it might go crazy when we go to Rome! He can deal with that, I am sure.'

And deal with it he did. The only real surprise of the night was that Mo didn't get on to the scoresheet when there were six goals scored. Roma turned the tie upside down, just as they had done against Barcelona in the previous round. They won 4–2 and so were only a goal away from taking the game into extra time. Jürgen Klopp had been spot on with his pre-match assessment of the hosts. He had warned: 'We have to work again in Rome, that is no problem. There would have been work to do if we won 5–0 because Roma would do everything to strike back. Roma need to score against us and we are not Barcelona. Barcelona is one of the two or three best teams in the world and won so many things in the last few years. We didn't, so we will fight with all we have for the result.'

And Roma boss Eusebio Di Francesco's warning had also proved relevant. Like Klopp, he had told reporters: 'Let me remind you once again the tie is not over and we have proved it. We have shown we can come back. We scored three goals at home against Barcelona, so we can do it. If any of my players does not believe we can win, they can stay away from the second leg.'

Of course as the showdown loomed ever closer the pressure cranked up on Mo. He was the main target of the paparazzi when Liverpool left the hotel for training and returned after it. Away from the training pitch, he spent his time relaxing, reading a little and speaking on the phone to his wife back home. He seemed immune to the pressure; he slept well and his countenance continued to be one of a pleasant, easy-going guy as he moved around Rome with the Liverpool entourage. Even on the day of the game Salah looked like a man who did not have a care in the world, although he listened as intently as his teammates when Klopp outlined what the match meant and what a victory would mean.

Jürgen emphasised the same theme when he spoke to reporters before the encounter in the Olimpico. He said that he had told his players that 'no one remembers losers' and that they needed to win so that they could get to the final and, hopefully, secure their legacy. An eternal legacy would have been engineered in part in the so-called Eternal city. Klopp said:

I don't think people are interested in semi-final losers, same as final losers. In football, as in life, if you are not ready to lose, you cannot win. You try everything to win – there are no guarantees that you get it – but it is the only chance that you try. If this team goes to the final it would be an outstanding achievement already. It is not the prize we want because if you go to a final then of course you have to think a little bit bigger, but it would be something we could not have expected at the start of the season.

We were not even qualified for the Champions League, we had to play a qualifier, and I don't know who else reached the semis having been a qualifier at the start. The boys really stepped up. They constantly saw the competition as an opportunity. There have been so many big developments this year. This team can still develop and we will bring in a few fresh legs as well because we need them for being on a high level constantly. A lot of things are really good but you must not be afraid that players do not know their responsibility to be successful. In the end, there will be a team at Liverpool at one point that wins silverware and we all hope that we are involved in that.

Klopp could have taken even more heart if his knowledge of English contenders in the Champions League had been better. His comment that 'I don't know who else reached the semis having been a qualifier at the start' drew wry smiles back in Manchester, at Old Trafford. For Man United had won the Champions League in 1999 after starting as qualifiers in the competition. A lucky omen lay just thirty-eight miles down the East Lancs Road, although Liverpool fans would no doubt not enjoy being reminded of the fact given their fierce rivalry with United.

The boss provided a rallying cry by claiming his team

were ready to make history and that they could come through their Roman passage successfully – and that it could be the start of something fantastic for Salah and the boys. He added:

> From the first minute I came in, you are confronted straight away by the history of this club. Did you ever hear a player who just signed a new contract not say, 'I want to win silverware?' They always say that. You cannot come to Liverpool and say, 'Obviously it's quite a comfortable situation so I'll have a few nice years of my career here.' We are Liverpool so somebody kicks our arses constantly. It is 'make the next step, make the next step, make the next step'. It is not possible in this club to stand still. We need to deliver and the good news is we have now a real group of players. I really think it is difficult to improve it a lot. They are at the best football age. Too young to say they are really experienced, but already that good that you think, 'OK, we could do something special.'

Liverpool have had some fantastic managers over the years and Klopp, after two years at the helm, was showing that he was ready to join the roll call of honour alongside the likes of Kenny Dalglish, Bob Paisley and Bill Shankly. This man was just the man the club needed to take it back to the real big time where they belonged. The man to 'knock Man Utd off their perch', just as Alex Ferguson had pledged to do to Liverpool when he joined the Old Trafford club in 1986. Except now it would be more a case of 'knocking Man City off their perch' given the quality they showed to win the Premier League with a points total of a hundred in 2018. Klopp had sold the dream and the vision that he had to Mo Salah. And the little man was now repaying him.

Salah's night in Rome at the back end of April 2018 would go down in history as the night he and this Liverpool team, and their manager, came of age. OK, they lost the tie and nails were being bitten at the end. But everyone, apart from probably diehard Roma fans, would agree that Liverpool and Salah were worthy victors over the two legs. And that Liverpool would pose more of a threat to Real Madrid in the final, basically because they had the world-class talent of Salah in their ranks. Roma had no one to match him. The fact that he destroyed them while playing for the team they sold him to probably rankled more than they would ever admit publicly. What had seemed like a good price, and a good deal, now had the air of a real clanger. Mo had been the Reds' record buy, but that fee now looked like it had been a bargain. And that misjudgement was hard for Roma and their fanatical followers to digest. Many of them wished Salah well after the match, but there were some who had booed him, and who would be glad if they never saw him again on an opposing team.

Roma had scored twice in the final four minutes because of the efforts of Radja Nainggolan, but it was not enough to force extra-time.

The end result meant Liverpool had triumphed by seven goals to six and would meet Real Madrid in the Champions League final on 26 May in Kiev, Ukraine. Liverpool had been beaten in the Champions League for the first time that season but Mo Salah couldn't really have cared less. In his debut season at his new club, he was in the final of the most prestigious club tournament in the world and would pit his skills against the man who was undoubtedly one of the best two players on the planet: Cristiano Ronaldo.

Mo said that it was 'the high point' of his career and he was 'so proud' to be part of a team that had reached the Champions League final. All his efforts, all his work through the years and his commitment to his profession had paid off in the best way imaginable. Sure, he felt 'sad' for his former teammates at Roma but said they had played well and were a great team themselves. It wasn't the end for Roma, he was sure of that. But for him and Liverpool he believed it 'was now the start of something' and he 'wanted to be part of it'. If they could go on and win the Champions League he was sure they could then use it as a launchpad for the Premier League the following season.

Klopp, meanwhile, was honest enough to admit that his team had been a little fortunate. He told reporters, 'We were lucky today, we know that. Roma are strong, we had them where we wanted, as they were wild, ran the risks and we went 2–1 up. All good. But then we didn't do enough on the counter, we didn't use the space that they gave us and we lost the game after going 1–0 up already. I know...we have to play much better than tonight. The good news is that we can play much better than tonight.'

Despite the 'off-night', Mo's new standing in the game did not take a dive. Indeed the Messi comparisons continued to be made but Mo had, typically given his humility, laughed them off, saying, 'It is certainly a good thing to be compared to a player as great as Messi, who has been at the top for as many years. But the only comparison really is the number of goals we have scored this season.' There was an argument doing the rounds that had a certain validity to it: that Salah had actually had a MORE impressive current campaign than Messi, since his goals came in the tougher climate of the English Premier League, while Messi was scoring against some teams in La Liga who were probably no more than mid Championship level. Salah's goals surely carried more weight and were, therefore, a more impressive tally than Messi's (or Ronaldo's come to that).

Dejan Lovren was certainly of the opinion that Mo was as deserving as the dynamic duo and, inadvertently, piled a bit more pressure on the little man's shoulders by saying so publicly. The defender told reporters:

Forty-three goals. F***ing hell. I don't know if this is the right time to put pressure on him but I believe he should be regarded as one of the best three in the world at the end of the year. He deserves it how he is doing right now. He deserves to be mentioned for the Ballon d'Or – when people talk about Messi and Ronaldo they should also talk about Salah. He deserves the credit but I think he deserves even more, to be honest. He is becoming the superstar. It looks easy what he does but it is very difficult. We help him, the manager helps, and this style of play helps him a lot. He didn't play that style before at Basel, Chelsea and Roma. They had different styles and this style suits him perfectly. Hopefully he can stay injury free.

It was certainly an interesting observation from Lovren that Liverpool's high-pressing style of play was more suited to Salah's talent than Roma's slower build-ups had been when he played in Italy. The three-pronged attack that Klopp employed at Anfield was made for Mo in that it was flexible, speedy and interchangeable. It replicated the system Pep Guardiola was using at Man City, where he often played Sterling, Sané and Jesus together. At Liverpool Mo was able to cut in from his favourite left wing but also had the versatility to play more central, since both Mané and Firmino were intelligent forwards who could move fluidly across the front line.

Klopp had helped Salah blossom by giving him the freedom to express himself in a team that loved to attack. Mo responded with the goal festival that propelled himself and Liverpool into the stratosphere. He had finally found his ideal club – the results, the goals and the personal accolades and honours he received at the business end of the season served to emphasise that was the case. Mo couldn't have been happier as he prepared for that meeting with Real Madrid in Kiev. Life didn't get much better than this for a footballer who many fans in England had written off after his time at Chelsea. When Liverpool signed him there was a general scratching of heads, with pundits and fans wondering how a man who had not shone at Chelsea could do so on Merseyside. But no one was doubting Mo Salah now.

Yet as the praise continued, Roma president James Pallotta provided an amusing anecdote about his Liverpool counterpart John W. Henry, which suggested the move might NOT have come about. Pallotta claimed that Henry had moaned to him about the fee for Salah and that the Reds only ended up with a 'bargain' because Pallotta soothed Henry over lunch! The Roma chief relayed the story to *ESPN.com*: 'I told him that because he was sort of bitching a little about, "Did we overpay? I think we overpaid," and I said "I'll buy you lunch," Well, when you look at it now, you can say it's an unbelievable bargain. The issue at the time was that when [director of football] Monchi came in, Salah wanted to leave, he had a year left on his contract so in another year you'd get nothing. He wanted to go back [to the Premier League] and prove himself, which he certainly has done.'

The deal was done much to Pallotta's chagrin, and to Henry's delight. The American now realised he had not only got a bargain, he had hit the bloody jackpot.

CHAPTER SEVENTEEN

THE GOLDEN BOY

Looking back over Premier League history, I couldn't find any footballer who had been more decorated with personal awards and honours than Mo Salah was in the 2017–18 campaign. You could tell just how crazy things were getting when Mo received one of the most unusual tributes I can recall for a professional footballer. Four days after the Premier League wrapped up it was revealed that a pair of Mo's boots would be exhibited at the British Museum in London. But not just as part of any old exhibition: no, they would be added to the world-renowned Egyptian historical collection amidst the statues of ancient pharaohs!

Mo's adidas X17 'Deadly Strike' boots went on display with the biggest collection of Egyptian objects outside of Egypt – which included the Rosetta Stone, a block of black 'grandiorite' stone, originally thought to be housed in an Egyptian temple, inscribed with three versions of an ancient decree that was issued during the Ptolemaic dynasty in 196

BC. Also in the collection is a 5,000-year-old sand-dried mummy, wall paintings from the tomb of Nebamun and sculptures of Ramesses the Great, the third pharaoh of the nineteenth Dynasty of Egypt. The boots went on public display the week before the Champions League final – to add to the build-up of interest. It showed just how popular Salah had become and the magnitude of his achievements, from an Egyptian perspective.

The display was to commemorate Salah winning the Premier League Golden Boot. Mo had already led his country to the World Cup finals in Russia in the summer of 2018 and this new honour reflected his standing in the game and in his native Egypt. Dr Neal Spencer, Keeper of the Department of Ancient Egypt and Sudan at the British Museum, said, 'This acquisition brings the British Museum's world-famous Egyptian collection right up to date. The boots tell a story of a modern Egyptian icon, performing in the UK, with a truly global impact. Displayed amidst the statues of ancient pharaohs, we now show the boots with which Mo Salah won the Golden Boot for Liverpool.

'Salah will shortly lead his national team, known as The Pharaohs, to the World Cup Finals. This acquisition builds on our recent project to acquire objects to tell the story of day-to-day life in 20th and 21st-century Egypt. From sport, to entertainment, worldwide trade to design, this collection is now accessible to all – like those from other periods of Egypt's rich history.'

Mo had claimed the Golden Boot after scoring in Liverpool's final Premier League match of the season. That goal took his total to a remarkable thirty-two in just thirty-eight games (and he actually achieved it in thirty-six, as he missed two games). This is the most goals scored by one player in a single thirty-eight-match season. 'This is very special,' he told Sky Sports after the final whistle in the Brighton win. 'It's always in my mind to help the team to win games, now we are in the Champions League next year and I have won the award, so I am very proud. It was always in my mind when I came back to England to give 100 per cent and have a great season. I am trying to improve every year so I am very happy. It's special to break the record here.'

In total, Salah scored against seventeen different opponents – another record, since no player has scored against more in the Premier League era. Tottenham's Harry Kane, who had won the Golden Boot for the previous two seasons, was second to Mo with thirty goals for the season. Manchester City's Sergio Agüero was third on twenty-one and Leicester's Jamie Vardy came third on twenty.

The Premier League provided a full rundown of precisely how the thirty-two goals were scored and other stats surrounding the marvellous achievement. Mo had scored a goal every 0.89 games, two with his head, five with his right foot, twenty-five with his left and one from the penalty spot. He had 144 shots, with sixty-seven on target, a shooting accuracy of 47 per cent, he hit the woodwork three times and missed 'Twenty-three big chances'.

That stat about 47 per cent accuracy will be one that Liverpool will have taken note of. It's good that a striker shoots on target, of course, but just imagine what the goals ratio would be if Salah became even more accurate.

He might be on course to be the first fifty-goal Prem marksman! Mo had also assisted ten goals, created ten big chances and provided eighty-six crosses for his teammates to hopefully capitalise on. In those thirty-six appearances he had been on the winning side twenty times and the losing team five times, with eleven draws. Maybe this is another area in which Liverpool could improve – turning three of those draws into wins would have earned them an extra six points and second place in the final league table above Man United on goal difference.

Mo became the second African after Didier Drogba (2006–07, 2009–10) to claim the prize and the third Liverpool player after Michael Owen (1997–98, 1998–99) and Luis Suárez (2013–14).

The man Mo beat to the award congratulated him after he was presented with the trophy and also set him a challenge for the following season. Harry Kane's thirty goals had been his best ever haul in a Premier League season and he felt that his and Salah's feats would push them both to do even better next time around. Kane told reporters:

It's good to have competition and it's great for the Premier League to have two players at the thirty-goal mark. For me, it was a target to improve on last year, when I got twenty-nine, and it was nice to get to that thirty-goal mark. Mo has done great this year, he deserves it, he deserves the Golden Boot. I am looking forward to the competition again next season.

I haven't seen Mo to talk with him. But this is what you want at the highest level – you want to be fighting for things and I think we pushed each other. He broke the record for a thirty-eight-game season and that is what I will try to do next season. For me, it is about doing it year after year. This is my fourth year now and the first time I have got to thirty goals in the Prem. Now it's about getting to thirty goals for the next two or three years. That's the aim. Any player wants to do it on a consistent basis and that's what defines a good player from a great player. Mo has done amazing and he looks like a great player. We'll see if we can both continue it next season.

Was there the slightest of niggles in there? Knowing Kane, no. He is as honest and straight-talking as they come in the game. Also, like Mo, he is one of the nicest guys on the 'circuit'. Some people had read into the line: 'Any player wants to do it on a consistent basis and that's what defines a good player from a great player' as being a dig but I don't think so. Harry was genuinely pleased for Salah although, being the fierce competitor he is, he also didn't like losing out, especially as he had set his heart on winning the award for a third consecutive time.

There had also been that business about Kane claiming a goal that looked like it had been scored by Christian Eriksen. Harry had 'sworn on his daughter's life' that he had got a touch and that it was, therefore, his goal. He was mocked mercilessly by fellow pros and fans, who said it was merely a case of Kane trying to up his tally so that he could catch Salah in the race for the Golden Boot. A few days after the goal was credited to Harry, he shared a video of himself in action at a golf course in rural Essex and compared himself to golfing legend Tiger Woods. He wrote: 'Taking the Tiger line! A great round in the sun at Abridge Golf Club.' That remark opened the door to many fans taking the mickey on social media. One fan said: 'Are u gonna claim the Masters Green Jacket and all other golf tours now (asking for Eriksen).' And another said: 'Claimed a hole in one?' While someone else added: 'He'll claim the ball gone into the hole', while yet another said: 'I heard the FA is gonna count that as a goal too.'

The Premier League goals accreditation panel reviewed the goal and decided that Harry did take a touch, and even Mo got in on the act, tweeting: 'Wooooooooh really?' Alan Shearer also tweeted, saying: 'I wonder if they will give me the other nine I also scored but were not given?' And Gary Lineker added: 'I was only ten yards away from Platt's volley against Belgium if that's near enough? Could yet be England's leading scorer.'

The sarcasm continued but Kane himself did not find it at all funny. Spurs boss Mauricio Pochettino said Harry would 'learn a lot' from the incident and that he was 'disappointed because he never wanted to create this'. Pochettino felt that his player had received a raw deal and said, 'Sometimes, it is a small or simple thing that becomes bigger and bigger and bigger and bigger and you cannot stop it. That was what happened. He is going to learn a lot from this. Of course he never thought that this situation was going to go on to such big things when he was so, so, so, so certain that he touched the ball. It's normal that he was a little bit disappointed because of course Harry and all of our players have Twitter, Instagram, everything. Tottenham fans will back Harry but other fans will kill him. People have opinions but that is normal.'

Kane's act was also backed by his Spurs and England teammate Dele Alli, who told the press that Harry had done nothing wrong and that the goal was his, not Eriksen's. Alli went on to say, 'Harry is an unbelievable striker and he touched it, so it is his goal. And every striker would and should claim it if it is his goal. You just have to ignore what everyone else is saying. He knows how good he is. I am sure everyone else knows how good he is.' Dele was asked if the criticism and jokes were unfair. He answered, 'I don't know how H is going to take it. It gives some people a chance to try to put him down, but playing with him every day and training with him I see how hard he works. He wants goals. Every striker wants goals. So he is [has] just got to ignore it and focus on himself, which I am sure that he will do as he is an unbelievable player and a great person as well. If it was me and I touched it, I would claim it as well.'

Kane also received backing from former Spurs striker Les Ferdinand, who worked with him as a coach. Les said, 'I think with most centre-forwards, if they get a nick, even if it's just a hair, you're claiming it. I worked with Harry and I know Harry and he's one of the most honest people I've come across in football, so if he says he got a nick, I'm believing he got a nick. You see it week in, week out, where the ball is going in and someone sticks a foot on the end of it to tap it in. He put himself in a position, he says he got a nick on it, so I believe he got a nick on it.'

The molehill probably did become a mountain and got a bit out of hand when Jordan Henderson and James Milner also poked fun at Kane, presumably to back teammate Salah in his push for the Golden Boot. Henderson had told BT Sport that Mo might try to claim all three of Liverpool's goals against Bournemouth and Milner then tweeted that the Egyptian international was waiting for the dubious goals panel to award him the goals scored by Mané and Firmino. But after all the talk, Mo knew that the best thing he could do, the only thing really, was get on with his job of scoring goals. Kane wasn't going to have the goal taken away, so Mo would just have to score more than him come the end of the season. Which is what he did – and which is why he won the Golden Boot and was honoured by the British Museum, no less.

The Golden Boot was just the icing on the cake in a season of awards for Salah.

There was a whole range of achievements throughout the campaign. The first award came at the end of August 2017. A few weeks into his new career in a new town Mo won Liverpool's Player of the Month award, such had been his immediate impact at his new club since arriving as the club's record incoming transfer buy. His three goals in five appearances had been plenty enough to convince the fans of his worth.

In September, he entered the record books by scoring for Liverpool against Seville. That goal meant he had become the first Egyptian to net on his Champions League debut for two clubs. Adding to that, a total of three goals in five games yet again meant he once more won Liverpool's Player of the Month. Then in October, he scored a goal that would endear him to his countrymen for ever. It had echoes of David Beckham's goal for England in 2001 against Greece at Old Trafford.

Back then David netted one of his greatest – and his nation's greatest – goals as the clock ticked down on England's hopes of reaching the World Cup finals in Japan and South Korea. So much rested on his shoulders as he prepared to take a free kick. His curling effort beat the keeper and sparked unadulterated scenes of joy on a scale not seen in the country since England reached the semi-finals of Euro 96. It was as if the nation's hopes rested on the ability of one man and Beckham delivered with a magnificent curling effort that gave the hapless keeper no chance. The goal came in the ninety-third minute; the final minute of a game that England had made such hard work of winning.

The Sun newspaper summed up the agony of a nation that day and the edge-of-the-seat hope as Beckham stepped up to take the kick, reporting:

With time running out, the Three Lions trailed the Euro 2000 champions 2–1 and a dreaded play-off showdown looked all but certain. Chance after chance came and went. Golden Balls himself skied many a free kick. Until the 93rd minute. The final minute of added time. The final kick. The final chance. Up steps captain Beckham. He may have missed a hatful of set-pieces already, but no-one in the country would ever want anyone else to take it. It was do or die. The pressure was incredible for supporters; just imagine what it was like for the Manchester United man on his home ground. A quick puff of the cheeks, a bending run up to strike the ball, a clean, curling effort...And before you could blink, the ball was nestling beautifully in the left corner of the goal. Cue ecstasy among the England ranks, throughout a buzzing Old Trafford in bars, living rooms and workplaces across the nation.

Beckham would go on to say it was one of his best ever goals and one of his greatest moments in football. The pundits, meanwhile, would say it was the moment he truly came of age as the captain of his national side. It had only been his genius that ended the nerve-racking feeling that this was not going to be England's day.

Similarly, in October 2017, Mo Salah had led his country into a must-win clash at home against Congo in a World Cup qualifier. As with Beckham, the eyes and hopes of a nation rested on his shoulders and he had a seething cauldron of support in the stadium itself in the Egyptian port of Alexandria. Cometh the hour, once again cameth the man. Liverpool's new idol scored twice in a 2–1 win to send the north African nation to the World Cup finals for the first time since 1990, when the tournament was held in Egypt. The capacity crowd went wild and acclaimed their man, just as Beckham's home crowd at Manchester United's stadium had done back in 2001. There'll be more of Mo's two-goal heroics in another chapter; suffice it to say that the win iced the cake of a wonderful October for the player.

THE GOLDEN BOY

Come November 2017, and Salah was at it again, breaking another record and earning another two awards. He scored against Southampton and that goal meant his nine goals in his first twelve league games had ended Robbie Fowler's record haul of eight in twelve, achieved in 1993. He also won Liverpool's Player of the Month award for the third time in four months and, more significantly perhaps, won the Premier League Player of the Month award for the first time. That win showed that acclaim for his work was spreading far and wide. After that disappointing spell at Chelsea, he was back in England, showing his true worth as a player. He had also become the first Egyptian player to win the award. Mo spoke of his honour at the win but stressed, as always, that it was the team that mattered most, saying, 'Each month I want to score many goals and help the team to win games. That month, I scored seven goals and it's a good feeling, but for me the most important thing is the result and we had good results that month.'

Mo scored twice in each of the victories against West Ham United, Southampton and Stoke City, and also netted in the 1–1 draw with Chelsea. It made him the Premier League's top scorer with thirteen goals thus far. Mo received the most combined votes from a panel of experts, Premier League captains and fans, to claim the prize ahead of six other nominees, namely: Burnley's Robbie Brady, Manchester City's Kevin De Bruyne and Raheem Sterling, Man United's Ashley Young, Chelsea's Eden Hazard and Arsenal's Shkodran Mustafi. The most significant name on that list of fellow pros he overshadowed was De Bruyne, because Mo and the Belgian would go on to battle for the big Player of the Year awards which were handed out at the season's finale.

The acclaim continued at a pace. December saw him voted the BBC's African Footballer of the Year. This was a great personal honour and no mean feat since Mo beat off some brilliant footballers to secure it. These were: Gabon and Borussia Dortmund (soon to be Arsenal) star Pierre-Emerick Aubameyang, Guinean and Red Bull Leipzig (soon to be Liverpool) ace Naby Keïta, Sadio Mané of Liverpool and Senegal, and Nigeria and Chelsea's Victor Moses. 'I am very happy to win this award,' Mo told BBC Sport. 'It's always a special feeling when you win something. I feel like I had a great year, so I'm very happy. I want to be the best Egyptian ever so I work hard. I always follow my own way and I want everyone in Egypt to follow my way. I would like to thank my Liverpool teammates and I also had a good season with Roma so I have to thank my teammates there and my teammates in the national team.

'Since I came here [to Liverpool], I wanted to work hard and show everyone my football. I wanted to come back to the Premier League since I left, so I am very happy.'

His boss Klopp was also delighted at the honour. He handed the trophy to Mo at Melwood and said, 'It's well-deserved. I am a really lucky person. I had the opportunity to work with a few outstanding players and I am happy that it is now with Mo. The good thing is that he is still young, there is a lot of space for improvement, a lot of potential still that we can work on, but that's how it should be. It's a big pleasure, to be honest, to work with him.'

Mo's win followed on from the previous year's winner

Riyad Mahrez, of Leicester and Algeria, and other luminaries such as Man City's Yaya Touré, who starred for the Ivory Coast. He also followed in the footsteps of fellow Egyptian legends Mohamed Barakat and Mohamed Aboutrika, who won the award in 2005 and 2008 respectively. Mo also said that he was honoured and happy to have achieved what they had.

In December he also matched his goalscoring feats at Roma with his nineteenth of the season. But the difference here was that he had reached that number of goals in twenty-four matches, whereas nineteen was his total for the WHOLE season in Rome (forty-one games). That showed how dramatically his game had improved in such a short period of time. It was also a tribute to Klopp, who had recognised Salah's knack for goalscoring by moving him further up the field and encouraging him to shoot when the net was in his sights. Klopp set it all up and Mo delivered. And how.

Christmas 2017 saw Salah receiving yet more presents as his fine form continued into the festive season and up to the New Year. Once again, he was Liverpool's Player of the Month. But he also notched up some scoring records on the way. He became only the second player at the club to have hit twenty-three goals in all competitions before the New Year, joining Roger Hunt, who achieved that in the 1961–62 campaign.

The New Year of 2018 started in a by now all-too-familiar pattern as Mo Salah won yet another honour. He was named Arab Player of the Year in a poll of journalists from Arab nations. The poll was launched by the beIN SPORTS channel on Twitter. Salah competed with Riyad Mahrez, and Syria's Omar Khribin, who plays for Al-Hilal in Saudi Arabia. Salah secured 51 per cent of the votes, while Khribin got 47 per cent, and Mahrez received 2 per cent. Khribin was named AFC Player of the Year for 2017, while Mahrez won the English Premier League's best player award back in 2016. January also had Mo flying off to Accra in Ghana to receive his African Player of the Year award. Liverpool showed a touch of class by sending him and Sadio Mané, who was runner-up, in a private jet. It was a gesture appreciated by both men and endeared them to Liverpool even more. The club clearly recognised their worth and valued their work.

February brought Salah his fifth Liverpool Player of the Month award, a feat unmatched by a player in his debut campaign. He was also adjudged to be the Premier League's Player of the Month for a second time. The level of his play could be seen by the fact that he beat off the challenge of Sergio Agüero, Eden Hazard and Mousa Dembélé. His four goals and two assists that month had earned the club two wins and a draw. Mo said, 'The players make it easier and the boss also makes it easier for me. It's nice to win it again especially because it's the Player of the Month of the Premier League, so that's good.' Mo's lethal left foot then earned him the accolade of yet a further Liverpool club record. The strike against West Ham, in the 4–1 win at Anfield, was the twentieth time he had scored in the league with his left foot. That overwhelmed Robbie Fowler's record of nineteen with his left foot in the 1994–95 season.

By March we at Fleet Street were running out of superlatives to describe his conquests as the records continued to tumble and the awards continued to arrive. He won the Premier League Player of the Month again, going down in the footballing history books as the first player to win it three times in a season. It was hardly surprising that he won again. He scored six goals in four Premier League games including the four against Watford – the performance of which he would say was his best of the league season. Salah also equalled Didier Drogba's record for the most goals scored in a Premier League season by an African player, with twenty-nine.

The award prompted his teammate Alex Oxlade-Chamberlain to publicly offer his praise and to say how much Salah had helped and inspired him to improve as a player and aim for the heights. 'The Ox' told Liverpool FC's official website: 'I can take so much from someone like Mo Salah. Just look at him this season. It has been relentless and when someone can go from – obviously he is a great player – but to be competing with Harry Kane and Sergio Agüero for top goal scorer is something you have to learn from. To put himself in that position is down to the mentality he has to work hard and get the best out of himself.'

Mo also won the club's Player of the Month award for the sixth time and earned a double accolade with those four goals against Watford. He had become the first Egyptian to hit a hat-trick in the Premier League and had scored more goals than any other Liverpool player in a debut season.

We were still drawing breath as April and May loomed, along with the biggest individual honours a Premier League footballer could achieve in a season. On Saturday 14 April, Mo scored in the 3–0 Premier League win over

Bournemouth at Anfield. That took his goals total to forty for the season – and he had become the first player to achieve that at Anfield since Ian Rush in 1987. He had also hit the 40-mark quicker than any other player. He'd got there in forty-five matches while George Allan had taken forty-nine, Jack Parkinson sixty and Robbie Fowler sixty-one. Salah also earned the accolade of 'Most games scored in a Prem season' – the goal against the Cherries was the twenty-second match in which he had hit the back of the net, beating the previous joint record of twenty-one set by Robin van Persie and Cristiano Ronaldo.

For the seventh time, he became Liverpool's Player of the Month and an extremely prestigious honour from the wider footballing arena also came Mo's way as he was named the PFA's Player of the Year. We were now talking major league acceptance. To win this prize means a great deal to every professional footballer as it is voted for, and awarded by, their fellow pros. Mo was the first Egyptian to win the coveted award and the seventh player to do so from Liverpool FC – following on from Luis Suárez (2013–14), Steven Gerrard (2005–06), John Barnes (1987–88), Ian Rush (1983–84), Kenny Dalglish (1982–83) and Terry McDermott (1979–80).

PFA members from the ninety-two Premier League and Football League clubs vote for their star man and Salah beat some pretty impressive rivals to lift the trophy. The other candidates up for the award were Man City's Kevin De Bruyne, David Silva and Leroy Sané, David de Gea (Man United) and Harry Kane (Tottenham).

Salah gave a speech after his triumph. He said, 'It's a big

honour, especially as it is voted for by the players and I'm very happy to win it. I didn't have my chance at Chelsea but I always wanted to return to England and show everyone my football. I left and came back a different person, man and player. My personal thing is to win something with the team. I always think about the team, I don't think about myself, so the most important thing for me is to win something with the team. We are very close now, in the Champions League semi-final, so hopefully we're going to win it.'

It was gratifying to yet again see the pure humility of the man shine through. The team was always the key in Mo's world. Whatever honour came his way delighted him and showed him his hard work was paying dividends. But he never failed to qualify his success by saying it was also down to his teammates and the work they put in to provide him with assists and encouragement. He added, 'The team helped me a lot, the way we play, they help me, they pass me the ball a lot. So the team help me a lot, honestly, to perform and be in that shape.'

He was asked at the presentation what it meant to be the first Egyptian to win the award. He said, 'Hopefully I am not the last one. I'm very proud to win and I've worked very hard.'

And what of his closing in on the Premier League goals record? At the time he was on his thirty-first of the campaign, tying the record for the thirty-eight-game season. Mo said, 'You're comparing your name with some great names. To break the Premier League record is something huge in England and all over the world. There are still three games to go. I want to break this record. Let's see what happens.'

Match of the Day host Gary Lineker tweeted his respect and congratulations to Mo. The comments by the former Spurs and England striker summed up the feelings of everyone who felt Salah had deserved to win. Gary tweeted: 'Congratulations to @22MoSalah on being named PFA Player of the Year. He's been superb, scored a multitude of goals and been a breath of fresh air to our football.' Mo's achievement was all the more special as he had beaten Kevin De Bruyne to the award. The Belgian had proved to be the best midfielder in the league by a mile and, in any other season without a record-breaker such as Mo up against him, would have won hands down. At the time, De Bruyne had provided more assists, with fifteen, and created more chances, with 104, than any other player in the Prem. He had also scored eight goals. Those are the stats of a star man and it made Mo's triumph all the more worthy because he had beaten off Kevin's brilliant challenge.

De Bruyne's boss Pep Guardiola had insisted before the presentation that his player should win, not Salah. Pep said, 'If he doesn't win, then congrats to the guy that wins. From my point of view when you are analysing the nine or ten months, there was no player better than him, in terms of the continuity, in terms of being there every three days of all competitions. Maybe the numbers say someone is better than him but this season, there has been no one better than him. That's my opinion but players can have another one. But in the end, in the summertime, we will be at home being champions.'

Well, he would say that, wouldn't he? And there is no argument that Salah and De Bruyne were the stand-out stars of the season. But Mo's ascendancy was also marked by the Football Writers' Association (FWA) Player of the Year award, which he won the following month. Again, he beat De Bruyne to the honour...the City midfielder must have been heartily sick of the sight of Salah lifting trophies by now.

The FWA put out a statement on Mo's triumph. It read: 'Mohamed Salah is the Football Writers' Association's Footballer of the Year. The Liverpool forward narrowly beat Manchester City midfielder Kevin De Bruyne in a ballot of over 400 FWA members, with the winning margin less than 20 votes. Tottenham striker Harry Kane was placed third. Between them, Salah and De Bruyne polled more than 90 per cent of the FWA member votes. The Egyptian, 25, becomes the first African winner of football's oldest individual award, which has been running since 1948. Salah will be presented with his trophy at the 2018 FWA Footballer of the Year dinner, to be held at the Landmark Hotel in London on May 10.'

Patrick Barclay, FWA Chairman, then revealed just how close the vote had been between Salah and De Bruyne and how the journalists had all been united in their belief that the duo were both world-class foootballers, and how blessed we were to have them in England. He said, 'It's been the tightest call since 1968/69, when there was a dead heat between Tony Book of Manchester City and Derby's Dave Mackay. Right up to the last week or so we thought it might happen again, so strong was the support for Kevin

De Bruyne. But Mo Salah's relentless match-winning form, exemplified by his two great goals against Roma, seems to have swung the vote by a very narrow margin. What a race it has been between two players who, in a relatively short time, have reached genuine world class. But Mo Salah is the worthiest of winners. He is also the first African to receive the award and we congratulate him on a magnificent season.'

It was revealed that other players to receive votes from FWA members were, in alphabetical order: Sergio Agüero (Man City), Christian Eriksen (Tottenham), Roberto Firmino (Liverpool), Nick Pope (Burnley), David Silva (Manchester City), Raheem Sterling (Man City) and Jan Vertonghen (Tottenham).

Once again, Mo showed his modesty by insisting on praising his teammates whom, he said, had played such a big part in his success, 'Roberto and Sadio have big quality. They always try to give me the ball and score. They are unbelievable on the pitch and away from it and I'm very proud to be part of the team and play with them.'

Two fans left messages of appreciation on the FWA site. Barnabas wrote: 'We Liverpool fans are very, very happy and we wish our best player to do more against ROMA 2morrow.' And Xeon added: 'A well-deserved achievement after a brilliant season from this world class player, Egyptian people should be so happy and grateful to have him in the national team. Congrats Mohamed Salah.' Salah had won both major gongs of the season by lifting the PFA and PWA trophies. By doing so, he followed in the footsteps of N'Golo Kanté, who also secured both individual awards.

Other fans were split down the middle about who should have won. On the Salah side, one said: 'As a neutral he has been the best player over the season – by a mile. KDB was matching him until Christmas but has not been at that level since. Kane has had another terrific season but for me Salah is the one player (along with KDB before Christmas) who has done things that have astounded me... having watched football for far too long.' While another fan, a regular at the Etihad, argued De Bruyne's case forcibly, 'Kevin D–B has more Premier League winners' medals than Liverpool!!! Medals not awards are what's counts, 21 points clear of Liverpool once our game in hand is played. No doubt Klopp will be given manager of the year for getting Liverpool to the semi finals of the European Cup (can't be the Champions League they're 28 years without winning one). KDB the all-round best player by far. 2 medals to zero.'

Fair enough, everyone has a right to their own opinion. Nonetheless, the two awards trophies would find a special place at Salah's home in the North West – and Klopp wouldn't win the Manager of the Year trophy...it would go to City boss Guardiola.

Mo would also be presented with two awards at Anfield – the Player of the Season and Players' Player of the Season. He then presented the fans a gift by saying this debut season was 'just the beginning' of his time at the club. Mo said, 'I'm very happy here, everything is fine. Of course I have got ambitions for the future with Liverpool. As you can see we had a great season, now we are in the Champions League final and everyone is excited. It is just the start. This is my first year here and it is the same for some other players. It is just the beginning.'

On the season's final day, Mo set one final record by scoring his thirty-second league goal of the campaign against Brighton. That meant he had overtaken Luis Suárez, Alan Shearer and Cristiano Ronaldo. As Ronaldo was arguably the greatest player to ever grace the Premier League, it showed just what an achievement Mo had managed. And he would still have the Champions League final in Kiev to gauge his own development against Real Madrid's Portuguese genius. In a season that had started so low-key and gone from highlight to highlight, there was – apart from that Champions League final – one last moment of glory for Salah to savour.

On 13 May, it was revealed that he had won the Premier League Player of the Season award. It had been an inevitable victory and one that was secured without argument from any side after he hit that thirty-second Prem goal of the campaign. After that difficult time at Chelsea Mo Salah had shown the footballing world just how far he had come. He had scored forty-four goals in just fifty-one games in all competitions for Liverpool in his first season. After being handed the final award, he commented, 'They say I didn't have success here the first time. So it was always in my mind to have success here in the Premier League. I am very happy. I am very proud to win it.'

With such remarkable goal numbers, and after claiming all the individual awards at the top of his trade, was it any wonder that word was emanating from Madrid that Zinedine Zidane was having sleepless nights worrying about Mo Salah – and how he might wreck Real Madrid's dream of a third successive Champions League triumph? The French boss of the most successful side of all time in club football knew a thing or two about class, and about players who had the natural technical ability to destroy rivals in seconds. He saw the danger that Salah presented to his team and the dream of retaining the trophy. He knew Ronaldo had the ability to open up the Liverpool defence and score. But he also knew that his own defence could be creaky and would be vulnerable to the pace of Salah, Mané and Coutinho. And it was the goals threat of Salah that was giving him sleepless nights. This boy was truly the real deal.

CHAPTER EIGHTEEN

LEGENDS INC.

When Jurgen Klopp bought Mo Salah, he was among the few in England who believed the player could become a complete striker; that his career would not see him play a mere supporting role on the left wing. Klopp gave clues to this in early press briefings but it mostly went over the heads of pundits and Fleet Street's finest. The other clues were in his goal record at Roma – that virtual 'one in every two games' strike rate. But it was not until the goals continued to flow, and flow, and flow, at Liverpool that we all realised an undeniable fact: that this boy was a goal machine, the very same complete striker that his new manager had always envisaged him being. Of course, Salah wasn't the first to become a goal idol of the Kop – he was simply the latest in a long line that included the likes of Billy Liddell, Ian Rush and, latterly, Luis Suárez.

Mo was following in the footsteps of some true legends,

and in many ways his breathless natural ability to find the net from any angle was a way of him continuing where they left off.

Yet Liverpool had struggled to find a deadly marksman of world-class stature in the period between Suárez leaving the club for Barcelona in January 2011 and Mo's arrival in July 2017. This was hardly surprising given the nature of the beast that was Luis Alberto Suárez, a striker who never gave an inch nor expected one, a player who was as controversial as he was brilliant. Mo didn't possess his snarling nature. While Suárez growled, shouted and fought with rivals, the agreeable Mo Salah preferred working with a smile on his face. However, both these top players possessed that single-minded desire to score goals and be the best in the world; that defining ambition was within them both. Suárez was signed by Kenny Dalglish after becoming one of the stars of the Uruguay national team's progress at the World Cup of 2010.

Just as Kenny himself had worked so brilliantly with Ian Rush, and Kevin Keegan had performed a similar partnership role with John Toshack, now Dalglish the manager saw much of himself and Keegan in the diminutive Uruguayan, who had nimble feet and a rare eye for goal. Luis signed for Liverpool on 29 January 2011, five days after his twenty-fourth birthday, in a deal that earned Ajax Amsterdam, the club that was selling him, £22.8 million. His credentials were there for all to see – these were the reasons why he had cost so much money, and why he was worth it.

At the end of the previous season in Holland, he had

scooped the Dutch Footballer of the Year award, after finishing the campaign with a remarkable thirty-five goals in thirty-three league matches (forty-nine in all competitions). The goal-scoring potential he would bring to Liverpool was underlined by the fact that in 2010, he joined luminaries such as Johan Cruyff, Marco van Basten and Dennis Bergkamp by becoming part of an elite club which had scored more than one hundred goals for Ajax in competitive matches – netting 111 goals in 159 appearances. He had also scored ten times in thirty games for his country, including three in the 2010 World Cup.

On Monday 31 January, it was revealed that Suárez had signed a five-and-a-half year deal that would keep him at Anfield until 2016. And Dalglish underlined his own assessment of how Suárez would fit into the new dream team he was building at the club by giving him the legendary Number 7 shirt – the shirt made famous by the likes of himself and Keegan. Former Kop hero Phil Thompson believed Suárez was a modern-day model from the Keegan/Dalglish prototype – just as Salah is now also being spoken of in such lauded terms. He said of Suárez, 'He excites me and he's a player between Kenny Dalglish and Kevin Keegan, that bundle of enthusiasm. Hopefully he can do it for Liverpool.'

Suárez knew that he was buying into legend when he signed for Liverpool, saying, 'It's a dream to be able to come and play here. Liverpool is a very famous club, the most famous club in England, and I watched Liverpool and English football as a boy. My aim is to work, to show the fans how hard I am ready to work. I want to put in lots of effort, to show people my capabilities. First of all I want to try to play as many games as possible and help move us up the table. My ambitions for the future are to do my very best for Liverpool, to try to learn more about English football and to become a champion.'

Dalglish paid tribute to his new signing and said it showed how ambitious the club were for success. He told *liverpoolfc. tv*: 'We're delighted. He's got a fantastic goalscoring record. He's played in the World Cup and scored goals, he's played for Ajax and scored goals. I think he'll really excite the fans and it's great credit to the new owners, John and Tom, who've put a stamp down. They promised there would be funds available during this. It's also a great reward for the supporters and the players who have been fantastic since I came in three or four weeks ago. All round it's a fantastic day for Liverpool Football Club. It should be and it will be warmly received.'

Suárez had become Liverpool's most expensive signing, his fee of £22.8 million dwarfing the £20.2 million the club had paid for Torres in July 2007. The other three most expensive players were Robbie Keane (£19 million in July 2008), Javier Mascherano (£18.6 million in February 2008) and Glen Johnson (£17.5 million in June 2009).

But they would all be eclipsed, firstly by Andy Carroll, and then by Mo Salah.

If Mo was looking back at the annals of Liverpool greats in his mould, he could do worse than spend a few minutes reading up on the legendary Billy Liddell, who, like Mo, began his Liverpool career down the left wing, before becoming the very model of the complete striker that Mo has become. Billy would earn his club the moniker 'Liddellpool' because of his regular brilliant exploits on their behalf. In the championship-winning season of 1946–47, he was darting down the left wing, scoring seven goals in thirty-four games. Like fellow Pool great Bob Paisley, Liddell was Scottish and the two would share a lifetime's friendship.

In his 1990 book, *My 50 Golden Reds*, Paisley would sum up Liddell like this:

Bill was always strong, even as a teenager, and was a naturally two-footed player. He also had good skills, but was so strong for a winger. In those days most wingers were fairly lightly-built players but Bill had absolutely no fear. He was a gentleman through and through. But he would also work on the pitch. He was a real workhorse but he had a nice touch as well. Sometimes he would use his strength to send defenders flying, but always totally fairly.

It is close between him and Kenny [Dalglish] for the title of the best player ever to have worn a Liverpool shirt. By today's standards, I don't think there is the money to buy a Billy Liddell.

Liddell was a one-club man. He signed for Liverpool aged sixteen in 1938 and retired in 1961, having scored 228 goals in 534 games and was the club's leading goalscorer in eight out of nine seasons from 1949 to 1958. By 1957 he had surpassed the club appearance record set by the great Elisha Scott. He became the club's oldest ever goal scorer, and after King Kenny, is the second oldest player to represent Liverpool. He died in 2001, aged seventy-nine.

He had become a legend for his exploits and he had been loved and respected by his colleagues at the club. Years earlier, Bill Shankly summed up Billy's physical strength, saying, 'Liddell was some player...He had everything. He was fast, powerful, shot with either foot and his headers were like blasts from a gun. On top of all that he was as hard as granite. What a player! He was so strong – and he took a nineteen-inch collar shirt!'

That is another aspect that links Salah with greats like Liddell, Dalglish and Keegan: their physical strength. For small men, Mo, Kenny and Kevin were incredibly strong and very difficult to knock off the ball. That aspect made them even more nightmarish opponents: not only could they kill you with their skill, they could also repel you if you tried the rough stuff.

Paisley was forever amazed by Billy's physical prowess, saying, 'Bill was so strong it was unbelievable. You couldn't shake him off the ball. It didn't matter where he was playing, though I suppose his best position was outside-left. He could go round you, or past you, or even straight through you sometimes!'

Even his English rival Sir Alf Ramsey, boss of England's World Cup winners in 1966, had only good words for this remarkable man. Talking about how he dreaded facing him in his playing days, Ramsey admitted, 'I always knew I was in for a hectic afternoon when I was marking Billy. The only way to try to hold him was to beat him to possession of the ball. Once he had it, he was difficult to stop.'

Three years after Liddell's death a permanent memorial to him was unveiled at Anfield by his widow Phyllis and fellow Anfield legend Ian Callaghan. The plaque pays tribute to a man who dedicated his life for Liverpool FC.

In 2006 he was acclaimed by Liverpool fans who voted him sixth in a poll entitled '100 Players Who Shook The Kop'. The poll was massive and emphatic – attracting 110,000 supporters, who all nominated their favourite Top 10 players.

Further acclaim befell Billy in November 2008 when he was finally inducted into the Scottish Football Hall of Fame.

After Billy retired two new goal kings emerged in the Anfield pantheon of fame. This time the Number 9 shirt would be worn by the little man while the bigger, more traditional target man would take the Number 8. Yes, step forward Ian St John and Roger Hunt – an Anglo-Scots partnership made in heaven that would propel Liverpool forward during the 1960s.

St John was another Liverpool great from whom Mo Salah could learn a thing or two about what it takes to earn a permanent place in the hearts of the Kop. Again, he was a compact, pocket rocket like Mo, and was just five foot eight inches in his football boots. Yet he had a terrific leap on him, a clever footballing brain, was very brave and he knew where the net was. He would also turn provider for Hunt as the years went by, as a result selflessly scoring less goals himself.

Ian St John was born in Motherwell, Lanarkshire, in 1938 and arrived at Liverpool FC in 1961 from his hometown football club. Bill Shankly splashed out £37,500 to bring the wee man south – a fee that was more than double Liverpool's previous transfer record. The twenty-three-year-old settled in quickly – so quickly that he became an idol of the Kop in his very first game!

In that debut, St John hit a hat-trick against Liverpool's city rivals Everton. It was not enough to save his new team going down 4–3 in the Liverpool Senior Cup Final but it was enough to have the fans chanting his name. Any player who scored a hat-trick against their bitter local rivals would have earned that accolade. This is something certainly worth aiming for, Mo!

'Saint', as he would become known, made his official debut in the 2–0 victory at Bristol Rovers in August 1961. At the time Liverpool were floundering in the Second Division, although that was all about to change under the auspices of Shankly, backed up by inspirational signings like St John and the grooming of local youngsters into the first team. They had been stuck in the Second Division for six long years but now with Saint in the team that was about to end. In his very first season at the club, they were promoted to the top-flight, finishing the campaign as champions, eight points clear of second-placed Leyton Orient.

Saint scored his first goals at the end of August 1961, grabbing a brace in the thirty-ninth and ninetieth minutes of a 4–1 win over Sunderland at Roker Park. His new strike partner, Roger Hunt, pulled off the same feat as Liverpool roared home. It was to be the start of a wonderful partnership that would take Liverpool to the very top. That debut season brought a goals return of eighteen from Saint in forty league matches.

His second campaign at the club was just as eventful – they finished eighth in the league but made the FA Cup semi-finals where only a defiant show by the brilliant Gordon Banks saw them lose to Leicester City. Saint's contribution saw him finish the campaign with a total of twenty-two goals in all competitions.

But it would be in his third season at Anfield that he really proved his worth – as the club finally won the First Division title again, for the sixth time but the first in twenty-seven long years. Ian chipped in with twenty-one league goals, the highest number he would ever chalk up in his time at the club. Liverpool had won the title with four points to spare over second-placed Manchester United, with deposed champions Everton third.

Liverpool fans are hoping Mo Salah propels them to similar league-title glory, ending their own drought of many years. He will be as legendary as Saint if he manages that feat.

The glory years continued for Saint as the following season he helped Liverpool to fill the one gaping hole in the club's list of domestic honours: the FA Cup. Not only did Saint help them lift the FA Cup – he won it for them. The final was an epic encounter between Shankly's Liverpool and Don Revie's Leeds United. With the score at 0–0 after ninety minutes, it became the first final since 1947 to go to extra time.

It was soon 1–1 but Saint brought the cup to Merseyside as he headed home from an Ian Callaghan cross. Leeds had no reply – Liverpool had won the FA Cup for the first time in their history, thanks to Ian St John, who finished his Liverpool career in August 1971. He had played 425 games and scored 118 goals for the club.

Kevin Keegan was another Kop idol in the image of Salah. He started out as a winger but became a fine forward, wearing the red Number 7 shirt with pride and distinction. Even though he was not the most naturally gifted player in the world, Keegan made up for it with his commitment and determination to win. That, allied with his talent, meant he became a massive star who was adored on the Kop and when playing for England. Yet when boss Bill Shankly initially watched him play, Keegan was a creative midfielder in the lower leagues with Scunthorpe. 'Shanks' had a similar role in mind for him at Anfield, with the plan that he would one day replace the long-serving Ian Callaghan in that role. But the boss changed his mind when he saw Keegan in action in pre-season training; he realised that Kevin, with his tricky skills and natural eye for goal, could become the perfect 'pocket rocket' forward à la Salah, Dalglish etc.

Keegan was signed in August 1971 from Scunthorpe. He was twenty years old and had cost £35,000 – it would seem like small change when he struck up what seemed an almost telepathic partnership with big John Toshack, and Shanks would later describe it as 'robbery with violence'.

Tosh, the big man, would win the ball in the air and plant it on the ground for the man who would become known by many as 'Mighty Mouse' to regularly lash home on the ground. In his six-year spell at Anfield he would win a clutch of top medals – including three First Division titles, two UEFA Cups, one FA Cup and the European Cup. The move to Liverpool also gave him the confidence to become a regular in the England national team and set him up for more glory on a Continental scale when he moved to

German outfit Hamburg in 1977 (he would be crowned European Footballer of the Year in 1978 and 1979).

But it was for his link-up with Toshack that he will always be fondly remembered at Anfield. The duo were unstoppable together and even earned another sobriquet from the football magazine *Shoot* – who dubbed them 'Batman and Robin' and took pictures of them in Dynamic Duo-style costumes. Maybe one day Mo Salah and Firmino will also do a Dynamic Duo photoshoot?

Keegan made his Liverpool debut on 14 August 1971, partnering Toshack up front after their impressive pre-season work together. Kevin scored after twelve minutes in the 3–1 First Division win over Nottingham Forest at Anfield. The team that day read: Ray Clemence, Chris Lawler, Alec Lindsay, Tommy Smith, Larry Lloyd, Emlyn Hughes, Kevin Keegan, Peter Thompson, Steve Heighway, John Toshack, John McLaughlin.

Shanks knew Keegan was a special talent and that he was the man he had been looking for up front. He now abandoned any plans to play him in midfield. It was a typical genius decision by a manager who was himself a genius. Just how good a decision it was became clear two years after Keegan had signed. During those years his partnership with Tosh continued to blossom and in 1973 the pair helped Liverpool to the Division One title, and the UEFA Cup. In the latter, Liverpool won the first leg 3–0 but went down 2–0 in the return in Germany. It meant the first leg triumph – with two goals from Keegan – was enough. Liverpool had won 3–2 on aggregate – and Keegan, who was the hero of the hour, had even missed a penalty.

The following year the Keegan/Toshack combination brought the FA Cup to Anfield as Liverpool beat Newcastle 3–0. As in the UEFA Cup final of the previous season, Keegan grabbed a match-winning brace. Of course, the match would also eventually be remembered for another reason: it was the last game in charge of Liverpool for the man who had gambled on Keegan and Toshack: the great Bill Shankly, who would be succeeded by coach Bob Paisley.

In 1977, his last season with Liverpool, Keegan helped the club to their finest hour: their first European Cup triumph. His mate Tosh was missing from the final line-up that wondrous night in Rome on 25 May. Tosh had got injured earlier in the campaign and had been forced to sit out the latter part of the season.

Of course, he was there in Rome cheering on his partner-in-crime against Borussia Mönchengladbach – and Kevin did not let him or the millions of Liverpool fans watching worldwide down. Eight minutes from time, with the score at 2-1 to Liverpool and nerves starting to jangle, Keegan darted into the German box only to be fouled by Berti Vogts. Fullback Phil Neal made no mistake with the ensuing penalty and Liverpool ran out 3–1 winners.

Keegan now departed for Germany, to join Hamburg. Later Toshack would pay tribute to him, saying, 'Myself and Kevin Keegan worked up a good understanding and as a partnership we flourished. We seemed to hit it off from almost day one and then got better and better as time went by.'

And Keegan said, 'Tosh was a wonderful player to play alongside. His aerial ability was fantastic and I always knew that he was going to win the high balls. From then on it was just a question of me reading which way the ball was going to go and from those situations we created many chances. I always admired Tosh's honesty as a player. He was a nice approachable lad and he did a really great job for the club during his time here.'

When Mo Salah looks through the Liverpool history books he will come across the duo who are arguably Liverpool's greatest ever strike combination – the brilliant Kenny Dalglish allied with the prolific goalscoring talents of Ian Rush. If Mo and Firmino get close to this combo's output and goals, they would certainly have earned their stripes and stars and a place in Anfield legend. To this day, Rush remains the club's record goalscorer, with 346 in 660 games during his Liverpool career. He also holds the record for the most goals in a season, hitting forty-seven in all competitions during the 1983–84 season. In the '100 Players who Shook the Kop' poll, Rush finished third, behind only Steven Gerrard (second) and, inevitably, Kenny Dalglish, who was in top position.

Rush signed for Liverpool when he was eighteen in April 1980, though he had to remain at his first club, Chester, until the end of the season as the transfer deadline had passed. Kop boss Bob Paisley splashed out £300,000 for his services – which was then a record fee for a teenager. Ironically, his Liverpool debut came on 13 December, standing in for Dalglish who was injured, and wearing his famous Number 7 shirt in a First Division fixture at Portman Road against Ipswich Town.

It was hardly a case of trumpeting the arrival of a

potential goal genius. Indeed *The Times* perfectly summed up the general disinterest in Rush's debut, with a piece highlighting the loss of Dalglish as a much more serious issue. *The Times* report stated:

> Dalglish has succumbed to a troublesome ankle injury. Obviously this is a serious problem for the Liverpool manager, Bob Paisley, who has been fearing just such a breakdown. Dalglish has a fine record of survival against all of the tough tackling that comes his way and perhaps it will be helpful for Liverpool to see how his first absence in three years affects overall performance. Rush, bought from Chester for £300,000 last season, plays his first game. Mr Paisley said: 'It was not an easy decision, but what swayed me in the end was that if I had picked anyone else it would have meant playing them out of position. I have replaced a striker with a striker.'

So 'Rushie' made his debut – but only because Bob didn't want to play another man out of position. From such inauspicious beginnings a legend was born, although Ian would initially be peeved at his lack of opportunities and even considered leaving the club. Paisley told him his time would come, that he should be patient, but that he should also be more selfish in front of goal. Ian did not need much persuading on that score! He eventually opened his goals account after nine games and became a regular in the side – as Kenny's partner rather than his replacement – in the 1981/82 season.

His first goal came on 30 September 1981, in the European Cup first round second leg tie at Anfield against Oulun Palloseura. Liverpool had already won the first leg away in Finland 1–0 and now they crushed their opponents 7–0, Rushie netting on sixty-seven minutes after coming on as a sub for David Johnson. He scored his first league goal on 10 October 1981, in the 3–0 win over Leeds at Anfield and a month later scored an even more important one – as far as hometown bragging rights went – in the 3–1 Anfield demolition of neighbours Everton.

The boy was on his way to becoming a man and to becoming a goalscoring Kop idol.

He ended the season as the club's top scorer, with thirty in forty-nine matches – of which seventeen came in the League as Liverpool won back the crown that Aston Villa had pinched the previous campaign. Rushie was also on target in the 1982 League Cup Final, grabbing Liverpool's third as they beat Spurs 3–1 at Wembley.

But his finest season would be the 1983–84 campaign when he hit forty-seven goals, helping Liverpool to a remarkable array of trophies – the League title, European Cup and League Cup. He won both the PFA and sportswriters' Player of the Year awards and his goal haul earned him the coveted Golden Boot, awarded to Europe's top goalscorer each season.

In the 2017–18 season, Mo Salah was desperate to beat Ian's forty-seven-goal record and put everything into his attempt to doing so. That he even came close is testament to his remarkable season and his remarkable knack for finding the back of the net, even from impossible angles. And here's a fact for Mo to consider. Liverpool's European Cup final win in '84 was all the more remarkable as they had to beat Roma in their home stadium (the Olympic stadium) – and do so in a tense penalty shootout, just as Mo and Co. had to keep their nerve to overcome Roma in that classic Champions League semi-final of 2018, which was also in the cauldron of the Olympic Stadium. Rushie scored the fourth penalty as Liverpool went on to win 4–2 on penalties (after the match itself had ended 1–1) and lift their fourth European Cup in eight years.

Liverpool's team was much changed from the one that had beaten Real Madrid to win the trophy three years previously. Ray Clemence, Phil Thompson, Terry McDermott and Ray Kennedy had gone and been replaced by Bruce Grobbelaar, Mark Lawrenson, Craig Johnston and, of course, Rushie. It read: Grobbelaar, Neal, Lawrenson, Hansen, A. Kennedy, Lee, Johnston, Whelan, Souness, Rush, Dalglish.

Rushie would tell *lfchistory.net*, that, yes, the '83–'84 season was his favourite in terms of goalscoring achievement, but that his favourite as a team player came two years later, adding that: 'As an individual it was maybe the 1983–84 season when I scored forty-seven goals but as a team it was when we won the double. To actually play in the first Merseyside cup final, against Everton. To be losing 1–0 at half-time and win 3–1 and score two goals. We had won the double. Everything rolled into one in this game, against the Everton team which was the second best team in Europe then.'

He would also tell the same website of his seemingly telepathic understanding with Dalglish, explaining that:

'We didn't speak a lot off the pitch but on the pitch we just had a thing that was natural. I knew what Kenny was good at and Kenny knew what I was good at. That was what made us work so well as a pair. Kenny wouldn't look up to see where I was, he would just put the ball into space and I just knew Kenny was going to put the ball there. The defenders were just left thinking, "how does he know the ball was going to get there." But we did know.'

And so to the final piece in the history jigsaw for Mo Salah, the man who was known as 'The King' on Merseyside, and the man he considers his own Liverpool idol and whom he would most like to emulate at the club. Yes, King Kenny Dalglish. Kenneth Mathieson Dalglish had arrived at Liverpool in 1977 with Bob Paisley, having had to fork out a British transfer record of £440,000 to secure his services from Celtic in Glasgow. Of course it turned out to be money well spent; a bargain if you looked at the service and honours Kenny brought. He was already a major star in Scotland when he arrived as Keegan's replacement – with Celtic he had won four Scottish First Division titles, four Scottish Cups and one Scottish League Cup from 1971.

At Anfield, he would comfortably surpass that haul, winning seven league titles, three European Cups and five domestic cups. As with Toshack and Rushie, the Liverpool fans initially had their reservations about the man who would become known to them as 'King Kenny'. This was hardly surprising considering the act he had to follow: Keegan was the best player in England and Kenny had a major job on his hands to persuade the Anfield faithful he could take on his Number 7 shirt with the same results.

But the man was a magician, a genius and the conductor of the orchestra, as Liverpool embarked on a period of domination in the domestic and European game.

Yes, he was as good as Keegan – yes, indeed he was better than Keegan. More naturally gifted and talented. He scored his first goal for the club on his league debut against Middlesbrough on 20 August 1977. Three days later he also hit the net on his first appearance before the Anfield fans, who would come to adore him in the 2–0 victory over Newcastle.

At the end of his first season, Dalglish had hit a total of thirty-one goals in sixty-two matches. The final one was the most important – it won the European Cup for the club as they beat Bruges 1–0 at Wembley. Two years later Rushie arrived at Anfield and the eighteen-year-old would eventually link up with Dalglish, who by then was twenty-nine, to form their wonderful partnership. The old head with the ultimate footballing brain, and the pace and goal-grabbing instincts of the young whippersnapper, combined to form a link-up that was irresistible and unstoppable. Kenny would score 172 goals in 515 games for Liverpool and would earn the accolade of being the club's best player ever. Indeed he had this accolade from fans, players and managers for the outstanding thirteen years that he graced Liverpool FC as a performer on the pitch.

In 1999, Alan Shearer and Michael Owen, no slouches in front of goal themselves, were asked by *Match of the Day* magazine to name the best strike force ever in British football. Inevitably, they plumped for the Ian Rush-Kenny Dalglish combo.

LEGENDS INC.

Owen selected two of his Anfield predecessors as Shearer reflected on the skills of his former Newcastle manager. 'Rush was a class striker; deadly around the box and with a scoring instinct,' Owen said. Shearer purred when he spoke about King Kenny: 'He would take the defender out of the game with a pass and put backspin on the ball so it sat up, inviting the shot. Class.' Peter Beardsley and Gary Lineker – who scored thirty-six goals together as an England partnership – were voted as runners-up, while Kevin Keegan and John Toshack came third.

Kenny Dalglish, Kevin Keegan, Ian Rush and Billy Liddell. Can Mohamed Salah live up to the standards he set himself in his debut season at Anfield and reach the peaks achieved by the likes of those four legends? They are the yardsticks by which he will be judged if he wants to become a Liverpool legend. After that wonderful first season, he is already an idol of the Kop. There is no doubt he has the talent to move up to their level if he can maintain the magnificent standards that he set during that unforgettable debut campaign.

CHAPTER NINETEEN

EUROPEAN CHAMPION

As he celebrated with his delirious Liverpool team-mates that June night in Madrid in 2019, Mo could have been forgiven for thinking it would have been even more perfect if Sergio Ramos had been among their vanquished foes. Now that would have been a case of real karma given the events of twelve months previous, when the Spanish bruiser had destroyed Liverpool's hopes of winning the Champions League with a criminal arm-grabbing manoeuvre that could have brought a bodily harm charge in the street, and was at least worthy of a freeze-frame treasure in the world of wrestling. He had tried hard, but it was not easy to forgive Ramos for his actions in Kiev. It almost looked as if the defender had targeted him, to take him out of the equation, and as a consequence he was condemned around the footballing planet as a rogue without a conscience. All Mo had from that night were tears as souvenirs, as he trudged despondently off the Olimpiyskiy Stadium grass with a damaged shoulder that would limit his effective involvement in the subsequent World Cup in Russia. So, yes, it would have been sweet to have looked Ramos in the eye in Atletico's stadium and watched his reaction to such a monumental defeat. But Mo is nothing if not resilient and, to his credit, made it clear on several occasions that he would not let the Ramos incident affect his game negatively once he had recovered from the shoulder injury. That night in Madrid would be the culmination of a breadth of work during the preceding season that proved he kept to his word. Indeed, some of his play was breathtaking, his attacking menace sometimes reaching the heights the mercurial Lionel Messi takes for granted. Mo was verging on impossible to halt when he set off on those mazy runs and the end result would often be the ball nestling in the left or right hand corners of the net.

It was a joy to watch the Egyptian at work; a privilege to be part of a mesmerising artist performing at his peak.

It was also a joy to witness redemption, with that Champions League triumph, for a footballer who is not only one of the greats of the modern era, but a lovely guy, too. A devoted family man, a kindly, religious man whose general demeanour is one of gratitude and appreciation at the fortune and lifestyle laid at his feet. Mo Salah always makes time for his fans, to sign autographs and to chat with them, and even makes time for the press, whom many of the spoiled kids of the Premier League walk by as if those members of the Fourth Estate are mere speckles of dirt on their pampered shoes. Not so Mo Salah. If anyone deserved success that 2018-19 season, it was Liverpool's Number 11.

If it wasn't for the brilliance of Pep Guardiola and his wonderful to watch Manchester City side, Mo would also have had a Premier League winner's medal in his hand. To finish the campaign on ninety-eight points and still lose out by a point was a killer, but Mo felt great pride that the boys had achieved that level of success. Liverpool became the first team in top-flight history to win as many as thirty games and ninety-seven points in a season and not win the title. Additionally, no side had previously lost just one game in a top-flight season and not won the title.

Winning the Premier League had become something of a holy grail for Liverpool FC. Their last top-flight title win had been back in 1989 and the pain was all the greater as their biggest rivals, Manchester United, won league crown after league crown as Liverpool struggled to recapture their glory days at the top. For Mo, the Champions League was his main aim, but he was honest, and generous, enough to concede he would not mind if that didn't happen if the club won the Premier League. He understood the passion that stoked both fans, players and management to bring the Premier League trophy to Anfield for the first time. In March 2019, before the team faced Bayern Munich in the Champions League last sixteen, second leg, he said, 'I will be honest with you, the most prestigious competition for me is the Champions League. But the dream for the entire city and the club is the league. So, I am happy to sacrifice my dream for their dream. But if we win both that would be great and this is what we are trying to do.'

But he also understood how difficult it would be to win the league as City had by now shifted into top gear. 'The competition is very tough and we have difficult games left as do they. All you can do is win your games and hopefully they will fail in one so we can win the title. My mind is sharp and there is pressure but I am strong mentally and we just have to keep going. We will see what we can do at the end of the season but mentally I am ready for everything.'

It would not be enough as City notched a remarkable fourteen league wins on the run to become champions for the second successive season. Yet it was certainly indicative of how close Liverpool now were to being top dogs in England. Mo had achieved that in Europe with them, now the aim was to draw breath, take City on again and, hopefully, with another year's experience of tangling with them at the top, take the glittering prize. But that was for the future.

For now, as Mo proudly showed off his Champions League medal to his family, he would rest up before the World Cup and contemplate what a season it had been for him; certainly, he had scaled the peak in his own career thus far. Looking back, he realised it had been a season that would guarantee him an eternal place in the glory annals of Liverpool FC and their fans. He had topped the appearances and goals charts, with twenty-seven goals from fifty-two games (including three as a substitute). Sadio Mane had pushed him hard in the goals hunt, with just one less from fifty games (one as a sub). But Salah had forged well ahead of Mane when it came to assists: making thirteen to his strike partner's five, with dynamic young full-back Trent Alexander-Arnold topping that particular chart, with seventeen assists.

Mo's haul guaranteed him a share of the Golden Boot award along with Sadio and Arsenal's Pierre-Emerick Aubameyang. Mo had scored more overall, but this honour was restricted to Premier League goals alone – with all three grabbing twenty-two apiece. Mo was ahead of the game when the final day of the campaign dawned, but his 'failing' was to not score against Wolves. In contrast, Mane scored twice and Aubameyang also grabbed a brace in the Gunners' 3–1 win over Burnley. It was the first time three players had shared the award since Jimmy Floyd Hasselbaink, Michael Owen and Dwight Yorke in 1998-99. That made it two Golden Boot wins in two years for Mo. He had triumphed the previous season with thirty-two goals, putting him two clear of Tottenham's Harry Kane.

The season that would end in triumph for Mo began the same way, with a thumping 4–0 win over West Ham at Anfield. Salah, naturally, used the occasion to open his, and Liverpool's, account with a relatively simple tap-in twenty minutes into the first half. The campaign started on 12 August and it would be the end of September before the team would drop a point, winning their first six matches and finally drawing 1–1 with Chelsea at Stamford Bridge at the end of that month. Mo had helped himself to three goals in that period, also netting against Brighton and Southampton as he found his feet again after the disappointments of the Champions League final loss to Real Madrid and a poor World Cup with his country. Returning to the city where he was now unconditionally loved seemed to revive him: it gave him renewed energy and hope, as if his batteries had been recharged. This was his home now, the years of wandering and wondering were over. He could stay at Liverpool for the rest of his career if he so chose, such was his growing legend. And that would be enhanced even further by the end of the season with the Champions League.

Two early disappointments blighted the start to the campaign. The first was that 1–1 draw at Chelsea, the second a 0–0 draw at home to chief rivals Man City. Sandwiched either side was a 2–1 home reversal to Chelsea in the League Cup (which no one seemed to care about) and a 1–0 defeat in Napoli in the Champions League group stage (which everyone did seem to care about – but which was countered by a marvellous 3–2 win over Paris St Germain in the same competition eleven days earlier). But it was arguably more disappointing to drop the points against Chelsea and City, both of whom could be labelled Premier League contenders. Mo was particularly downcast after failing to break through against City, whom he knew would be a tough nut to crack if they were to beat them to the title. He told friends it was a match he thought they had to win – and should have won – but at least there was still a long way to go. It was a marathon, as the old footballing cliché went, and not a sprint, in the quest for the big one. There was also the fact that Guardiola had paid Liverpool the ultimate compliment by sending out a team set up to not lose. A yet rarer sight in top-class football it is harder to visualise given the Spaniard's utter devotion to attacking at all costs.

And it could have been worse for Liverpool had Riyad Mahrez not ballooned the ball over the ball when City earned a late penalty. Some Fleet Street pundits voiced concern that Salah had lost his golden touch. That he didn't look the goal poacher he had been the previous season. OK, the City encounter wasn't his finest moment but he still put in a shift and the Kop appreciated his efforts, continuing to chant his name. He had scored three times in eleven games in all competitions and, yes, maybe he was a little rusty after playing constantly, even when he was recovering from the Ramos-inflicted injury, and could probably have done with another couple of weeks' rest. There is also the inevitable mental toll after such an injury setback as an elite player works his way back into form, maybe worrying that it may have taken something away from his game.

Salah has never struck me as that kind of footballer. He is a naturally positive, engaging character whose whole demeanour suggests he looks forward rather than backwards. Someone who keeps believing in his abilities and that he can remain at the top of his game for many years. He doesn't sulk and rarely complains. This is a footballer who just gets on with it and lets his range of sublime skills do his talking. And so it was as the international break loomed in October 2019, providing Mo with a chance to work his magic for his country and then return to Liverpool and step up a gear.

Mo scored as Egypt walloped Eswatini in the African Nations Cup and now hit a particularly fine vein of form upon his return to Anfield, finding the net four times in the next three games. He began by hitting the winner in the 1–0 win at Huddersfield in the league, then grabbed a brace as Liverpool trounced Red Star Belgrade 4–0 in the Champions League group stage at Anfield, and rounded off with another goal in the 4–1 triumph at home over Cardiff in the league. It was a powerful retort to those who had questioned him and he would get even better as the season shaped up. From a stats perspective, the brace against Red Star meant Mo had scored fifty goals for the club in just sixty-five appearance. That initial £36.9 million fee paid to Roma for his services in the summer of 2017 was beginning to have the feel of a bargain. Mo exited Anfield after his goals against Red Star buzzing. He was starting to hit the net regularly again and now felt ready to push on and aim for that second Golden Boot. Was it a huge weight lifted off him? Not really, as he had never doubted himself, but it would be fair to say he walked a little lighter that night – and Klopp was certainly in no doubt that nothing had changed. He bristled when asked about Mo's goalscoring so far this season, telling reporters, 'It's good that we can maybe stop talking about that a little bit. I was not in doubt, he was not in doubt, but if you are constantly asked about it, you think something is up.' Confirmation that the press now believed again came from a comment from my friend Charlie Wyett, of *The Sun*, who felt some aggrievement that Salah had been subbed on seventy-three minutes, 'The only regret was that he was not still on the pitch when the club was awarded a second penalty and it was missed by Sadio Mane, who then completed the scoring.' The win put the team top of their Champions League season. The campaign was beginning to open up for them and Salah.

It would be a happy Christmas for Salah. After that goal against Cardiff, he had netted nine times by Boxing Day. The highlight of that period was a hat-trick recorded away at Bournemouth on 8 December, as the boys romped away with at by four goals to nil. The result meant Liverpool had equalled their record of seventeen Premier League games unbeaten, set in 2008. It sent them to the top of the table, yet Salah once again showed how unselfish a player, and person, he is by refusing to accept his Man of the Match award. Instead, he insisted it be handed to James Milner, whom he believed deserved it more. Mo explained the gesture in this way to Sky Sports, 'I will not take it. Congratulations on his amazing career. He deserved it today. I hope we'll win something together.'

Klopp was more effusive about his star man, making it clear he felt Mo deserved all the praise that came his way. Jurgen said, 'He was brilliant, absolutely brilliant. From the first moment if we could play in-behind he was there. Obviously when he is not there, we don't have a lot of speedy guys other than Sadio and Mo. We all know how big his desire is to score goals, so another match ball for him, it's nice. Mo scored a fantastic second goal. They wanted to make a little tactical foul, but he stayed on his feet. Whatever you do in a football game, you need somebody to finish it off and what Mo did with his two goals in the second half was exceptional.'

Cherries boss Eddie Howe was also generous in his praise of Salah in defeat, saying, Bournemouth boss Eddie Howe described Salah as 'one of the best in the world', going on to say 'Salah looked very good, razor sharp and we struggled to handle him. He played more centrally and did well from that position.'

The year of 2019 got off to a bad start at Man City's Etihad Stadium. Liverpool lost their only league match of the campaign, 2–1, and you could argue that the defeat cost them the title as they lost out by just one point – and the Blues claimed all three in the crucial clash on 3 January. Mo didn't get on the scoresheet but was involved in arguably the most contentious decision of the night when City skipper Vincent Kompany lunged at him as he sped towards goal. It was a sure red card but the defender was only served a yellow. If Kompany had gone, Liverpool may have earned a draw which, in turn, would have affected the final league table and even the title's final destination. That yellow card would become the decision fans everywhere would have liked to have seen subjected to VAR when they were asked for their top twenty in a poll conducted by Sky Sports at the start of the 2019-20 season. Liverpool star Jamie Carragher said, 'It was a pivotal game in the title race last season.'

No matter. Mo and his team-mates exited Manchester feeling disappointed and fatigued after losing such a key match. The loss ended Liverpool's twenty-match unbeaten run and cut their lead at the top of the table to four points. That still gave them daylight but suggested there would be no room for further setbacks given how City were now powering forwards under the persuasive direction of demanding Guardiola. Klopp was just as ambitious as his counterpart but had the ability to defuse tension than Pep seemed to lack. With Pep, it was constant use of the whip, whereas Jurgen preferred a more balanced act of carrot and stick. City's players would often come out with public soundbites of being grateful to work under his leadership; that he would teach them to be better players. Klopp's men relayed the same sort of attitude of gratitude, but also relayed stories of how the German was a superb man manager who was always there with an arm around the shoulder when required. Guardiola was much more of a cold fish.

It was likely Klopp would be the best motivator after such a defeat. If Guardiola had lost, he would have been much tougher and critical on his players. Klopp knew his men had given everything and, on the way back to Merseyside that night, told them to go easy on themselves. To relax, take the next day off and spend time with their families or friends. There would be other days and City would also hit obstacles, he said. They still led the table, and the outcome was still in their hands. It was one defeat, and that was it. Put it behind you and let's move on.

Klopp said more or less the same, telling Sky Sports, 'We were unlucky in our finishing moments. Unluckier than City, I would say. They had periods where they dominated the game and everybody felt the intensity. But we came back and had big chances. It is always like this. You have to score in those moments. When Aguero scores, there is no angle. In similar situations we didn't score. It was not our or City's best game because we both made it difficult for the other team. I have already said to the boys this is OK. We lost it but it will happen. Tonight it is not nice but it is not the biggest problem.'

No, the biggest problem was that City refused to buckle in the face of Liverpool's intense pressure. The two teams had slugged it out like prize fighters, each daring the other to crumble week in, week out. After that defeat at the Etihad, Salah put in almost superhuman efforts to lead his team to the title. He knew full well how important claiming the crown was to the club: to the fans, especially. In the four weeks following the City defeat he hit the back of the net four times and seemed to be on a personal mission to drag Liverpool to the finishing line and that elusive title. It wouldn't be enough but his goals won key matches. On 14 April, he netted in the 2–0 win over Chelsea at Anfield and what a goal it was. Some claimed it was the goal of the season – and that wasn't far off the mark. From a good twenty-five yards out, Mo thundered the ball into the top corner to make it 2–0 and secure the victory. It was his nineteenth Premier League goal of the season and his twenty-second overall.

Mo declared himself 'very happy' with the strike, but added that 'the most important thing is the win and the three points' – which left Liverpool top, two points clear of City, who had a game in hand. Klopp said he was 'so proud' of Salah and described his goal as 'just amazing'. Even Chelsea boss Maurizio Sarri added his voice to the praise for the Egyptian, saying he was 'the difference' and, when asked if he would like him in his team, the Italian nodded and offered up a wry smile and said, 'But too expensive to buy!' Which, coming from a Chelsea manager, was quite something. A fortnight later, Mo grabbed a brace in the 5–0 demolition of Huddersfield and concluded his Premier League goals campaign with one in the impressive 2–0 victory at Tottenham in the penultimate league game. Liverpool concluded their league season eight days later by beating Wolves 2–0 at Anfield but, agonisingly, it would prove not enough to win their first top-flight title in twenty-nine years.

EUROPEAN CHAMPION

Guardiola's City finished their campaign with that astonishing run of fourteen successive wins. It was a crushing blow but for Mo it was more than compensated by the wonderful Champions League triumph. He had always maintained that for him the Champions League was *the* prize that mattered most. He knew about and understood the club's obsession with winning the English league, but as an outsider now on the inside at Anfield he always maintained, when quizzed, that Europe was his personal holy grail. Mo had played in Europe and witnessed at first hand the drive to win in continental matches with Roma. While in Italy, he had viewed Juventus' push to lift the Champions League with a certain admiration, if also a touch of natural envy.

In August 2019, two months after he helped Liverpool become champions of Europe, Mo publicly insisted that the Champions League is more important than the Premier. His stance came after Guardiola set out his priority for the new season, saying winning the Prem was his main aim. Guardiola told Goal.com, 'The Champions League is seven games, you can win the Champions League but the league is every three days in the same month.

I'm sorry but it's much more important what these guys have done the whole season.'

But Mo disagreed with that point of view, saying the Champions League is a more difficult competition to win. He said, 'I think if you give him a choice to choose which one, he would choose the Champions League. That's my opinion. I'm not talking about him, but my opinion. It's the biggest competition in football, so everyone wants to win it. Every coach, every player wants to win it, dreams of winning it. So, of course, the Premier League also is something big, but still the Champions League is the biggest competition.'

There was also the issue of redemption after that mauling by Ramos led to Mo's premature exit from the final of 2018, and Liverpool's subsequent defeat. That injustice fired Salah up every time he put on a Liverpool shirt in the Champions League the following season. He kept it at the forefront of his mind, determined to inspire the team to go one step further in the new campaign. Salah helped the team to the runners-up spot in their qualifying group – Group C – behind winners PSG. Italian side Napoli finished on the same number of points and Liverpool had kicked off at Anfield in the deciding match – and final match – of the group against Napoli knowing they had to win by two goals or win and keep a clean sheet. Mo Salah hit the decisive goal while keeper Alisson Becker also played a key role by defying the Italians with a couple of crucial saves. Salah's winner came as he fired home coolly just after the half-hour mark. Salah was the toast of the city that night – and admitted his goal was 'one of the best of his career as there was so much dependent on the result' – but his goalkeeper was also rightly feted by Klopp. The manager said, 'The goal Mo scored – what a goal, unbelievable. But the save Ali made – I have no words for that. It was a lifesaver. It was wild and there were lots of counter-attacks but we were ready for that. That is Anfield live and in colour. Wow, what a game. I am not sure a manager could be prouder of a team than I am.'

To be fair, it hadn't been a convincing return to the competition for Liverpool as they lost all three away matches. Home form, and the famous Anfield roar, had yet again seen them emerge victorious against the odds.

But the runners-up spot left them at the mercy of a draw that could see them face one of the favourites in the Round of 16. Fortune did not seem to favour them – they drew Bayern Munich, one of the favourites to win the tournament. Luckily, this was not the Bayern of old or, more precisely, it was the old Bayern as in an ageing team. Flying wingers Arjen Robben and Franck Ribery were in the final year at the club and a rebuild would surely be uppermost in the minds of the club's top brass. Having said that, the traditional German spirit and fight was in abundance as they scrapped to a 0–0 draw at Anfield. The downside was that the hosts had not won, the upside was they had kept a clean sheet, so any score draw in the return leg would put them through to the last eight. It was worrying that they had lost all three of their group stage games but surely that bad run had to come to an end some time?

It did, and impressively so. They overpowered the famed German machine 3–1 in their own Allianz Arena, in what was their best performance of the current campaign. Strike partner Mane stepped up to the plate with a brace and the man mountain who is Virgil Van Dyke iced the cake with the third. A Joel Matip own goal was the only consolation for the distraught hosts, who were not used to be dismantled in this manner on their own turf. It was a salutary lesson in how the pendulum was swinging towards Liverpool under Klopp's direction. The club had cemented their place among Europe's elite yet again and their reward was to draw arguably the weakest team remaining in the competition in the last eight.

They had been brave in their attacking intent in Munich and fortune now favoured them as they were paired with Porto. No mugs, but certainly nothing to cause sleepless nights on Merseyside. It proved to be a fairly routine passage to the semi-finals with a 2–0 win at Anfield followed by an emphatic 4–1 victory over in Portugal. Salah was on the scoresheet in Porto and later admitted he had revelled in leading his club into the last four. The 6–1 aggregate showed how one-sided the tie had been, with Mo also setting up a goal in Porto, combining well with Mane for the Sengalese to hit the target and set off the avalanche on the half hour mark. Mo made it 2–0 twenty minutes after the interval, with a cool finish after an assist from the ever-improving – and ever-impressive – Trent Alexander-Arnold.

Afterwards, asked who he would like to play or avoid in the last four, Mo refused to be drawn, merely stating that all the teams remaining would pose a difficult challenge, but one he believed they could overcome. Before the two matches against Porto, their manager Sergio Conceição had claimed Liverpool were the best team on the planet – and claimed he wasn't indulging in any mind games. Klopp had laughed off the suggestion but admitted they were 'very good'. Well, the draw for the semis couldn't have been more testing if that aim was to be achieved. Out of Barcelona, Tottenham and Ajax, the Catalans were clearly the most dangerous team left in the tournament. With Lionel Messi and ex-Reds striker Luis Suarez, not to mention ex-Reds midfield ace Phil Coutinho, the task couldn't have been more daunting. A 3–0 hammering in the Camp Nou in the first leg had many pundits, and even some Liverpool fans, cursing that the game was up. There would be no final redemption for Salah this year.

But Liverpool are a football club moulded from adversity and tears, whose history is one of resilience and glory; one whose heart as well as talent has meant they can never be written off. The 2005 Champions League 'Miracle of Istanbul' win over AC Milan and the triumph in the 1984 European Cup over Roma in their own stadium in Italy provide two of the most prominent examples of this remarkable stoicism and heroics. So, most Reds fans believed all was not lost; that a miracle could still happen, Messi or no Messi. And the signs of Liverpool's strength up front had flourished at time in the Camp Nou: Mo had hit the post after a Firmino effort was cleared off the line and it could be argued Liverpool were the better team, despite the demoralising result.

Certainly, watching Messi and Suarez laugh and smile in the warm-up at Anfield, there was a feeling that they felt they merely had to turn up and they'd be in the final. Suarez should have known better: his night, and indeed whole ninety-minute showing, was one that lost him much love within Anfield, as he indulged in a snarling repertoire of play-acting, unpleasant tangles with his former team-mates and general moaning and groaning. And for what? At the end of the night, he'd crashed out of the Champions League as Liverpool stormed to a tremendous 4–0 victory.

It was all the more impressive as Salah and Firmino both missed the match through injury. A patched-up, battle weary Liverpool still had too much for Barca – and had the last laugh on Suarez.

Salah would be fit for the final. No way was he planning

to miss out after the previous year's heartbreak. He declared himself ready and raring to go and that this year he planned a much different outcome. It helped that Real Madrid would not be their opponents again. Instead, it would be an all-English affair – but not against Manchester City, as most punters had predicted earlier in the competition. No, Tottenham would be the opposition in the first Champions League final of their history. Of course, they couldn't be dismissed out of hand, especially after their stirring win over Ajax Amsterdam in the semis. But they were no City.

Klopp confirmed he had a virtually fully-fit squad before the match at Atletico Madrid's new stadium, telling the *Liverpool Echo*, 'We will have all available players on the bench apart from Naby Keita, so that gives us different opportunities and solutions. But I hope something similar will not happen again. Salah's injury was not the best thing that ever happened in football. People will probably call it experience. We are completely different team from last year. For this team, it is the first final.'

Two minutes, just two minutes, was all it took for Mo to shake off the cloud that had hung over his head for twelve months. Moussa Sissoka provided the opening for the penalty that Salah gratefully converted. The Spurs midfielder foolishly handled the ball to deflect a cross by Mane in the box after twenty-two seconds. It was Mo's first kick of the night – and a glorious one at that. Mo hammered the ball into the middle of the goal as the hapless Hugo Lloris dived to his left. It was 1–0 and there would be no way back for Spurs, who looked ponderous and one-dimensional on the night. Divock Origi, the hero against Barca, was on target again, to make it 2–0 with three minutes left. It was all over – and the shouting was about to begin as the delirious Reds and their fans celebrated.

Salah cried tears of joy after the win and told BT Sport, 'Everyone is happy now. I am glad to play the second final in a row and play ninety minutes finally. Everyone did his best today, no great individual performances today, all the team was unbelievable. I have sacrificed a lot for my career, to come from a village to go to Cairo, and to be an Egyptian at this level is unbelievable for me.' Later he summed up his emotions on social media. In an Instagram post with a picture of him with the trophy he wrote, 'Believe, work hard and it'll happen.'

And that just about sums up Mo Salah, the little Egyptian Liverpool fans had taken to their hearts. At the start of the 2019-20 season, he then helped the club lift the European Super Cup as they overcame the challenge of Chelsea, on penalties after a 2–2 draw in Istanbul. Could he yet inspire them to the World Club title, and the Premier League. Well, he would give it his best shot. Whatever was to follow, his legend was assured at Liverpool FC. His adoring fans worldwide hailed Mo Salah after his exploits in Madrid and Istanbul: King of the Kop – and now King of Europe.

ABOUT THE AUTHOR

FRANK WORRALL is Britain's No. 1 sports biographer and writes exclusively for John Blake Publishing. He is the author of nineteen books on sport, including the bestselling *Jamie Vardy: The Boy From Nowhere, Roy Keane: Red Man Walking, Anthony Joshua: King of the Ring, Rooney: Wayne's World, Celtic United: Glasgow and Manchester, Lewis Hamilton: Triple World Champion – The Biography* and *Rory McIlroy – The Biography*. Rock star Rod Stewart once hailed Celtic United as 'the last good book I read'. Frank's website frankworrall.com has details of all his books and he can be found at @frankworrall on Twitter.